Once, having been asked by the Pharisees when the Kingdom of God would come, Jesus replied, "The Kingdom of God does not come with your careful observation, nor will people say, 'Here it is,' or 'There it is,' because the Kingdom of God is within you."
Luke 17:20-21 (NIV)

Prelude:

THE KINGDOM OF GOD - SALVATION, SIGNS, AND SERVICE

Rev. Dr. Scott T. Arnold

SHINE Publications
Quincy, Michigan 49082

Copyright 2012

www.preludeKingdomofGod.com
www.comefollowjesus.com
Scotteagle777@gmail.com

Dedication:

This book is dedicated to Rev. Forrest R. Gilmore, my grandfather, who was a faithful pastor of American Baptist Churches for over 50 years in New England. He served as Pastor of the Phoenix Baptist Church in Phoenix, Rhode Island, First Baptist Church of North Attleboro, Massachusetts, First Baptist Church of Leominster, Massachusetts, First Baptist Church of Salem, Massachusetts, and First Baptist Church of North Saugus, Massachusetts.

Throughout his life Forrest demonstrated his joy and commitment to Jesus Christ by serving faithfully in the cause of God's Kingdom with passion, love, faithfulness and grace. He exhibited a cheerful joy while giving God glory. Forrest lived for the purpose of reaching people with the Gospel and of building up the church. He believed in representing the Kingdom of God through faith and service to Jesus Christ. He preached from God's Word with intelligence, humor and compassion. On the occasion of celebrating his 50th year in ministry he approached the old pulpit at First Baptist Church of Salem and pointed at his fine silky white hair saying: "There may be snow on the roof, but there is still fire in the furnace. I believe in Jesus Christ; He is the greatest." This testimony represented a lifetime of gratitude in knowing and serving Jesus Christ. I dedicate this book to my Grandfather Gilmore as I consider his trust and reliance upon God's Sovereign care.

During our first two years of ministry after seminary Marilyn and I lived in New England, we met with my grandfather Gilmore twice a month. During this time he imparted the gift of wisdom through his experience and encouraged me to stay faithful and fervent for the gospel of God's Kingdom in Christ. I thank God for this time of mentoring, a time to "pass on the torch". Quite often he would remind me of the importance of working together with other churches and clergy, and of how large God's Kingdom is. Most of all, he loved Jesus. The spark in his Irish eyes revealed this truth and the presence of God's grace. Before he died he told me that he wanted me to do his memorial service, but he told me not to call it a "funeral" but to understand it as a "coronation". I was curious as he continued to explain. "I look forward to finishing the race. I run not for a temporary crown, but for the crown of righteousness that Christ bestows to those who run with faith, trusting in His perfect grace." In my grandfather's memorial service we sang "He Leadeth Me" and "Faith is the Victory". As I dedicate this book to my grandfather, Rev. Forrest Gilmore, I do so knowing that he and others are in the Kingdom of Heaven. Together they are praying for us here on earth to seek Christ and His Kingdom first and foremost.

Why "Prelude"?

Originally the title of this book was to be: "The Kingdom of God: Salvation, Signs and Service." The idea: to share a hope-filled and joyful response to God's Holy Word in the Bible by lifting up Jesus Christ as the Messiah King. Then, while two thirds into writing this book, I had a dream that I could not ignore. In this dream I had a conversation with three people. Each one looked closely into my eyes and said: "I see the word 'prelude' in your eyes." When I woke up from this dream I began to pray about what this meant. I felt the Lord lead me to Psalm 40:

> ³ He put a new song in my mouth, a hymn of praise to our God. Many will see and fear and put their trust in the LORD. Psalm 40:3 (NIV)

"Prelude" describes the ministry of preparation through praise, prophecy, prayer and preaching. John the Baptist prepared the way for Jesus' first coming. The Church has been entrusted with the responsibility of preparing the world for Jesus' Second Coming. A "Prelude" is a song of preparation; it is a witness to the greater presence of God involving a message of hope with thoughtfulness and reverence. The lives of Christians are to be a "Prelude" whereby God the Creator/Father, the Lord Jesus Christ/God's Son and the Holy Spirit/Counselor are worshipped here on earth. Psalm 40:3 affirms that believers "see" the Lord now by faith. God's promises prepare us to behold His unfolding plan; we gain vision for His present and coming Kingdom. This has been revealed throughout Scripture with both Old and New Testaments maintaining an ongoing Spirit-filled witness. The message of this song of "Prelude" is in summary: ***The Kingdom of God shall transform humanity and history in the culmination of Christ's coming in glory and majesty***. The prophetic apocalyptic Word given to Ezekiel, Isaiah, Daniel, Paul, Peter and the disciple John in Revelation are each a direct Biblical "prelude" to Christ's coming reign. The whole of Scripture is a "prelude" to the full revelation of God's Kingdom that is unfolding and is still yet to come.

Jesus said that "the Kingdom of God is within you" (Luke 17:21). When one lives their life as a "Prelude" (or example) of God's Kingdom being a present reality through faith, a person grows to become someone whose purpose is centered upon Christ's current leading as they also prepare for Christ's future coming glory. Is "Prelude" in your eyes, heart, mind and soul? A life that is a "prelude" prepares the way for the risen Lord. Jesus is ready to change lives; He starts by calling each person by name and then fills the hearts of those who repent and believe with new life through the Holy Spirit. From spiritual regeneration, one's faith and vision is of God's Kingdom. Then truly, the Kingdom of Christ the Lord and Savior is within you. A new song, poem, painting, deed of kindness, idea, or expression of truth and grace is within your heart and mind, manifested and magnified through a life of praise and worship to God and loving service to others. The "Prelude" of God's Kingdom abides and grows within believers to then be expressed in praise and living witness.

In regard to the Kingdom of God involving salvation, signs and service, the object of this study is to affirm the faithful sovereignty of God and the redemptive Lordship of Jesus Christ. The application point of this book is to inspire and edify believers so they may grow together in their understanding of God's Kingdom and grow together in their faith and service to Jesus Christ. This study is, therefore, written as a witness to Christ with reflections, questions and input that will aid in explaining biblical truth to those who question the reality of hope in God's Kingdom.

The prayer of this author is that skeptics, agnostics, and even proclaiming Christians would open their hearts and minds to know and serve God with a greater vision of God's Kingdom. Ultimately all people will give account to the inevitable authority/reality of God's Son, Jesus Christ. The priority of Jesus, who called people to "seek first God's Kingdom", challenges humanity to consider two questions: "What is our nature and identity?" And, "Where is God in the equation of our life's purpose and direction?"

Understanding what the "Kingdom of God" is, and anticipating its increase and fulfillment, are probably two of the most important biblical and theological pursuits of studying Holy Scripture. Once a person grasps how vitally important commitment and service to God's Kingdom is, then one's vision and purpose for life can, upon repentance and faith, be transformed by an infusion of God's grace and truth. Growth of faith in Christ will translate into outward expressions of God's Kingdom through compassionate and faithful service. In this way people become living representatives and personal signs of the Kingdom of God. God's saving grace and majestic power are revealed in and through such personal transformation and service. When the Body of Christ (the Church) is at work, incarnate (in the flesh) within society, the world then witnesses the renewing hope of the gospel of God's Kingdom here and now, with a taste of what is yet to come.

The key passages examined in this study shall be from the Gospel of Matthew and the Book of Psalms. The teachings of the "Sermon on the Mount", the parables of Jesus, and the signs of God's Kingdom revealed in Jesus ministry all herald the presence, potential, and promise of God's Kingdom through Jesus the Christ. The Psalms were inspired by God as He was moving through His Spirit and His messengers to bring people into worship and wonder before His majestic throne. Within the tabernacle and temple, and within the heart of worshippers, the Psalmists learned to see the world from God's point of view. Prophetic writings will also be referred to as they also speak of God's present Sovereignty and coming reign that shall hold all people into account and that God's Kingdom is both present and coming in fulfillment.

Worship is experienced in the present as we learn to see reality with vision that is framed and focused upon God and His Kingdom. God revealed then, and reveals to people today, the presence, power and hope of salvation, His Holiness and righteous judgment and His power to forgive and redeem. The Old and New Testaments are bridged and fulfilled through Jesus Christ in the Biblical vision of God's eternal and everlasting Kingdom. While this Kingdom exists beyond time and space in the realm of Heaven, this Kingdom is also now present in the hearts of believers and is represented through the witness of the Church (those who truly follow and serve Jesus Christ).

Scripture gives us the promise that while God's Kingdom has yet to come in fullness on earth, when it does come there shall be an unmistakable appearing and arrival of Jesus Christ again, at that time He shall come in power and glory (Matthew 24). Prior to Christ's return there shall be extensive trial and intensive tribulation throughout the world (Matthew 24 and Daniel 9:20-27). Even so, those who are wise and responsive to God's call shall receive Jesus Christ the risen Savior for redemption. They shall shine brightly in advance of the Age to Come. After this time of intense witness, and Christ's return, God's Kingdom shall replace the governments of the nations of men (Daniel 12:1-4):

> [1] "At that time Michael, the great prince who protects your people, will arise. There will be a time of distress such as has not happened from the beginning of nations until then. But at that time your people--everyone whose name is found written in the book--will be delivered. [2] Multitudes who sleep in the dust of the earth will awake: some to everlasting life, others to shame and everlasting contempt. [3] Those who are wise will shine like the brightness of the heavens, and those who lead many to righteousness, like the stars for ever and ever. [4] But you, Daniel, close up and seal the words of the scroll until the time of the end. Many will go here and there to increase knowledge." **Daniel 12:1-4 (NIV)**

Upon God's glorious revelation of His Beloved Son, every knee shall bow and every tongue will confess that Jesus Christ is Lord (Isaiah 45:23 and Romans 14:11). With hope and vision renewed by God's Spirit working in our midst, in our very times, the Church must go beyond mere survival and maintenance and serve the noblest cause of furthering God's Kingdom in Christ. We do not build this Kingdom by sheer will, but humbly serve with the realization that it is Christ and the Spirit of God who are building the Church. Kingdom citizens are being identified, reconciled to God, and sanctified. Salvation is the ongoing work of God's beloved Son Jesus Christ, and the Church is called to participate in preparing people to receive the Gospel of the Kingdom now. Likewise, we are to have a vision for the fulfillment of God's Kingdom to come daily, in sufficient grace. In the future we trust in God's grace to be fulfilled through the utter transforming power that is integral to God's Sovereign righteousness as the Creator/Redeemer when Christ Jesus returns.

Prelude: The Kingdom of God: Salvation, Signs, and Service

Book Outline

Dedication	5
Why "Prelude"?	7
BOOK OUTLINE	11
VISION 1: GOD'S COMING KINGDOM	13
VISION 2: A Story of Stars	21
VISION 3: Providence and Airplanes	31
VISION 4: Faith Steps to Follow Jesus	39
Overview of the Encounter Experience	41
Purpose of this Encounter	43
Bible Encounter Outline	44

Chapter Title:	Scripture:	Page:
1. "God is Enthroned"	(Psalm 47; Psalm 48; Matthew 18:1-4)	45
2. "God is Glorious and Majestic"	(Psalm 8; Psalm 24; Matthew 17:1-5)	61
3. "God is Mighty and Merciful"	(Psalm 29, 33, and 61; Matthew 18:10-14)	75
4. "God is Building His Kingdom"	(Isaiah 62; Revelations 3:11-13)	89
5. "The Ambassador of the King"	(Matthew 3:1-12; II Corinthians 5:17-21)	103
6. "The Kingdom of God is Near"	(Matthew 4:8-17; Psalm 84)	113
7. "Seek A Kingdom of Righteousness"	(Matthew 5:17-20; Psalm 72)	123
8. "Please God in Secret Service"	(Matthew 6:1-4; II Corinthians 5:9-10)	133
9. "Treasure the Kingdom of God"	(Matthew 6:19-24; Psalm 62)	141
10. "Judgment in God's Kingdom"	(Matthew 7:1-12; 20:1-16 and Psalm 67)	153
11. "The Great Mercy of the King "	(Matthew 8:1-17; Psalm 57)	163
12. "The Great Forgiveness of the King"	(Matthew 9:1-8; 18:21-35; Psalm 32)	171
13. "Service in the Name of the King"	(Matthew 10:1-42; Psalm 145)	183
14. "The King Who Suffered"	(Matthew 21:33-46; Psalm 22)	195
15. "The King Who is Victorious"	(John 20:1-18; Psalm 91)	205
16. "Invitation to God's Kingdom Party"	(Matthew 28:18-20; 22:1-14, Psalm 93)	215
17. "The Return of the King "	(Revelation 1:1-8; 22:7 Psalm 96)	229
Three Principles of "Prelude"		241
About the Author		243
Current Books and Resources by Dr. Scott T. Arnold		245
BIBLIOGRAPHY		247

VISION 1: GOD'S COMING KINGDOM

    In January of 2010, when earthquakes rocked the island of Haiti and a collective cry of humanity was moved with concern and compassion, I began to have intense visions while battling pneumonia. For several days the visions were relentless and overwhelming. At first I considered the possibility that my struggle with pneumonia, that had landed me in the hospital, had left me in a partial state of mental delirium. Yet each time that I closed my eyes, while being awake and conscious, I saw visions. I came to believe and trust that God was revealing something important to be shared, and since these visions I have seen their connection to visions and teachings in the Bible regarding God's Kingdom. Though most of this book is written from a sermon series that I preached in the winter of 2009, there are insights and visions that have come since that time as God has continued to reveal the importance of having His Kingdom be my primary desire and priority.

    What I saw at first with closed eyelids (even before going to the hospital) were moving and dynamic colorful images of the earth being formed. I watched with awe and wonder as the earth was being molded and then powerfully modified. Mountains were rising and falling as geography was altered in rapid lapsed-time. Oceans, seas, lakes and rivers roared and flowed as sunlight and moonlight moved and danced in colorful array. The earth was filled with the awesome glory of the Lord.

While having these visions I was physically struggling, and with coughing and lung pain it seemed futile attempting to sleep. However, these visions continued to amaze and flood my mind. I felt overwhelmed and yet inspired. I was deeply humbled as I watched these things unfold in my mind's eye. What I saw in these visions directly compared to the creation account in Genesis 1:2: *"And the earth was without form, and void; and darkness was upon the face of the deep. And the Spirit of God moved upon the face of the waters."* I wondered if Moses, who recorded what God revealed to him in writing Genesis, saw something like these visions as he was inspired to write the creation account.

After about a day of these initial creation visions, I began to see development in the growth of vegetation followed by the creation of a wide variety of creatures, beautiful, colorful and vivacious. In a splendid and moving series of events (most of which by now are far too complex to even describe) I eventually I saw the emergence of people and their many faces. There were people from every race, tribe, nation, and age. They would appear to me close up as individuals and sometimes in groups. At first it was intimidating and intense. These visions of people continued for the next day and a half, every time I closed my eyes. This kaleidoscope of people gave me an overall impression of awe and wonder. I grew to gain appreciation, concern and respect for being human and for the biblical perspective that we as humanity are created in the image of God. Yet not all the visions were beautiful; some faces were ugly and disturbing. Some of these visions were even mixed with seeing beings that were non-human as we would be familiar with, yet these beings appeared to be intelligent or human-like. I wondered if some were alien, angelic or demonic beings. Was I losing my mind? The whole experience of seeing these faces every time I closed my eyes prevented me from sleeping and drew me toward God in prayer. Whether all these visions were from my imagination, or whether my imagination was being informed by God, is a matter of debate and reasonable deliberation. However, when wrestling with the question of why there is supernatural phenomena that intersects our psyche and physical conditions I will choose to trust that God is not absent and can be discovered within and beyond our meek and moldable minds.

Between the times of being alert with my eyes open and resting with my eyes closed, these visions continued as a steady stream as often as I closed my eyes. Suddenly, amidst these relentless and fascinating visions, there was an interesting turn of events. People started turning and gazing in the same direction, their orientation had shifted in unison. They began moving together as if summoned or called. When I looked to see what everyone else saw, I beheld an extremely large city, one that no human construction was capable of making. This luminous city was like a large mountain of geometric shining precious stone, bright and reflective, with walls that loomed tall and wide. I had no doubt that it was the New Jerusalem, the City of God. I remembered Ezekiel and how he was given visions to write down and share. For Ezekiel, the succession of divine visions culminated in the following account:

> *² In visions of God he took me to the land of Israel and set me on a very high mountain, on whose south side were some buildings that looked like a city. ³ He took me there, and I saw a man whose appearance was like bronze; he was standing in the gateway with a linen cord and a measuring rod in his hand. ⁴ The man said to me, "Son of man, look with your eyes and hear with your ears and pay attention to everything I am going to show you, for that is why you have been brought here. Tell the house of Israel everything you see."* (Ezekiel 40:2-4 NIV)

As God's vision continued in my own state of weakness and reliance, I saw the nations' peoples as they processed toward this immense city of radiant stone. There were many moods and expressions revealed in the spectrum of faces of the people. Some were rejoicing while others looked somber and anxious. What I first saw, as I was being slightly lifted above from the crowd, was a wide dispersed sea of humanity funneling forward along a wide highway. Eventually the movement became concentrated into an urban boulevard of people walking toward the great city. I watched as waves of people from different nations (all dressed in their ethnic, national or native garments) moved along as if in a parade. With the spectacle of this diverse movement of people heading toward the city, I would find myself caught between tears and laughter, being moved with concern and even amusement. More often I would cry with a sense of grief and compassion as not everyone was happy or at peace. I saw a diversity of Africans, Europeans, Asians, Indians, native tribal peoples, Aussies, Latinos, Americans, Middle Easterners, and then the people of the tribes of Israel with rabbis walking proudly and rabbinic scholars with glasses donning black and white suits while riding bicycles. Various priests strode forward; there were Greek Orthodox, Roman Catholic, and then the Coptic priests with their full beards and robes. This was all so vivid as I lay wondering and amazed in my hospital bed. Every time I closed my eyes the vision continued. The climax to this vision was close at hand.

As people entered the large city, brightness showed on their faces. I continued to watch the people in their procession. Some exhibited hope while others exhibited anxiety. The parade of humanity made their way through the streets toward a common destination. At this point my vision was lifted to where I was looking high above the city with a vantage point high above its center. There, in the midst of the city, was a lush large open garden park with an incomparably bright light shining within it. People were gathering here, I felt overwhelmed with joy and awe. In the middle of this meeting place I saw what looked like an open temple and a throne with a bright cloud and rainbow over it. Since it was dusk, the luminous colors of twilight gave way to starlight. Bright and glorious, the light from the throne shined the rays of God's peace and serenity, a beacon for the people of the world to come to. (If I were to estimate how large this open garden area was I would guess that it was about 20 miles wide and 40 miles long. It seemed as though I had been elevated to thousands of feet above the city's center from a view similar to that of being at the height of a small aircraft.) From high above I could see the overall picture of people coming into the city and approaching the luminous throne.

With this last image staying in my mind, my heart was racing. The vision concluded as it slowly faded from my mind. In that moment I was simultaneously filled with God's peace and a reverent sense of awe. After having gone through three and a half days of such intense and interesting visions, my mind now rested, and I was finally able (by God's grace and mercy) to sleep peacefully.

Since that time, I have pondered these visions and their meaning and have asked God for wisdom and understanding related to His coming judgment and Kingdom. I believe that in the creation visions I was shown God's Sovereignty and Majesty. In the visions of people, creatures, angels and demons I was shown a glimpse of all who must appear before God pertaining to the matters of judgment and salvation. In the vision of the procession that led to the City of God, I believe that I was being shown a time that is coming, the very time of Judgment when all nations shall be brought to the New Jerusalem and shall appear before Jesus Christ.

A few weeks after this vision, I was teaching a class in our church. The Scripture passage for us to read and study was from when Jesus taught His disciples about the end times in the gospel of Matthew (ch.24-25). As we read this passage, the vision the Lord gave me was once again reaffirmed in Christ's own authoritative words of prophecy regarding His own eventual enthronement that will involve His judgment of humanity.

> *^{31} "When the Son of Man comes in his glory, and all the angels with him, he will sit on his throne in heavenly glory. ^{32} All the nations will be gathered before him, and he will separate the people one from another as a shepherd separates the sheep from the goats. ^{33} He will put the sheep on his right and the goats on his left.* **Matthew 25:31-33 (NIV)**

This foretelling of Jesus about Himself was that of being the anointed divine/human King whose inevitable reign shall be consummated in power and glory. The responsibility of Christ is completed in both judgment and salvation. People shall be gathered before Jesus from every nation, and the Lord Himself shall judge each and all in order to separate sheep (Grace and faith-filled followers) from goats (disobedient and rebellious humanity).

All people are being called in Jesus' Parable of Separation to prepare for God's coming Kingdom. I was convinced of this as I started writing this book a year before I had the visions that I described here (which accompanied my battle with pneumonia). For months I had put this project on hold while working on several other writings in my spare time as a pastor. Now, with urgency and persistence, and with renewed and clarified vision and purpose, I share these visions and the Bible Study that have undergirded this journey of discovery. As you read this book or study it together with others, take time to explore what the Bible reveals about the process of how God shall bring His Kingdom into a greater manifestation on earth, ultimately culminating in Christ's return. Take time to carefully examine and consider the revelation of the Scriptures of the Old and New Testaments. The Holy Spirit, and the very Word of God, shall disclose the very nature and reality of God's Kingdom to anyone who earnestly seeks. From God's revelation, the invitation of Jesus Christ to each person is to respond in faith and obedience. To do this we are called to prioritize faith, citizenship and service for the Kingdom of God. May we prepare for Christ's coming rapture of the church and be faithful to endure times of tribulation and trial that shall precede (are a prelude to) Christ's coming in power and glory. The coming enthronement of Jesus Christ, and the restoration of Christ Jesus as King for Israel and the world, is the hope and culmination of God's promise in Scripture. In God's sure promises in Scripture, people may know a hope that will engage their hearts and minds. Believers (and even skeptics) shall be stirred and inspired by the Spirit of God. By faith, we are called to respond to Christ's compelling call to salvation and service, discovering the immanence of our Lord's Second Advent and the urgency of believing and sharing the Gospel of God's Kingdom.

May we come before the Holy Scriptures with openness to the Spirit of God so as to discover God's call and application of what it means to be "Kingdom" citizens who serve in Jesus' name. While probing the Bible for knowledge of God's Kingdom and while also considering God's moving hand in human history, there is something even more profound that Jesus came to offer and reveal. The most important truth of God's coming or existent Kingdom, Jesus said, is that: "*...the Kingdom of God is within you.*" Luke 17:21. This factor of responsibility, awareness, potential and faithfulness is affirmed by Jesus' prayer for people to discover God's Kingdom here and now. We are not to passively wait for the day that God establishes His Kingdom in Christ's return to judge the peoples of the nations. The prayer that He taught His disciples *was: "Thy Kingdom come, Thy will be done, on earth as it is in heaven"* Matthew 6:10.

Jesus taught that the Kingdom of God exists eternally whether we see it or not. The seed of God's Kingdom is planted within our souls by the very reality of God making us in His image. However, for this seed to grow it must first crack open (die to its static state), sprout, grow, develop and mature. The health of our spiritual condition, and our relationship with our Creator/Father God, is therefore the issue at hand as Jesus confronts people with His identity and mission of salvation.

God's Kingdom, therefore, has always been a reality, and was established from the beginning of creation and throughout creation's existence and development. This Kingdom has also been manifest and evident through God's interaction with humanity. God's Sovereign Kingdom is patiently being revealed in our lives personally and corporately, eventually culminating in a full manifestation that is possible only through God's gift of grace imparted through faith in Jesus Christ and the transformation of God's Holy Spirit. Beyond what we see, God's Kingdom is wonderfully at work in quiet and simple ways that mold, fill and shape our souls. God's Kingdom is likewise coming in a greater fullness of glory and power as well, in a way that will transform all that we know, and this promise and purpose of God is specifically going to be fulfilled in the Second Coming of Jesus the Christ, the Messiah. Before Jesus comes in the ultimate fulfillment of God's Kingdom, Jesus has begun to reign within and through the lives of those who receive Him, who believe in Him and honor His name. The joy of believers is to live in fellowship with Christ, this while anticipating God's Kingdom to come. God's people live in the present reality of a Savior who inhabits their hearts, their worship, their communities, and their service to others. The way that believers are to live shall reveal that Jesus is present and that His love is real. In spite of our shortcomings, the Lord will cause our lives to be a "prelude", a "taste" of what He is preparing for all who will believe, follow and trust Him.

VISION 2: A STORY OF STARS

    The river was flowing steadily underneath me as I gazed up into the starry sky. The rugged wooden footbridge that I had laid down upon provided a unique vantage point to the heavens. The first stars were coming out in the twilight as frogs, toads, and crickets sang upon the banks of this tree lined trout stream in Wisconsin. Even so, a thick cloud covered my thoughts on that clear September night in 1982; I felt that I had failed in many ways to serve God. What more could I do to impact the little inner city church I was helping in and a northwest side neighborhood of Chicago that so needed God's touch of grace? Was I completely sure of God's call to serve Him through urban ministry? Thoughts returned to a symphony of flowing water in the sound of this little stream that swiftly moved underneath me as I looked up to the starry canopy beginning to appear up above. I hoped that somehow the creation in all its beauty could sweep my concerns away in a current of cleansing. My hometown friend Daryl had gone upstream to cast his fly with skill for the many trout that were rising to feed upon the river's surface. I chose not to fish any more that day because I knew that I needed some direction from the Lord.

Fishing was a nice distraction, but it did not solve my need for being still before God.

Praying, I asked God what His specific purpose and calling was for my life. All the sounds of creation along a wooded riverside did not contain a direct message from the Lord; the presence and voice of the Lord was veiled at first. Eventually, as I waited and watched, enjoying the light of the moon and the deepening indigo of the heavens, my heart was being prepared as each new star appeared. Then, to my wonder, in a sweeping arching flash, a meteorite streaked across the starry night sky. I felt the power of God's presence move in order to penetrate and stream through my soul. I was still as I listened with awe and joy. What I heard was a firm voice within me saying: "I love you; you are my child." This very word from God spoke unconditional, unwavering, love into my soul. In this poignant stillness I listened carefully. "I am calling you to go and preach the gospel to all the world, to people in cities and to those in the countryside." "Fear not, I will be with you always", were the Lord's concluding words of encouragement. The voice of the Lord was firm, warm and strong. My heart was greatly strengthened and my soul was blessed. The Lord had come to me in a beautiful and profound way. This was a very personal message from the creator and redeemer of my life. I have often looked back at that moment as a defining call from God, a clarification of His will to participate in the work of His Kingdom. Internally I reaffirmed that God's Kingdom is more than a vain hope, or a concept of religion, it is a reality that is entered into and pursued by faith.

When looking up to the stars in heaven one can certainly be humbled by the majesty of creation. There is a growing realization among the scientific community that the evidence for intelligent design extends from the vast expanse of the universe to the details found within specific and minute biological, molecular and atomic structures. The patterns that define creation speak of a Creator. The way in which God the Creator exercised sovereignty through the initial act of creating, and the way that God maintains sovereignty through continued interaction with the creation, is essential in understanding God's prior and ongoing revelation. God actively communicates and reveals His very nature in infinite ways, and God calls upon humanity, made in His image, to respond in faith and be reconciled and renewed through spiritual transformation. God's Kingdom is focused upon bringing salvation and redemption to humanity. More than a renewal of the past, God is bringing new life, resurrection, a covenant of grace and truth into alignment with His Sovereign care.

There are many claims as to what to believe about God and His Kingdom. Not many are accurate, biblical, or inspired from God's Spirit. While there are those theologies about God and His Kingdom that arise from God's various means of revelation, there are contrasting and manipulative formulations that arise from man's inventions or misinterpretations of God's revelation. The Holy Bible provides an unparalleled inspired and authoritative vessel of God's Word that will help us to examine the revelation of God. The Bible provides historical, empirical, and personal experiences of God that speak to all subsequent experiences of God. May our goal be found in the pursuit of serving, magnifying, and giving honor and glory to the Lord and King, Jesus the Christ, the Son of God. In this matter of glorifying God may we grow in the way in which we live by "Kingdom of God" values. People who abide by the Word and Spirit of God will inevitably shine a brighter witness of their relationship and understanding of God, His nature and His Kingdom. God's intent is that we become spiritually alive through being renewed with an identity and nature in Jesus Christ that is transforming and fruitful. Jesus Christ calls people to believe in Him and pick up the cross of service; we may begin participating as citizens of God's Kingdom.

When God said: "Let us create man in our image" (Genesis 1:26-27), God was creating the broader human community from the one Divine Community (the Holy Trinity). This initial revelation of God in Genesis raises two essential truths: We are created in the image of God, and that image involves our purpose and identity within the fullness of creation and community as God intends. More simply, we were designed by our Creator for communion and citizenship within His eternal Kingdom. However, the problem is, the corruption of man's goodness by evil, as originating from the personified temptation and perversion of Satan, makes salvation essential. God's redemptive Kingdom work has been therefore active since man's corruption and fall.

Challenging questions must be raised regarding the free-will that God has given us. How does free-will relate to God's plan of making us to be stewards of this earth? How does free-will factor into our redemption from evil? Also, how does free-will enter into the establishment of justice, righteousness, and the accountability held to all people before God? In all this, it will be important to explore how we live according to God's revealed guidance. There is hope in becoming citizens of God's Kingdom in the present tense, discovering transformation as we become "living signs" of God's kingdom through faith and the way we live. There is deeper purpose to be found in exploring and experiencing the kind of service God calls us to offer and render in obedient and faithful action. When we behold the needs of people, and consider our own needs, we are invited to be moved with the understanding of God's redemptive compassion. According to Jesus, Kingdom service is essential (Matthew 25). The sheep (God's Kingdom citizens) and the goats (those not of God's Kingdom) are distinct because of their actions and devotion. Those who actively responded to the needs of the hungry, naked, homeless, sick, imprisoned, and lonely have evidenced the heart of God's compassion and are welcomed for doing the work of God's Kingdom.

In writing this book my intent is that it will reflect something that is genuine and life-changing. Therefore, I come humbly before God, sharing the work of God's Kingdom through Jesus Christ that has brought salvation and direction for my life. This journey began as I was immersed in the community of faith at Memorial Presbyterian Church in Midland, Michigan and was nurtured in the basics of the Christian faith in my home. Yet not until I began to seek after God's heart, and recognize that I had only a superficial relationship with God, did I become aware that something was missing. While seeking God as a junior in High School, God began to reveal His Word, presence and truth to me through Jesus Christ. One Sunday, I went forward to pray with others during an invitation. We didn't have these invitations too often, but I felt compelled to go up no matter what others might think. These steps were bigger than I could have known, as I did not realize the implications of surrender into His loving arms. There was a "warmth" and "revealing truth" that moved within me in that moment of commitment and prayer. My life was never to be the same as Jesus had come into my heart and life. I was born again as a child of God.

Remembering all these times has helped me to see how Jesus has always been there for me as friend, Savior, Lord, Righteous King and Prince of Peace. God's grace was received in that transforming moment of repentance and faith, and has always been sufficient, no matter the challenge in life or lack of faithfulness on my part. I keep learning what it means to humbly serve Jesus, and He guides me with His word of truth and life. Christ reigns with authority and mercy; in Him I find peace and strength. What I learned then (and what I continue to observe) is that Jesus empowers and equips His disciples with the Holy Spirit. This precious gift of the Holy Spirit is also from God our Heavenly Father; it is given when we are born again and adopted spiritually into our inheritance into God's family and Kingdom. My prayer is that we may honor and glorify Jesus Christ by living in the way of God's will so as to be ambassadors of the Kingdom of God.

By the grace of God, Christ has called me to serve as a pastor of four different churches in twenty-eight years of ministry. From inner city churches, to suburban and small town churches, God continues to call me to develop a deeper understanding of His Kingdom. My theology (faith understanding) continues to develop in the essentials of Christ's calling and Great Commission of evangelism and discipleship. God calls out to people in diverse places to believe and become distinctive (salt within the world). By faith and obedience to Christ we become pleasing to God as active citizens His Kingdom. Peter said it well as he encouraged the church to consider their identity of holiness as the Body of Christ:

^{9}But you are a chosen people, a royal priesthood, a holy nation, a people belonging to God, that you may declare the praises of him who called you out of darkness into his wonderful light. ^{10}Once you were not a people, but now you are the people of God; once you had not received mercy, but now you have received mercy. (I Peter 2:9-10 NIV)

The best and worst in people, in churches and in secular communities, should not make us stumble in pride or hesitate to serve because of doubt and frustration. God is at work for His Kingdom's completion and is bringing about something that, when revealed in fullness, shall answer all questions and reveal all mysteries. In the midst of the range of beauty and brokenness that we encounter or experience now, may we grow to understand that the Kingdom of God is in our midst, is "at hand" as Jesus proclaimed. The Kingdom of God is both present in the witness and souls of believers, and yet it shall come in the complete fulfillment of God's promise through Christ's return in transforming glory and saving power.

Being a cancer survivor, I understand what it is to face death and what it is to receive God's healing touch. I know what it means to walk in the "valley of the shadow of death." I am also deeply humbled and grateful to have experienced the bright and healing presence of the living Christ. Jesus is the "Light of salvation". People struggle with the cancer of sinfulness and corruption. All the while, Jesus is knocking on their heart by the witness and prayers of those who care and are faithful in prayer and loving witness. I too have tried to minister to others from my own struggles, sin and imperfection. In all of these times and trials I have learned to trust (and have discovered) how Christ's strength and grace is at work. The Kingdom of God is eternal, and yet we continue to discover how the Kingdom of God is a "work in progress". What an amazing consideration! God's call is for us to be participants. God desires that we receive and extend His grace and mercy. This good work is rooted in the good news that He has ordained through Jesus Christ His Son. The beloved Son of God reigns in the hearts of all who believe and receive the Gospel of God's saving love and forgiveness. What a challenge and engaging mission! God has given us the opportunity to joyfully and meaningfully explore what it means to be disciples who share salvation. We are given an identity of the Kingdom by becoming the "living signs" or "living stones" of Christ. We are knit or held together by God's Spirit as we grow in serving unselfishly for the sake of God's great and glorious Kingdom.

There is nothing more inspiring and transforming for personal faith than to receive the revelation of God's Kingdom in Jesus Christ. While Christ Jesus is Lord of life now, He shall transform all things in a time yet to come. This revealed hope is pervasive throughout Scripture. The light of God's truth and grace comes through knowing Jesus Christ. The Lord is risen and resident within believers. Jesus' words ring true within the heart: *"The Kingdom of God is within you."* Jesus teaches His disciples to pray with focus: *"Thy Kingdom come, Thy will be done on earth as it is in Heaven"*. The eschatology of Jesus (His vision and the realization of God's coming Kingdom) affirms the Sovereignty of His Heavenly Father while also giving hope for the full arrival and power of God's Kingdom to be established in completion upon the earth.

This perspective of the immanent presence of God's Kingdom was particularly true in the words of warning and judgment for Israel in the Old Testament, and it was also personally evident in Jesus Christ the Messiah, the Son of God. Jesus Christ's presence did not, however, equate into power and glory exclusively. Indeed, Jesus came to serve as the Suffering Messiah-King, the Prince of Peace, the reconciler and mediator between God and man. The Kingdom was truly evident and manifest in His being and through His ministry. In God's Providence of mercy, the Kingdom was not to arrive in full bloom but as a seed which sprouted and grew. The full power and glory of Christ is reserved until the age of the church shall be concluded. At that time both Gentile and Jew will be joined, grafted as one, on the vine or tree of David (Romans 11). Both shall receive the completion of God's plan of salvation. In the fullness of time Jesus came in grace and truth, and in the fullness of time He shall come again in power and glory. Until then, God is preparing believers to become faithful and responsible citizens of His Kingdom. Trusting Jesus for the culmination of God's plan of redemption and judgment is a matter of faith. Living with a faith that is centered and focused upon God and His Kingdom is of utmost importance for salvation. Such vision gives believers discernment and wisdom to know what their ultimate purpose is, who they serve and to whom they are accountable to.

Those who assume that the Kingdom of God is a creation of religion or an invention of man have accepted short-sighted, ignorant and misguided humanistic philosophies. Too often people believe in their false assumptions about God because they are deceived by the lies of those who oppose God and His Kingdom. The result of believing lies is a disconnection from the truth, a distance from what is real and life-giving. God is the architect, master planner and builder of His Kingdom. Historically, the kings and prophets of Israel often failed to lead Israel to be the example and witness it was called to be, "a light unto the nations". The emperors of ancient Rome failed to create a sustained united Republic during the time following Christ's death. Afterward, the Holy Roman Empire founded under Constantine compromised and corrupted Christianity through "state religion". Over the following centuries, colonizing European nations often failed in their attempt to represent Christianity as they were overwhelmingly motivated by greed, power and the conquest of resources and peoples. Christian missionaries who brought the message of salvation in Christ could not always counter the corruption of monarchs and merchants who viewed their colonies as a means for building power and wealth. In Western civilizations and Eastern civilizations there have been rulers and religious leaders who have temporarily assumed a god-like status. Each and every temporal ruler has inevitably died and been replaced. Man's kingdoms and governments are corruptible and insufficient. The religious intertwining of church and state has historically wrought havoc. Even the best expressions of faith, that give witness to the liberty of conscience within those who follow and serve Jesus Christ, are met with persecution, suspicion and indifference. Nonetheless, the Gospel has gone forth in word and witness.

Through proclamation and prophetic actions, in hope and faith that God's Sovereignty will be represented and manifested, faith-filled followers of Christ are empowered to shine in the way that God calls them to live in peaceful responsibility.

Paul wrote with such awareness, realism and vision: "For freedom Christ has set us free" (Galatians 5:1). The human soul is designed for communion with God, and therefore needs salvation from the pervasiveness of willful sin that has resulted in separation and brokenness. We need to be set free from ourselves; that is, to be free from greed, foolish pride, self-reliance, ignorance, fear, prejudice, self-justifications and false assumptions. The work of God's redeeming power through Christ is to set us free from sin, from our corrupted nature. When Jesus is received within, the old rule and stronghold of sin is crucified. The process of transformation and salvation begins by faith and is completed by the sufficient grace of God for those who believe and obey Jesus Christ.

Human governments cannot provide freedom and welfare indefinitely. In a limited way, human institutions are still used by God as temporary agencies that have a role to provide order, ethical accountability and a degree of social and moral compass. Meanwhile, governments and institutions of man can be positively influenced and led by people of God-centered faith or good-will. This should not presume that an institution or government would ever be assigned equality with God or a God-like status. No creation or institution of man should seek to divert or possess the loyalty and devotion that must ultimately and exclusively belong to God's sovereign reign. Governments and those who lead or serve within them are called to respect and protect such freedom that allows for religious liberty and moral accountability. Freedom of religious expression and conviction is one of the key foundations within the advocacy of faith and devotion to God and His Kingdom. While government is a caretaker or steward of human society, God alone is the author and sustainer of life, love, truth and grace, salvation and spirituality. Government's role is, therefore, to protect the religious freedom of people to seek and serve God in mutual and moral respect.

The Kingdom of God is, therefore, above all human government, and this includes all monarchies, democracies, republics and forms of governance. Even so, the transcendence of God's Kingdom has been constant, stalwart, and influential during all of man's imperfect governances; it has indeed been working above, in, and around the kingdoms of this earth. Therefore, in a spiritual sense that undergirds existence, the Kingdom of God is a matter of historical significance, of present importance, and of great future hope and promise. Man's governments are flawed, imperfect, and subject to frustration because of humanity's' bent to sin and corrupted condition. However, God's Sovereign reign is not restricted by human faults. God is at work to redeem and reconcile lost humanity in a patient and persistent work of grace.

Thankfully, the Kingdom of God is not fully dependent upon our initiative. This does not mean, however, that the call of God to serve for His Kingdom is any less urgent or necessary. We discover, in earnest, that "God's Kingdom shall come and His will shall be done on earth as it is in Heaven", according to His planning, timing and infinite grace. The Apostle Paul spoke of this as he wrote to the church in Rome: ***"It does not, therefore, depend on man's desire or effort, but on the mercy of God."*** (Romans 9:16).

Wonderfully, God welcomes and involves those who respond to His invitation and call to salvation and service. We are called by the Most High to become ambassadors of His grace and truth in Christ. The Gospel of the Kingdom of God is quite simple and yet has profound results: "Repent and believe, for the Kingdom of God is close at hand". Responding in faith to Jesus' invitation will compel and engage His followers to receive the hope that is born of Christ and the new life ignited by the Holy Spirit of God. The Kingdom of God is not far away, it is right before us, and is at work within us, even now as we serve and wait through diligent and vigilant actions of love and mercy.

VISION 3: PROVIDENCE AND AIRPLANES

"Last call for flight 788" blared from the overhead speakers in front of the Detroit flight gate at the Dallas/Fort Worth airport. I had two hours to wait before the next connecting flight would complete my trip back home to the "Motor City". I wondered if it was too late to get on board, or even if they had room. The young lady speaking into the microphone looked at me and asked: "Are you getting on board this flight?" "Well, it all depends; I am scheduled to go on the next flight." "Sir, we have room for you on this flight if you would like to board," the hostess said, "but your luggage will come on the later flight." I prayed about it briefly and felt God's direct affirmation to go ahead. When God gives you directives, be ready for a specific mission. That's often the way the Spirit moves when you live according to a "Kingdom of God" perspective.

Soon I was being led down and up the ramp over to board the plane. I crossed the threshold of the aircraft and looked down the aisle to see many faces gazing in my direction. I considered that I was probably the last person to board. I was wrong. After sitting down in the back in an aisle seat that had an open seat next to me, I looked up to see a fast moving businessman. He knew the layout of the airplane and looked in my direction. He seemed disappointed as he realized that he would sit between me and the person near the window. As he came closer I offered him the aisle seat, but he declined my offer. I'm not sure if it was the "International Ministries" hat I was wearing or if it was something goofy about my appearance that had him anxious. Either way, I believed that this guy had come on this plane as a matter of divine appointment. Through a variety of conversations I realized that while he talked about his children, he did not say a word about his wife. In one topic we discussed the enjoyment of lawn mowing and how the grass in Texas wasn't very green or appreciable like the grass we have in Michigan. In that moment, as I was attentive to wait upon God's leading, the Holy Spirit put a memory and thought into my mind to share. I told him about a riding mower I once had with a motor whose screws vibrated loose because the screw-heads were mounted upside down. With words of application I shared: "Life is like that mower engine. I find I must take time to keep the relationships 'tight', otherwise things will loosen and fall apart." After a slight pause I noted that he was listening, so I continued: "I have learned that marriage and family relationships take constant maintenance and attention, especially in this "upside down" world. If one doesn't watch out, the screws will come completely loose and the engine will need to be rebuilt or replaced." After I had made this observation the man became very quiet. Then after a long three minutes he said, "Yes", "Thank you for sharing that." We didn't have much more of a conversation on the flight after that, but when we landed, even as we taxied up to the terminal, he was quick to call home and talk with his wife. I smiled and prayed: "Thank you God." Of course, I also had called my wife Marilyn and enjoyed hearing her bubbly voice.

One would think that my mission was completed that day. But God works on many more dimensions than we often imagine. After all, God is the ultimate multi-tasker. So when we arrived in Detroit's American Airlines terminal I did not proceed to claim my baggage. I sat down to have dinner in a restaurant and waited in the lobby two hours for the baggage to arrive on the next flight. As I pulled out my laptop to check email, I noticed that there were only two people in the large terminal. Next to the seat where I sat there were a few greeting cards, a pen and a jacket. After a few minutes, a tall casually dressed man in his 40's came and laid his canvas briefcase down carefully as he sat down to write upon his stationary. Eventually we struck up a conversation.

Where are you from I asked? "I live in California", he said. "I am on my way to see family in Virginia". "I'm from Michigan." I said. "I caught an earlier flight back, but now I am waiting here for my baggage to return." "Why were you in California?" he asked with interest. "I was at a convention of churches." Then I added, "My sons went with me but came back home on an earlier flight today." "Did you go anywhere sightseeing when you were out there?" he inquired politely. "Yes, the highlight of our time was a day at Yosemite National Park." Then in my heart I felt God's leading to say more. "The most moving thing happened as we came into view of Yosemite Valley." He perked up, "Yes, I've been there before." "Well, you may recall that as you approach the valley there is a stretch of road where for about 5 seconds you can see the glory and beauty of the El Capitan cliff and Bridal Vail Falls, but then the view is obstructed by a mountain as you wait another 10 minutes in expectation for the view to reappear. After going through a very long tunnel, all of a sudden you see the glorious valley vista fully revealed before your eyes." I could see by now that the man was highly engaged in the story. I continued, "I was not prepared for what I began to feel. It was at that moment, I remembered my father who had brought me there with my family many years ago when I was 13 years old. He died about four years ago, and now in view of this spectacular place I remembered my Dad and felt his nearness in a wonderful way. I felt not only his presence, but the healing presence of God." I looked over to see that this man's eyes were welling up with tears. God's Spirit kept me sharing the story, "Then, an inspiration came to me. In this life we may catch a glimpse of the glory of heaven, and because of our hope, we long to go to the place of God's preparation in heaven. Ultimately, we must trust that someday, through the passage of death, we will come through death's tunnel by God's grace into the vista of the glorious Kingdom of Heaven. In that place of God's Heavenly Kingdom there is an even more beautiful valley where the fountain of life pours forth and we are joined again with those who went before us."

A poignant silence told me that God's presence was strong and that the man was living through a trial. Then he told me, "You have no idea how powerful that story is to me at this moment. My father just died and I am on my way home to be with my family at his memorial service. I am a believer, and just a few years ago my dad became a believer. He made a lot of mistakes, but he came to know Jesus and received the grace of God. The vision you just shared with me has just reaffirmed God's promise of salvation and renewed my hope in His Kingdom to come." We both looked at one another in amazement with a bond of peace that is born through shared understanding. We considered the means by which God worked to allow this divine appointment. By His providential direction, God had encouraged each of us. The inspiration and revelation of God's Kingdom was powerfully present and affirmed through a work of the Holy Spirit. This event served to remind me once again that God is constantly revealing His goodness; He involves us in the purposes and plans of His Kingdom. Oh, and by the way, when I went to check on my luggage, it had actually arrived on the first flight after all. God does have a great sense of humor and timing. God has many reasons for us not to know certain things. His plan in unfolding before us and faith is essential.

When I consider the hand of God at work, I wonder why so many people think of the Kingdom of God as being something either far away, non-existent, or beyond our comprehension. Jesus saw the Kingdom of God much differently than this, and so did the prophets and people of faith who preceded His coming. The vision and teaching that Jesus Christ gave us was both revolutionary and profound, He understood that the Kingdom of God was "at hand". This was particularly true in who He was as the Son of God incarnate, but it was also evident and revealed in Christ's way of living. Indeed, what God has shown us in Jesus Christ is that the Kingdom of God is deeply personal and all-encompassing of life and our existence. Jesus showed humanity that the Kingdom of God is not to be restricted to either place or time. Jesus revealed the truth that God's Kingdom is at once eternal and present, transcendent and immanent. The Kingdom of God is therefore not static, but dynamic, transformative and redemptive.

Participation and citizenship in the Kingdom of God comes, therefore, as an opportunity of grace and as a response of faith. Through faith one may not only acknowledge God, but also receive the life-giving infusion of God's Holy Spirit that establishes the reign of God within one's soul. This reign of God within one's soul dispenses abundant grace and administers forgiveness for salvation. The reign of God imparts life eternal and shines forth the light of God's guiding counsel in Word and Spirit. Because of this counsel, inspiration is available and the study of Holy Scripture is not merely academic. One becomes aware that the "Word", the Bible, is *"God-breathed"* (II Timothy 3:16). The Kingdom of God is understood, therefore, as a powerful reality that transforms people through the authority of God's Living Word, revealed through God's

Son Jesus Christ. Furthermore, God's Son Jesus continues to give the Holy Spirit, and insight into the Scriptures, to believers for the ongoing work of God's Kingdom. The beauty of participating in God's Kingdom is that it unfolds before us as we are given vision, purpose, counsel, direction, patience, faith and joy for living.

Therefore, for those who believe and obey God, there is reward in the continual development and eventual realization of God's Kingdom. However, for those who deny God and His Kingdom, who continue in disbelief and disobedience (even though God gives ample opportunities for faith and obedience, and showers people of doubt with innumerable blessings), to these there will be eventual judgment that is void of the prospect of God's gift of grace in Jesus the Savior. The holiness of God shall not be mocked. No one shall enter the Kingdom of God without faith or upon their own merit. For indeed *"all have sinned and fallen short of the Glory of God"* (Romans 3:23), and only through receiving the gift of God's saving grace in Jesus Christ will anyone be received into the Kingdom of Heaven.

In the fullness of time, God will establish His Kingdom on earth in the coming millennial reign of Jesus Christ. The view of the Kingdom that Jesus taught was simultaneously personal and corporate, intimate and universal. In teaching His disciples to pray, Jesus taught His disciples to trust His Heavenly Father's Sovereign Kingdom plan: *"Thy Kingdom come"* (Matthew 6:10). Jesus also guided his disciples to discover faith and the presence of God's Spirit moving in their souls: *"The kingdom of God does not come with your careful observation, nor will people say, 'Here it is,' or 'There it is,' because the kingdom of God is within you"* (Luke 17:20-21 NIV).

Throughout Scripture, and within life itself, we note that there is an ongoing tension involved with how God's Kingdom is both present and yet is also not completed. Christ has already accomplished a great work of salvation on the cross, yet the full work of salvation in yet to come in the believer's resurrection. Believers receive the blessing of communion with God through prayer and the reception of grace, however believers also experience the dilemma of suffering and pain along with everyone else within this life. There are many tensions or paradoxes that exist in which faith is required. God has sent His Son into the world that we may believe in Him and through faith become citizens who are reconciled to His eternal Kingdom. Still, we live with a

Kingdom that is "already" but is also "not yet". Biblical scholar and theologian George Eldon Ladd wrote:

> "Our problem, then, is found in this threefold fact:
> (1) Some passages of Scripture refer to the Kingdom of God as God's reign.
> (2) Some other passages refer to God's Kingdom as a realm into which we may now enter to experience the blessings of His reign.
> (3) Still other passages refer to a future realm which will come only with the return of our Lord Jesus Christ into which we shall then enter and experience the fullness of His reign." [1]

In every way God's Kingdom is eternally existent because His reign is timeless, confined neither to past, present or future. God's Kingdom is also more than a matter of God's position of sovereignty. God's Kingdom exists in a realm that intersects with our realm of creation in a way that we may experience the blessings that come from God's Kingdom in Heaven. Yet we note that the fallen condition of humanity combined with the existence of evil has brought about a form of bondage, decay, and corruption within the realm of creation. God has therefore put into place a plan of redemption for creation since the fall in the garden. Man, being the crown of God's creation, is destined through God's work of salvation to be brought into the glorious freedom of the coming Kingdom of God. Christ shall come again to establish the fullness of God's redemptive reign. Until then, we are called to participate in God's Kingdom in three ways:

1. Through receiving and proclaiming the Gospel of **salvation** in Jesus Christ.

2. Through living in a compelling way that represents God and shines forth a witness that reveals believers as being living "**signs**" of God's Kingdom.

3. Through faithful and unselfish **service** that grows from God's calling in our lives to love the Lord our God and our neighbor as ourselves. By doing so God will help us bear spiritual fruit for His Kingdom.

The united Lordship of God and of His Son Jesus the Christ is a relational living-reality to those who believe in their hearts and minds. This shared Lordship extends to all the heavens and applies to the ends of this planet earth

---

[1] Ladd, George Eldon. "The Gospel of the Kingdom" Grand Rapids, Eerdmans p. 22

upon which we live. Though there are those who seek to denigrate God and deny His existence, this does not impinge upon His authority and power. God's rule is established from His eternal and unchanging nature of goodness and righteousness. Though all subjects of creation are given freedom, and this freedom allows for creative or variant behavior from God's good and holy will, God's kingdom remains established and secure no matter the choice of the Creator's subjects. God works in and through History to uphold and establish His Kingdom on earth and throughout the heavens. God's keen interest is to dwell in peace and love in our hearts and minds. God calls us to covenant with Him and one another in respectful and fruitful relationships and community.

The reality of sin is not to be quickly dismissed as a psychological or physiological development in man's evolution. The root of sin and evil are spiritual, coming from the disobedience of Satan and man's choice to follow or reject evil's influence. Beginning in the Garden of Eden and over time, the existence of evil and the movement of human corruptibility have allowed for a dynamic drama. God's Kingdom stands in contrast to the temporary principalities of evil and the imperfect kingdoms of man. God's redemptive work is nonetheless consistent and constant. God is at work to reconcile humanity and all affected creation through the work of salvation, this involves bringing justice through the work of judgment. God has ordained His One and only Son, Jesus Christ, to join Him so as to mediate and administer this great work of re-creation and redemption. Through Christ, the Servant-King who obediently went to the cross for our reconciliation and redemption, God established a new covenant relationship for humanity. Ultimately, the prayer Jesus taught His disciples: "Thy Kingdom come, Thy will be done, on earth as it is in Heaven…" will be fulfilled conclusively. The call of God is not for people to wait passively for His Kingdom, but to wait with expectation and involvement, to join in the work of God's Kingdom here and now.

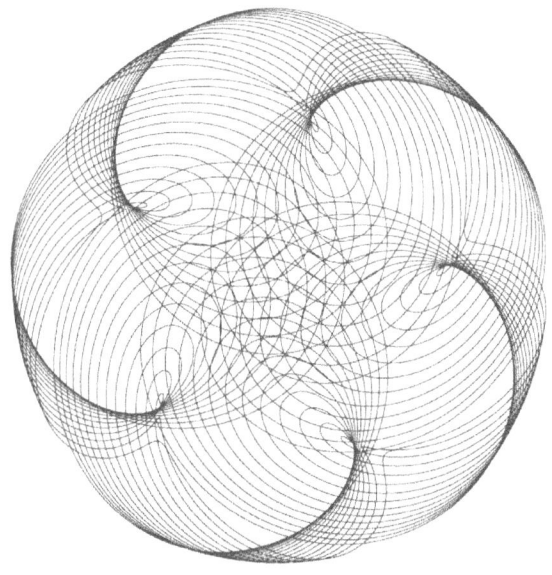

VISION 4: FAITH STEPS TO FOLLOW JESUS

Imagine walking up a long and challenging trail through woods and climbing rocks until your guide brings your group to a vista that opens before you revealing at once both the peril of height and the splendor of vast beauty. The mountain pass you stand upon sweeps down to a lush valley that extends down to a broad plain and a sparkling bright sea and city in the distance. You stand in awe and fear; at once your knees are wobbling between the reality of danger and the ideal of potential. Your faithful guide speaks to you and the group with both excitement and warning. Behold your destination! Have courage, you must take careful steps for we are at the highest point of the trail. You look down to see that you are a few feet away from destruction if you were to fall, yet you are excited with the vision of the encircling mountain range and the valley below. In this moment you must decide to step forward trusting the guide, the alternative would be to shrink back and safely go back the way you came. One way leads to life transformed, the other way to safe retreat and subtle death. In your anxiety, you look to the guide and seize the hope of opportunity that beckons you. The outstretched hand of the guide invites you to set aside your past and your fears. At a pivotal point between reality and hope the decision is to trust the guide and walk by faith. God's Kingdom is before you, the past has taught you to trust the guide, the Good Shepherd and Overseer of your faith and life.

When one has a dream like this, waking up with a mix of feelings, one has the sense that the vision was given for a purpose. When this vision was given to me recently, I recognized that the guide was Jesus Christ our Lord and that He was speaking not only to me, but to others upon the trail, that is, the church as His disciples. His Kingdom vision is before us, we are called to steps of faith that will allow us to follow Jesus into God's grace and glorious Kingdom. The danger is real, but so is the Lord who leads us to take the steps that lead past our perilous fears and sins.

Remember those times in your life when the peril of taking steps of faith was real, yet faith was necessary to move beyond the narrow gap of danger into God's place of goodness and grace. There is a Chinese set of characters for the word "Crisis", it is composed of three symbols. The symbol on the left is "Danger" and the symbol on the right is "Opportunity". The symbol in the middle connects these two and resembles a cross with an upward arrow inside. Could it be that when we look to the cross with an upward point of view of faith that our dangers turn into opportunities? Through faith in Christ we are led to the doorway of truth and grace into a new reality and hope.

The Chinese Symbol for Crisis

Danger   Opportunity

This reality of crisis can be true of the times we face threatening realities that we experience as obstacles, broken relationships, failure, rejection, loneliness, depression, pain, mortality and evil. Jesus came to lead us through those moments of doubt, danger, difficulty and fear. He calls us to keep our focus on Him and take steps that will help us go up, through and beyond the gap/bridge of crisis. The doorway of hope lies beyond the initial danger. Focus upon Christ is what leads us through adversity, danger, temptation or distractions.

A friend of mine, Brad Parrish, was teaching a class on Spiritual Gifts and told a story of visiting the eye doctor. He mentioned that going to the eye doctor was far less threatening than going to the dentist. The eye doctor turned off the lights and asked him to follow His instructions. He told him to look up at the little red light while he shined a bright light into the pupil to examine each eye carefully up close. In the midst of the exam, Brad looked down at the eye doctor and into the bright light. The eye doctor commented, "You looked at me didn't you?" "Yes I did", he confessed. "How much longer will it take for my sight to be restored in that eye?" "About ten minutes or less", the doctor replied. Humbled, Brad had to wait until his retina recovered. In reflection he observed, "Discipleship is like keeping your eye on the red dot. When we don't we can easily be blinded by our own tendency of disobedience."

If we follow Christ's leading we will be able to use our Spiritual Gifts to glorify God, but when we allow ourselves to take our focus off of the red dot (the sacrificial love of God in Christ) we can too easily be blinded by the world or by the critical examination of God as He looks into our souls. In the power of His grace, God can restore and guide our vision.

Overview of the Encounter Experience:

This encounter Bible Study on the Kingdom of God will focus primarily upon the Gospel of Jesus Christ from Matthew along with writings from the Psalms, Isaiah, John, 2 Corinthians and Revelation. The first four chapters will focus upon God as enthroned in majesty, might and mercy. The fifth, sixth, and seventh chapters will focus upon Jesus as the Christ, the promised and anointed Messiah whose Lordship is revealed from Heaven and whose presence brings hope for God's rule of righteousness for humanity. Chapters eight to thirteen follow the path of discovery and discipleship for those who walked with Jesus then, and also for we who trust and obey Jesus Christ now.

Chapters fourteen through seventeen focus on the passion of Jesus, the ministry and service of His death and resurrection, and His call for believers to proclaim and embody the Gospel of His reign until He returns again in power and glory to fulfill God's Kingdom plan on earth.

Warner Sallman: "Christ's Return"

Purpose of this Encounter:

To glorify God and to help further an understanding of the nature and working of God's eternal Kingdom. To encourage people to believe and trust God for salvation in Jesus Christ, become ambassadors of God's Kingdom, and increase in service to God in every aspect of life.

Three Key Principles of "Prelude"; Living as Citizens of God's Kingdom:

1. **Receive salvation** and citizenship in God's Kingdom by faith in the authority and sacrificial love of Jesus Christ. As the Servant King He forgave and ransomed us on the cross, and rose three days later victorious over sin and death.

2. **Become an ambassador (sign)** of God's Kingdom as you follow, grow, and serve the Lord Jesus Christ as disciples.

3. **Give glory to God** the Creator/Father in **service** His Kingdom as ambassadors of reconciliation and agents of righteousness through faith and obedience to Jesus Christ.

Format for each encounter unit:

1. Title, key verse, purpose of study
2. Prelude: (Introduction to the study)
3. Scripture passages and outlines of key passages
4. Exploring the Scriptures
5. Bridging into today
6. Questions for group discussion
7. Closing idea, concluding thought, story or reading

Note: The scriptures cited will come primarily from the
New International Version. (Zondervan Corporation, 1981)

"The Kingdom of God: Salvation, Signs, and Service"
Bible Encounter Outline

Page:	Chapter Title:	Scripture:	
1.	"God is Enthroned"	(Psalm 47; Psalm 48; Matthew 18:1-4)	45
2.	"God is Glorious and Majestic"	(Psalm 8; Psalm 24; Matthew 17:1-5)	61
3.	"God is Mighty and Merciful"	(Psalm 29, 33, and 61; Matthew 18:10-14)	75
4.	"God is Building His Kingdom"	(Isaiah 62; Revelations 3:11-13)	89
5.	"Ambassadors of the King"	(Matthew 3:1-12; II Corinthians 5:17-21)	103
6.	"The Kingdom of God is Near"	(Matthew 4:8-17; Psalm 84)	113
7.	"Seek A Kingdom of Righteousness"	(Matthew 5:17-20; Psalm 72)	123
8.	"Please God in Secret Service"	(Matthew 6:1-4; II Corinthians 5:9-10)	133
9.	"Treasure the Kingdom of God"	(Matthew 6:19-24; Psalm 62)	141
10.	" Judgment in God's Kingdom"	(Matthew 7:1-12; 20:1-16 and Psalm 67)	153
11.	"The Great Mercy of the King "	(Matthew 8:1-17; Psalm 57)	163
12.	"The Great Forgiveness of the King"	(Matthew 9:1-8; 18:21-35; Psalm 32)	171
13.	"Service in the Name of the King"	(Matthew 10:1-42; Psalm 145)	183
14.	"The King Who Suffered"	(Matthew 21:33-46; Psalm 22)	195
15.	"The King Who is Victorious"	(John 20:1-18; Psalm 91)	205
16.	"Invitation to God's Kingdom Party"	(Matthew 28:18-20; 22:1-14, Psalm 93)	215
17.	"The Return of the King "	(Revelation 1:1-8; 22:7 Psalm 96)	229

1
GOD IS ENTHRONED

(Psalm 47; Psalm 48; Matthew 18:1-4)

> **Key verse:**
> *How awesome is the LORD Most High, the great King over all the earth!* - Psalm 47:2

Purpose of Study:

The focus of this chapter's study is the awesome majesty of God and His enthronement over the entire universe. The Kingdom of God began alongside of creation as God exercised His Sovereignty by implementing His providential and great master plan. The pre-incarnate Christ, the beloved and only begotten Son of God, was with God the Father and the Holy Spirit from the beginning of creation. Intelligent beings within creation are designed to worship God the Creator, Christ Jesus His Son the Redeemer and the Holy Spirit. Worship of God is the most appropriate and natural response man can give.

Prelude

Praise God for His Sovereignty! God is enthroned over the universe! Words of praise and adoration fill our formal and spontaneous worship, affirming the attributes of God, the presence, power, and covenant of faith that God initiates and maintains. Deep within the soul of humanity there is something life-giving that God brings into focus and births into reality through His Holy Spirit. The first PRELUDE to God's Kingdom is WORSHIP. "To worship God" means "to give ultimate worth to God." Worship of the true living God leads us into a supernatural experience of communion and transformation. Given this definition of worship, and the malaise of our corrupted spiritual condition, we have a clue as to why a part of our nature chooses hate, war, destruction, violence, greed, prejudice, perversion, vice, oppression, injustice, and inequality. The reason for our corrupted sinful state is that we shifted worship away from God and toward the elevation of self or something else other than the true Creator/God. The fall in the Garden has led humanity to a severe consequence, a pollution that only God's imparted grace can cure and that genuine worship alone can purify.

How long will God allow evil to have a form of temporal reign? More specifically, we speculate upon how the persistence of sinfulness makes it more difficult for people to believe in God and respect His sovereignty. The free will that our Creator has granted to all humanity makes for a dynamic interplay and creative challenge. Still, we are loved and created with potential good, made in the image of God (Genesis 1:26-27). How then does free will work in respect to the reality of the Sovereignty of God? What is God revealing through the allowance of free will, be it good or evil? Does this also reveal something important about the nature of God and His Kingdom? How do humans, angels, and all creatures great and small relate to the authority of God and His Kingdom? Since God's Kingdom includes we who are subject to His reign, what is our involvement or responsibility? What are the consequences for those who deny God's sovereignty or disrespect His authority? What are the rewards for those who seek God's will, consult His Word and follow His Holy Spirit?

Further questions reflect the need to seek, find, and know the nature of a God/Creator who is both intimately personal and infinitely powerful. Could it be that God is both mighty and merciful? Could it be that God is enthroned above us and yet desires to be enthroned within us by our faith? Could it be that the dynamic nature of God's Sovereignty speaks to the realization that His Kingdom is not imposed, but is implicitly interwoven into the fabric of all existence? The answers to these questions are revealed to us when we respond in faith to God's presence. God's truth and grace lead us as we humble ourselves to follow through on His ongoing invitation to communion, friendship, faith experience and a response of active obedience to His pervasive and persuasive Lordship.

The witness of those to whom God revealed Himself to in the Bible (and since then) has been to affirm the existence of God, His loving nature, righteousness, holiness and majesty. A comprehensive picture includes the primary moving force of the King and Creator of the Universe bringing life, hope and redemption to reveal, expand and refine His eternal Kingdom. God is the Creator/King who has set forth a redemptive plan. Therefore, God has not only created us, God desires to reconcile us and save us from our sin, redeeming the very masterpiece that was scarred and broken by willful sin. Jesus said: *"Unless you change and become like little children, you will not be able to enter the Kingdom of Heaven"* (Matthew 18:3). In a very personal way, God is to be honored and enthroned by people who commit their hearts by faith to glorify and serve God and His Kingdom through their actions.

Worshipping God involves the synthesis of inquiry, devotion, sacrifice, service, discovery and knowledge. Through a worshipful perspective God's Kingdom can then become a more vividly expressed reality, not only within our hearts and minds, but also within the sphere of life's relationships and responsibilities we are given to influence. Participation in the Kingdom of God requires faith and trust in Jesus Christ, God's Son. Jesus said, *"I am the way, truth and life, no one comes to the Father except through me"* (John 14:7). How well we relate to God's sovereignty, God's Son Jesus and the Lord's invitation to allow His reign to be manifest in and through our lives, is where startling variance exists among even those who claim to have faith. While problems arise because of man's rebellious nature, the hope of God is given in the form of His covenant and promises. Like Abraham who looked out among the stars of the night and heard the voice of God speak to Him, so too we may inherit eternal blessing and serve with the hope and promise of God's eternal Kingdom.

The Kingdom of God was a key reality within the experience and history of the people of Israel, and consequently was a predominant theme of the Old and New Testaments of the Bible. Kings and rulers discovered first-hand that there is a God who moves and acts to intervene above man's own temporal rule and authority. The sovereign Creator God holds all people accountable, giving individuals and nations the choice to freely believe or rebel. Even with this freedom, the plans of God and His Kingdom cannot ultimately be thwarted, and God's sovereign justice cannot be avoided. In the fullness of time, the presence and working of God's Kingdom gave rise to the intervention and incarnation of God's Son Jesus Christ, born of the "root of Jesse" in the human lineage of King David. Jesus, therefore, came to fulfill and reveal God's Kingdom plan.

Jesus began by preaching the good news of the Kingdom of God as being "at hand". Jesus' was sent to love, teach and suffer as the Messiah who perfectly reveals God's truth and grace, His Lordship is designed to reign within human hearts. This mission was established through the Church and extends to a future time when Christ will eventually return in glory and power to be enthroned over all the people and nations and creatures of the earth.

While there is a great deal of speculation surrounding the details of how God will establish His Kingdom through Christ's second coming, the reality and promise of God's present and coming Kingdom is secure. Because Jesus saves, one need not speculate whether faith in Jesus Christ can qualify them for citizenship in God's Kingdom. However, over-speculation about Eschatology (the study of the end times and the coming of God's Kingdom) can sometimes distract and disengage believers from currently living-out the principles of God's Kingdom right now. Jesus preached with an urgency of the Kingdom of God as He began His ministry. This urgency should indwell all who realize that God is enthroned, and that He has a book of life where all of what we do is known, and Christ's very word of life and grace can be written above and alongside our names. Salvation involves a process, a journey of trusting in the Lord and His Kingdom plan.

The reality of accountability before our Creator/King should inspire humility and commitment because we realize that our very lives shall come before Christ's judgment seat.

> [9] So we make it our goal to please him, whether we are at home in the body or away from it. [10] For we must all appear before the judgment seat of Christ, that each one may receive what is due him for the things done while in the body, whether good or bad.   - **2 Corinthians 5:9-10 (NIV)**

Jesus called us to participate in sharing the good news of God's Kingdom, this call to become faithful and Spirit-filled participants will change our worldview, and in turn, our actions. While a change of worldview is important, it still does not address the matter of corruption within one's soul or society. This is why salvation is needed, and why God has provided His Son as Savior and Lord. In the midst of humanity's struggle for survival, meaning, and purpose there is an underlying search for something satisfying, a deep longing for spiritual and physical transformation. God's promise is fulfilled in Jesus Christ, through His life, death and resurrection. Jesus revealed that the Kingdom of God is "at hand" by embodying grace and truth. The very presence and working of God is intended to lead people to open their hearts to believe, be transformed by grace and then to serve with faith to trust in God's words of loving promise and truth.

Beyond our own struggles with sin and battles with evil, we must trust that God is greater and that His Sovereign reign will change us. Those who believe are being remade in God's righteousness, as His children, all within the realm of a Kingdom that has no end. God knows all about us, our struggles and heartaches. There are times we find it difficult to understand or believe this, especially when facing tragedy and loss or when dealing with illness or depression. God does not leave us; He calls us to grow in faith and love. Trusting the very presence of God's anointed Son, Jesus the Christ, is essential to fulfillment and calling within God's Kingdom.

One weekday in early January at church I was nicely interrupted by the man who runs the school release Bible class for children. He asked if I could help chaperone the older elementary children. I walked over to the school and escorted the children over to the church by foot (in Quincy the school was just a block away from the church). I watched him work with the children as he introduced the Bible memory verse "Glory to God in the Highest, and on earth, peace, good will toward men" (Luke 2:14). While he was finishing up, he had children come up one at a time to read and then recite this verse. They had a difficult time remembering. The first one recalled the Luke reference, "Luke 2:14…umm…", but she could hardly remember what words to start with as she began "Glory… in the highest… on earth, peace…" Then another child tried to help as she said: "Luke 2:14, peace on earth, and good will to all." Several children eventually did get it right with further instruction, but the part that they seemed to find difficult to remember and state was "Glory to God in the highest". The point was that "God" was missing from their recitations. I would have thought that this may have been more familiar to the children right after Christmas as the proclamation of the angels to the shepherds. But then again, I wondered if the story of Christ's birth had been as well told and repeated as I had assumed. In reflection, as I walked with the children back to their school, I thought of how this very statement "Glory to God in the highest" is crucial. Either we join the angels and creation in giving glory to God at Jesus' birth or we deny the opportunity and dismiss the invitation. So often we end up glorifying something else, or even ourselves, in place of God and His most direct and personal revelation. Too often we as humanity violate the first of God's Ten Commandments given to Moses and Israel (Deuteronomy 6:5), and we negate the commandment of Christ to *"Love the Lord our God with all our heart, soul, and mind and to love our neighbor as ourselves"* (Mark 12:30). The reason peace on earth is fragile and good will toward fellow humanity is inconsistent is due to the break in our relationship with God. Our condition and relationships will change when the priority of giving "glory to God in the highest" is foremost. Children will understand this when adults live out their worship in lives that glorify God. True and lasting peace and goodness is God's design for our redemption and restoration. God's beloved Son Jesus was given and offered for all the people of this world. God's personal invitation through Christ the Lord is to "repent and believe" in God's Kingdom that is "at hand" (Matthew 4:17). The essence of life is to give worth to our creator, this elemental factor is so often missing.

That same day (when the older children came to our church for release Bible class) there was a boy who was not feeling well in his stomach. He was afraid to call his mother because the last time he did she was very mad with him. I prayed with him and then I said: "Talk with your mother about how you are feeling, if she is upset with you then just tell her "Mom, I love you."" The boy perked up and smiled. I encouraged him to consider what his mother might be going through, and to forgive his mother if he needed to. In the midst of this I realized my limitations; I was not going to be able to do much more than give the boy encouragement to believe and put his faith into action. Many times God calls us to believe and trust Him, and put our faith into action. Encouraging others involves genuine faith and hope. God allows us and others space to work things out. His Kingdom reign is not absent in the midst of our seeking and struggles. In fact, His reign is working itself out in our lives and in the lives of those for whom we are to encourage.

Some years ago, I had blood tests done to check how I was doing in my fight with Non-Hodgkin's Lymphoma. The doctor noticed that I had an elevated level of certain proteins that are associated with my type of cancer. Perhaps my time of being in remission was over, I thought. He explained that eventually this type of cancer returns, so he ordered CT scans, and an MRI for nagging pain and dizziness that I was feeling in my head. Several weeks later the test was completed and the results were in. The finding was that my cancer had not resumed, but that I had something rare in my brain, "Arnold Chiari Malformation". This condition is caused by there not being enough room in the back of the skull; the result is that the brain pushes out from the cerebellum into an area where it partially blocks the flow of spinal fluid at the brain stem. The symptoms sometimes include dizziness, imbalance, vertigo, nausea, neck aches and fatigue. I was talking with my brother Paul about this (he is also a pastor) and we speculated if this "pain in the neck" was from many years of dealing with people in pastoral ministry. We laughed, but then I remarked "I know God will help me deal with this and will give me strength."

God helps us in these times of adversity. When we seek to advance the Kingdom of God we often are met with opposition and obstacles. In those moments we deal with pain, limitations and anxiety we also recognize that Satan wants to discourage or derail us just as he tried to distract and discourage Jesus and His disciples. In life's challenges we are called to trust that God is sovereign, all knowing, and all able to make us stronger through the trials and troubles. All the more, faith in God brings us victory and builds the character and integrity of God's Kingdom within us, and even through us. A malformation in the brain, a cancer, a limitation, an illness, a weakness or whatever imperfection it is that is within us cannot ultimately deter the formative work of Christ and the Spirit of God if we are open and willing to be healed and changed.

God's Kingdom is Infinite and Intimate

Have you ever wondered how big the universe is when looking up at the stars at night? Then, looking down at the sand on a beach you realize how many grains there are. God has created an awesome universe, and has even given us the ability to speculate upon the wonders and beauty that we behold. We grow to appreciate the intricacies and mechanisms of what He has created. Snowflakes, autumn colored leaves, the patterned feathers on a bird, the soft fur on an animal, the many interrelated organs that function together in our human body, the various habitats with their complexity of life upon this earth, the mind-bending distances just within our galaxy, and the billions of other galaxies. The whole universe gives evidence to the intelligence revealed in God's creation. When considering how all of this is interrelated, that there is structure, definition, and beauty to what we see individually and collectively, it is then by faith we may come realize that God is revealing something about Himself and His Kingdom. God is enthroned and affirms His creation by saying "It is good", then affirms our worth as created in His image by saying "It is very good".

We affirm that God did not simply make us as machines. We have a relational and personal connection to His creative order and plan of redemption. God's Kingdom is not like the lifeless models of reality that take purpose and beauty out of the equation. Such mechanistic theories cram in evolutionary speculations like "random selection" or the "spontaneous generation of life" as if there is no work of creation or intelligent designer. Contrary to such a mindless muddle of meaningless mush, God's creative order brought forth a world that He made for His children and all creation to enjoy and find meaning in. This is not a virtual world, but an actual Kingdom wherein our own existence is authenticated through communion with God and one another. God's Kingdom is a reality that includes everything and allows for freedom of thought and choice, while still maintaining cohesiveness and virtue. God's Kingdom is big enough to allow for doubt and skepticism, yet holds all people into accountability of thought and action.

Through the adventure of living, God's design is that people can find answers if they genuinely seek the truth. God is always revealing His truth. God's creative work and nature are bigger than we can imagine, and still we can use our empirical tools and scientific techniques to observe the patterns in life in which God communicates His intimacy, imagination, provision and infinite personal care. God is constantly and consistently revealing Himself to us, and wooing us to understand not only His love but also His Kingdom plan that shall redeem us from sin's destructiveness and the temporal existence of evil.

God's Kingdom has been existent and evident through people of faith in both the Old and New Testaments of Scripture. Yet the ultimate prophecy and promise of God is for His Kingdom to be manifested upon the earth in a way where evil is fully defeated and sin is completely overcome. The fulfillment of God's Kingdom on earth was, and is, and shall be, through Jesus Christ the Messiah, the Servant King.

> God's reign expresses itself in different stages through redemptive history. Therefore, men may enter into the realm of God's reign in its several different stages through redemptive history. Therefore, men may enter into the realm of God's reign in its several stages of manifestation and experience the blessings of His reign in differing degrees. God's Kingdom is the realm of the Age to Come, popularly called heaven; then we shall realize the blessings of His Kingdom (reign) in the perfection of their fullness. But the Kingdom is here now. There is a realm of spiritual blessing into which we may enter today and enjoy in part, in reality the blessings of God's Kingdom reign." [2]

Scripture Passages
(Psalm 47; Psalm 48; Matthew 18:1-4)

PSALM 47

For the director of music. Of the Sons of Korah. A psalm.

[1] Clap your hands, all you nations;
   shout to God with cries of joy.
[2] How awesome is the LORD Most High,
   the great King over all the earth!
[3] He subdued nations under us,
   peoples under our feet.
[4] He chose our inheritance for us,
   the pride of Jacob, whom he loved. Selah
[5] God has ascended amid shouts of joy,
   the LORD amid the sounding of trumpets.
[6] Sing praises to God, sing praises;
   sing praises to our King, sing praises.
[7] For God is the King of all the earth;
   sing to him a psalm of praise.
[8] God reigns over the nations;
   God is seated on his holy throne.
[9] The nobles of the nations assemble
   as the people of the God of Abraham,
for the kings of the earth belong to God;
   he is greatly exalted.

I. God's Throne is Exalted
(Psalm 47:1-9)

A. Adoration before God's Throne (1-2)
B. Thanksgiving before God's Throne (3-4)
C. Praise before God's Throne (5-9)
 1. God is present (5)
 2. God is praised in songs (6-7)
 3. God is proclaimed as reigning (8-9)

---

[2] Ladd, George Eldon, "The Gospel of the Kingdom" p. 22-23.

PSALM 48

A song. A psalm of the Sons of Korah.

¹ Great is the LORD, and most worthy of praise,
 in the city of our God, his holy mountain.
² It is beautiful in its loftiness,
 the joy of the whole earth.
Like the utmost heights of Zaphon is Mount Zion, the city of the Great King.
³ God is in her citadels;
 he has shown himself to be her fortress.
⁴ When the kings joined forces,
 when they advanced together,
⁵ they saw [her] and were astounded;
 they fled in terror.
⁶ Trembling seized them there,
 pain like that of a woman in labor.
⁷ You destroyed them like ships of Tarshish shattered by an east wind.

⁸ As we have heard,
 so have we seen
in the city of the LORD Almighty,
 in the city of our God:
 God makes her secure forever. Selah
⁹ Within your temple, O God,
 we meditate on your unfailing love.
¹⁰ Like your name, O God, your praise reaches to the ends of the earth;

 your right hand is filled with righteousness.
¹¹ Mount Zion rejoices,
 the villages of Judah are glad
 because of your judgments.
¹² Walk about Zion, go around her, count her towers,
¹³ consider well her ramparts, view her citadels,
 that you may tell of them to the next generation.
¹⁴ For this God is our God for ever and ever;
 he will be our guide even to the end.

II. God's Reign is Manifested
(Psalm 48:1-14)

A. In His Holy City (1-3)

B. In the strength of His Holy City (4-8)

C. In His Temple in the Holy City (9)

D. Throughout the Earth and to all people (10)

E. In the New Jerusalem and Israel. (11-14)

Matthew 18:1-4

¹ At that time the disciples came to Jesus and asked, "Who is the greatest in the kingdom of heaven?" ² He called a little child and had him stand among them. ³ And he said: "I tell you the truth, unless you change and become like little children, you will never enter the kingdom of heaven. ⁴ Therefore, whoever humbles himself like this child is the greatest in the kingdom of heaven.

III. God's Kingdom is Humbling
(Matthew 18:1-4)

A. God humbles the proud (1-2)
B. God changes the humble (3)
C. God rewards faith and humility (4)

Exploring the Scriptures

The two Psalms here (Psalm 47 and 48) are both songs of God's enthronement from the "sons of Korah". These men were temple servants who led praise and singing but were also like porters in serving those who came to offer their meat sacrifices in the temple. It is interesting to note how the sons of Korah were called to approach both their practical duties of preparing sacrifices and their inspirational call of offering praise. Both of these duties were sacred acts, each being a "prelude" to worship. God used these humble servants to prepare and inspire God's people toward the meaningful sacrifice of prayer, offering, praise and adoration. The message is one of preparation of one's heart and reflection upon one's need prior to exaltation of God and praise in affirming God's presence in the Holy Temple of Jerusalem. The emphasis here is that God's greatness and grace must be sought and relied upon within God's covenant of love ("hesed") and peace ("shalom"). Through humility we are rightly positioned to perceive the magnitude of the Lord's kingdom and the wonder of His might and mercy. It is then, with such preparations and perspective that we may partake fully in the spectrum of petition and praise in worship that honors God's powerful sovereignty over all creation, over the earth and over our lives.

God manifested His presence throughout biblical history and has continued to manifest His presence. While this is true, there is a greater manifestation yet to come that is spoken of through the prophets and psalmists. The full manifestation of God's Kingdom shall be fulfilled in the second coming of Jesus Christ in a future millennial reign. These Psalms were written to give the people of Israel, and believers from all nations, hope for the eventual full manifestation of God's Kingdom on earth. Because there have been, and will continue to be, counterfeits who will claim to be the Christ, it is important for us to take note of what the real Kingdom of God will be like when the Lord returns. Jerusalem will be the center of Jesus' reign upon the earth, and all nations will come and stand in awe of the Lord within the great New Jerusalem, the City of Zion. In Psalms 47 and 48, praise that began in Israel's history will continue until the future manifestation of Christ Jesus and His rule upon the earth. These Psalms prepare us for that event, reign and future worship. There is an exciting, yet humbling, sense of awe. It won't be the current Jerusalem structure with political leaders taking the reins. The location will be the same, but the city itself will come down out of heaven from God. Jesus will reign in power and glory. There will be a radical change upon the earth and even in the heavens, such that all things shall be made new.

Revelation 21:1-5 (NIV)
[1] Then I saw a new heaven and a new earth, for the first heaven and the first earth had passed away, and there was no longer any sea. [2] I saw the Holy City, the new Jerusalem, coming down out of heaven from God, prepared as a bride beautifully dressed for her husband. [3] And I heard a loud voice from the throne saying, "Now the dwelling of God is with men, and he will live with them. They will be his people, and God himself will be with them and be their God. [4] He will wipe every tear from their eyes. There will be no more death or mourning or crying or pain, for the old order of things has passed away." [5] He who was seated on the throne said, "I am making everything new!" Then he said, "Write this down, for these words are trustworthy and true." [6] He said to me: "It is done. I am the Alpha and the Omega, the Beginning and the End. To him who is thirsty I will give to drink without cost from the spring of the water of life.

The wonder of it all is that God takes a personal interest in redeeming those who place their trust in Him. God is planning an extensive overhaul and renewal of the universe and earth. We of faith are being prepared for this, much like a bride prepares for her groom. God is planning to make His dwelling place visible and tangible upon the earth. After God Himself wipes away our tears and takes away our pain, we will open our eyes to a brand new order where everything is made new! This is God's promise and our peace. Our preparation is to read the words that were written down and then live them out with faith that trusts the promises of God. Our readiness becomes complete as we worship and serve God through drinking from the truth and grace of Jesus who is the "Spring of living water". To complete God's work and will of redemption and reconciliation we share the good news of Jesus with the world. Salvation is right at hand in Christ, and our worship and service for Him and His Kingdom begins, and is made complete, by faith and obedience.

The passage from Matthew 18:4 is a reminder that we often approach God's Kingdom from faulty assumptions, expectations and desires. Jesus addressed the question of "Who will be the greatest in God's Kingdom?" with a gentle, yet firm, critique of most people's presumptions. By placing a child before them, Jesus reminded them that before God they are to become as little children, free of pretense and open to the truth. The Kingdom of God is not like the kingdoms or systems of inequality of this corrupted world where position and title are abused. Jesus taught that what matters to God is that we would be willing to humble ourselves to trust God, let go of selfish ambition, serve others and be faithful to God's guidance. The Kingdom of God manifests itself now through believers who are willing to follow Jesus as they die to selfishness; this is the ultimate expression of devotion, compassion and trust where Christ is best represented to the world in faith. The renewal of God's Holy Spirit leads us toward genuine spiritual transformation. The living water that Jesus gives us through faith and obedience springs up. Salvation is received, worked through, and made real in Christ-like witness.

Bridging into Today

Praise and adoration of God the Father, Jesus Christ the Son and the Holy Spirit (now and in the coming Kingdom of God on earth) gives believers joy, great hope and encouraging vision for the future. God's Kingdom will be a greater reality in the return of Christ Jesus the King. What will it be like when

He returns to reign from within the New Jerusalem some day? The worship of Israel in the past was inspired with a vision and hope for the eventual reign of God on earth in a tangible and transforming way. God has come to us in Christ, He has called people to acknowledge and experience the righteous rule of Jesus internally. Through faith put into actions, believers are to live in preparation (as a "prelude"), trusting that the righteous rule of Jesus shall come to transform the earth upon His return. Christ Jesus shall establish the fullness of God's Kingdom above all nations, principalities and powers.

Jesus is the Messiah; the King who gave himself for God's lost children throughout the earth. Jesus came to first establish God's Kingdom in the hearts and souls of all who humble themselves in faith and obedience. Jesus will also come again to establish the fullness of God's Kingdom upon the earth in every respect.

Evidence of God's Kingdom is seen through the lives of those who are willing to approach God with the "faith of a child". Manipulative politicians and false prophets will make promises of bringing peace or prosperity through man-directed means. One illustration of this came recently as a pastor had a stranger knock on his door. They went on to tell the pastor about how a certain political party and many others in high office were part of a communist plot to take over America. This person went on to tell the pastor that the reason this was succeeding was because religious leaders were not doing enough to inform people of this conspiracy. The pastor then told this person that the solution to the world's problems will not come through political means, or by the vigilance of those protecting freedoms, but that the ultimate hope for the world is the return and reign of Jesus Christ. The person at the door then told him, "But even Jesus turned over the tables in the temple in anger. If people just sit on their Bibles things are going to get worse and God won't be happy with that." The pastor thanked the person for trying to warn him and then stated: "Jesus' approach was humble, and besides we are not just sitting on our Bibles, we are seeking to live the way Jesus lived and do those things that represent His Kingdom. The fullness of His Kingdom will come only upon His return." After the person left, the pastor considered how worked up people can get when they are on a crusade.

History has shown that after centuries of concerns and crusades by many well-meaning people the underlying tendency of humanity has been to try to force the hand of God. Much can be learned from those whose Christian faith was exhibited in non-violent actions of trust in God. Leo Tolstoy, a Russian believer in the mid 1800's, witnessed the brutality of Russian Czars and landlords. He wrote a book, "The Kingdom of God is Within You."[3] His plea was for Christians in Russia to stop using force and violence, for believers to stop wielding swords and guns. His point is still relevant, especially as centuries later the witness of Christians has been compromised by violent tendencies and compromising alliances with corrupted principalities and powers. Without deep faith in God, the kind that produces patience and a perspective of discerning God's work and timing for His Kingdom (both present and coming), believers err in judgment and compromise their witness.

Jesus gives the promise of the Kingdom of God's inheritance to those who believe and follow Him through humility and trust. To receive this promise we must also trust and follow the Lord as our Good Shepherd into the "promised land". This requires acknowledging our need to be led and redeemed by God's one and only anointed and appointed Son, and then through Christ we are called to trust in God's sufficiency of grace. Taking the hand of Jesus that leads us, and being open and responsive to the Holy Spirit, we can follow, bless others and be blessed. The secret of greatness in God's Kingdom is not found in how clever or creative we can be, neither will it be fulfilled in how observant or analytical we may be about the times and troubles we note are preceding Christ's return. What God desires for us, and what will be rewarded or granted through grace alone, is found through trust and obedience to God our Father, Jesus Christ the Lord and the Holy Spirit. The community of trust within the Trinity of God invites us into communion, leads us to faith and inspires appropriate action.

Questions for Group Discussion

1. What makes for a good king, national leader, president or mayor?

---

[3] Leo Tolstoy, "The Kingdom of God is Within You" 1894. Written in Germany as Tolstoy sought to distinguish the true church from the state compromised Russian Orthodox Church.

2. How have kings, governmental leaders, or corporate leaders abused their power?

3. What hope did Israel share with the world about the reign of God in Psalms 47-48?

4. What is the role of praise within the community of believers and within daily life according to Psalms 47 and 48?

5. In what ways did Jesus humble His disciples? How are we humbled to be more childlike in God's presence? Remember a time of prayer or praise, help or healing.

Closing Idea

The more one believes in God's Kingdom reign, the more their faith vision is improved in order to discover the reality that God's Kingdom is "at hand" and "at work'. Furthermore, as one grows in faith their desire for service in God's Kingdom will increase. Life has lasting fulfillment and meaning in connection to God's existence and revealed care, this is seldom a promise for more comfort and ease. People who grow in grace and Christ's peace will likewise increase in expressions of gratitude to God. The sacrifice of praise will lead to a "costly grace" in which life is purposefully being transformed by God as we consistently choose to love the Lord and others by celebrating His redeeming power and choosing His righteous will. This will mean putting to death our corrupted selves, the sinful nature. Then it is that we grow spiritually and relationally deeper to live with a song in our hearts that the world will listen to. The call and challenge is to let your voice and faith expression ring strongly with gentleness, patience, gratitude, appreciation, respect and kind joy. This is how one's life becomes a melody of love, a PRELUDE of God's Kingdom.

Consider doing something that is outside of your comfort and will require a measure of sacrifice. Pray about finding God's peace in the midst of doing His will or acting your faith out in a radical kind of compassion, forgiveness or mercy.

2

GOD IS GLORIOUS AND MAJESTIC

(Psalm 8; Psalm 24; Matthew 17:1-5)

> ## Key verse:
> ⁵ While he was still speaking, a bright cloud enveloped them, and a voice from the cloud said, "This is my Son, whom I love; with him I am well pleased. Listen to him!"   Matthew 17:5

Purpose of study

Chapter two will consider how God calls people into communion and worship. This study will explore the implications of two psalms (Psalm 8 and 24) that emphasize the importance of people beholding and proclaiming the glory and majesty of God. God calls people into His presence. God calls people to affirm His name and qualities. His children then discover the life-altering power of praising their Father God as the Sovereign ruler and redeemer over all creation. The rise of faith in God leads people into life-changing experiences and encounters. From the awareness of being upon "holy ground", and with a sense of wonder and hope, the responsive expression of God's children is Spirit-filled praise and adoration. Genuine worship will lead us to confessions of repentance and joy. In those moments of profound personal and corporate worship, God's Kingdom is manifested. The very Lordship of Jesus Christ is revealed. Believers affirm Christ by responding in faith, receiving God's grace, heeding Christ's call, embracing God's word of truth, humbling themselves for healing and preparing their hearts for a ministry of transforming love.

Prelude

The people of Israel in the Old Testament spoke glowingly of their encounters with God. Moses wrote of the "burning bush" (Exodus 2 and 3) and of being invited by God to take his sandals off and step onto holy ground and into the Lord's holy presence. God had touched down upon the earth and so Moses was called to remove anything that would desensitize him to God's footsteps and voice that resonated upon the ground of his being. Moses responded to God's call to worship and service for his people saying: "Here I am, Lord". It is interesting to note that God did not appear to Moses until the King of Egypt had died and the time for Moses' mission had come. Moses was told by the Lord (whose name Yahweh meant "I am that I am"), that He had heard the voice and cry of His people. Before God would call Moses to deliver the people of Israel, God called Moses to come and experience the Sovereign Glory and Majesty of the Lord in worship. The worship Moses experienced was humbling, life changing and empowering. Later, after Moses had returned to Egypt and God worked to deliver Israel from bondage and rescue them from Pharaoh's army, God would lead them to this same mountain where Moses had worshipped before. Moses could testify through His praise how God had fulfilled His promise and plan. Worship for Moses preceded and concluded a chapter of God's amazing work. So too, God calls us to prepare for His work through worship and to celebrate His work through worship. In this sense worship is both "prelude" and "gratitude".

The Psalms arise from worship and are inspired as people consider the Sovereignty and Majesty of God. In their oral tradition the people of Israel would recount the worship inspired experiences of Abraham, Isaac, Jacob,

Joseph, Moses, Miriam, David, Elijah, Isaiah, Ezekiel and Daniel. From this great tradition of worship, believers in the New Testament likewise gave witness through the gospels of their Divine encounter and experiences with Jesus Christ, the Son of God. His teaching and miracles gave evidence to His identity, ministry and Kingdom authority. Consistently and compassionately, Jesus revealed a glimpse of His Divine nature and Kingship through His incarnate presence. In Matthew 17:1-5, God the Father/Creator spoke to Peter, James and John directly telling them that Jesus was His Son. While Jesus was transfigured before them, with Moses and Elijah at Jesus' side, God spoke with endearment and endorsement about His Son Jesus to the disciples. Indeed, God's beloved Son was worthy of being worshipped along with the Heavenly Father. Because Jesus is worthy of our praise and worship, we must trust that He is also able to reveal Himself to people around us. Jesus is able to disclose His Word and presence independent of man's efforts, but most often the Lord chooses to work in and through His disciples, inspiring and empowering believers through the Holy Spirit by the gifts, grace and truth God imparts.

One day I was visiting a family in the hospital where an elderly woman's husband was dying. The nurses and doctors had spoken with the family about the patient's guarded condition. In praying, I asked the Lord to reveal His will and grace to the family and their loved one. That afternoon, the patient managed to open his eyes, squeeze his wife's hands, and move his right foot. In the past, his wife told me, he had very little interest in matters of faith and religion. Now, however, with his fragile condition and with an open heart, he responded positively to every word of truth from Christ and promise of Scripture that he heard. He opened his eyes, though they had been closed shut for a few days; he focused with interest upon each person. With tears and a smile faintly upon his brow and cheeks, joy was conveyed. Though there was a tube in his mouth and his hands were restricted, yet he could still move his right foot. That afternoon in the hospital, with his wife and son at his side, he responded by tapping his toe in affirmation to the questions I asked him. He was indicated that he had entrusted his life to Jesus Christ as King and Savior.

The next morning the Critical Care Unit called me to meet with the family again as the patient's condition had worsened. The wife of the patient spoke to me as I came in to the room: "Pastor, the Lord woke me up last night with a vision. I saw Jesus walking in heaven in bright glory amidst God the Father. The Lord Jesus came up to me and touched me and told me that it was alright now to let go of my husband and that it was now time for him to come home." She went on to tell me that right next to Jesus there was a dove and that it looked like one of her husband's mourning doves that he had raised and that had recently died. As she continued to describe her vision of Jesus in heaven she told me how beautiful, bright and glorious Jesus appeared and how much peace she felt. She affirmed that she was now ready to trust her husband over to the care of Jesus who would bring him to heaven.

That afternoon, with continued reading from the Scriptures (John 14, Romans 8, 2 Corinthians 4 and 5, and Psalms 121 and 23); the husband responded enthusiastically by moving his right foot with every verse. With every meaningful truth that he heard from God's Word it was as if a deep chord was struck within him. His soul walked upon the tender trail of prayer, guided by God's word of promise, praise and proclamation. Though weak in body, he listened and his soul danced lightly with a willing heart. In that day of divine grace and providence he took a giant step of faith into the spiritual dimension that knows no bound of gravity. By faith his soul received the graceful hand of the Great Shepherd. Once lost, now found, this stray was led word by word and step by step over the gap that spans between us and God. Upon these moments of grace, a journey was secured in simple faith and responsive joy. Together we were treading on holy ground. Christ the Lord was there. The Savior's ministry was complete as this man finished life with the promise of Jesus now secure: "I will come back and take you to be with me that you also may be where I am" (John 14:3 NIV).

Life is sacred. We need vision to behold God in His glory and majesty within our everyday journey. When we humbly welcome those moments, we enter into awareness of God's manifest presence. We then may positively respond to Christ's transforming gift of salvation and redemption. Holy ground is all around us. The question is whether our hearts and minds are open to believe and behold this truth so as to receive God's grace, mercy and righteousness. This chapter's passages from Psalm 8, 24 and Matthew 17:1-5 all involve people worshipping God in His holiness and glory. Their response of awe, trust, and obedience inspired a bright horizon of hope as to what God was doing in their midst to bring about His reign and righteous Kingdom. The same holds true for those who worship today. We are invited to come and approach God with awe, trust, and obedience. In humility, we place our hope in the Lord, witness His works and give worth to His manifested Glory. God's might, majesty and mercy sustains and transforms all existence and we are forever moved in joyful, grateful praise.

Scripture Passages (Psalm 8; Psalm 24; Matthew 17:1-5)

Psalms 8:1-9
For the director of music. According to *gittith*. A psalm of David.

¹ O LORD , our Lord, how majestic is your name in all the earth!
You have set your glory above the heavens.
² From the lips of children and infants you have ordained praise because of your enemies,
 to silence the foe and the avenger.

³ When I consider your heavens, the work of your fingers, the moon and the stars, which you have set in place, ⁴ what is man that you are mindful of him,
the son of man that you care for him?

> I. God's Majesty and Glory is proclaimed. (Psalm 8)
>
> A. God's Name is glorified above all. (1)
> B. God's praise is ordained from children (2)
> C. God's creation humbles us. (3-4)
> D. God's redemption empowers us (5-8)
> E. God's Kingdom extends to all the earth. (9)

⁵ You made him a little lower than the heavenly beings
and crowned him with glory and honor.
⁶ You made him ruler over the works of your hands;
 you put everything under his feet:
⁷ all flocks and herds,   and the beasts of the field, ⁸ the birds of the air,
and the fish of the sea, all that swim the paths of the seas.

⁹ O LORD, our Lord, how majestic is your name in all the earth!

Psalms 24:1-10

[1] The earth is the LORD's, and everything in it, the world, and all who live in it; [2] for he founded it upon the seas and established it upon the waters. [3] Who may ascend the hill of the LORD? Who may stand in his holy place? [4] He who has clean hands and a pure heart, who does not lift up his soul to an idol or swear by what is false. [5] He will receive blessing from the LORD and vindication from God his Savior. [6] Such is the generation of those who seek him, who seek your face, O God of Jacob. Selah [7] Lift up your heads, O you gates; be lifted up, you ancient doors, that the King of glory may come in. [8] Who is this King of glory? The LORD strong and mighty, the LORD mighty in battle. [9] Lift up your heads, O you gates; lift them up, you ancient doors, that the King of glory may come in. [10] Who is he, this King of glory? The LORD Almighty-- he is the King of glory. Selah

Matthew 17:1-5

[1] After six days Jesus took with him Peter, James and John the brother of James, and led them up a high mountain by themselves. [2] There he was transfigured before them. His face shone like the sun, and his clothes became as white as the light. [3] Just then there appeared before them Moses and Elijah, talking with Jesus. [4] Peter said to Jesus, "Lord, it is good for us to be here. If you wish, I will put up three shelters--one for you, one for Moses and one for Elijah." [5] While he was still speaking, a bright cloud enveloped them, and a voice from the cloud said, "This is my Son, whom I love; with him I am well pleased. Listen to him!"

II. The Hope of God's Kingdom (Psalm 24)

    A. The hope of all the earth (1-2)
    B. The hope of salvation (3-6)
      1. Holiness by mercy (3)
      2. Holiness by repentance (4)
      3. Holiness by vindication of grace (5)
      4. Holiness by seeking God's face (6)
    C. The hope of Christ's coming (7-10)
      1. Be alert (7)
      2. Be aware (8)
      3. Be ready (9)
      4. Be assured (10)

III. A Glimpse of the King of Glory (Matthew. 17:1-5)

    A. Following Jesus' lead (1)
    B. Seeing the face of God in Jesus (2)
    C. Seeing Jesus as the Christ (3-5)

Exploring the Scriptures

David wrote many songs for worship. He began Psalm 8 by addressing God through the personal name "Yahweh", "I am that I am". David then also addressed God as our Lord "Adonai", the name of God as the sovereign Lord having dominion over all nations and creation. In this way David led the people to understand that God is both their personal creator and redeemer, yet even above all this, God is supreme and sovereign Lord over all peoples. Israel was called by God to be a blessing to all the nations. God inspired Isaiah to write: *"Listen to me, my people; hear me, my nation: The law will go out from me; my justice will become a light to the nations"* (Isaiah 51:4). God gave the Torah (teaching of the law and commandments, primarily through the first five books of the Bible) to the Jews. This law was fulfilled through the Messiah, Jesus the Christ, the Son of God who was also the promised Servant King for our salvation. In Psalm 24 the emphasis is upon preparing God's people for worship in God's Holy Temple. Holiness is what God requires for our participation in worship. Holiness is possible only through repentance before God. Our hope for transformation and entry into God's Kingdom is possible only through the righteousness and holiness accomplished by the atoning sacrifice of Jesus on the cross, and this work of grace was authenticated by the power of Christ's resurrection. From this work of sanctification, which leads to the believer's future glorified resurrected state, the believer looks forward to the eventual return of the King of Glory and the opportunity to behold our Lord and Savior face to face in His majesty. Meanwhile, the world that exists without hope or faith in God's Son Jesus would like to avoid and deny this coming reality of the Lord's very personal and extensive judgment and reign.

In the context of Matthew 17:1-5, the disciples Peter, James and John were invited by Jesus to join Him up on Mt. Herman near Caesarea Philippi. Here Jesus revealed His bright heavenly glory as the Son of God, the Messiah. Moses and Elijah also appeared and talked with Jesus, not as equals, but as those who stood by His side ready to serve Christ as their Master and King. Peter sensed the significance of this moment and in suggesting that they build booths, Peter makes the connection to the "Feast of Tabernacles". This Jewish festival remembered how God was faithful to shelter His people as they had wandered in the wilderness, but it also looked forward to the fulfillment of God's blessing of provision in the coming of God's Kingdom on earth. Peter jumped to the conclusion that perhaps at this time Jesus would retain this glorious presence. After a time of preparation and consecration through celebrating the Feast of Tabernacles, Peter imagined how glorious and triumphant Jesus would be as they would descend the mountain and bring forth the Kingdom of God. Peter was right that Jesus would bring in the Kingdom of God, but the way and means for Jesus to do this was not at first through force, power or political overthrow and social revolution. The Kingdom of God would first be established within people's hearts, within believing souls through Jesus' work of salvation on the cross. The Kingdom of God was not to be established through force, but by faith.

Bridging into Today

Never under estimate the power that is released from God when people are humble in prayer and open their hearts in praise and petition. These Psalms affirm that God is exalted over creation while still being interested in every detail of life, with concern for every living creature. God is especially concerned for humanity, created in His image. Through worship we discover that the Lord our God is personal and profound, intimate and infinite.

Worship is open, therefore, to all who humble themselves before God. Infants praise God in their delightful and playful babble and sages worship God in their words of woven silk. The simple, fun and innocent songs of young children are used by God to silence those who oppose the Kingdom of Heaven. God displays His glory all around us through creation, in the vast and deep heavens and upon the intricate and interwoven systems of life and ecology. God cares for small flowers and birds, and even all of us "odd people" with various idiosyncrasies and ideas. God is intimately and passionately involved and at work to redeem life on this earth; but not with imposition and force as His preferred tool, but with invitation and engagement that respects will and personality. People can still relate to these Psalms now as then because true worship is timeless. True worship involves focus upon the timeless King of glory who came to reign within our hearts and over our lives. Worship is designed to be our first and foremost priority; this was God's command from the beginning. Worship is meant to be non-stop, a way of life oriented to the transforming Spirit of God (as revealed in the Father and through the Son, Jesus the Savior and Christ).

The same hope of Israel for a messiah to reign upon the earth is the same hope of Christians who look forward to the millennial return and reign of Jesus. It is important for us to understand the nature of Jesus' reign so as not to be misled by false messiahs who would seek glory for themselves. When Jesus comes in full glory and power it will be unmistakable and complete. Salvation is given through faith in Jesus. Through Him salvation is secure. By the righteousness that is His to authorize, the Kingdom of God shall escalate and culminate in the worship of God's people. All worship eventually leads people to God's very presence in the coming Holy City and Temple built by God in the New Jerusalem. In God's plan, Christ's righteousness and holiness will be accompanied by His majesty and glory. His service as Triumphant King and Righteous Judge will honor and reflect the glory, grace and truth of God our Heavenly Father.

Worship is therefore vital for God's people to maintain perspective and hope. Worship is also vital in the work of God's Holy Spirit to reveal truth and inspire faith. When we worship God in "Spirit and in Truth" now, we are being prepared for even greater life-transforming encounters with God. Genuine worship will equip us to respond to His call and leading as we serve for His Kingdom. While people will see Jesus face to face some day in His full Glory, worship begins now as we seek His merciful and encouraging presence, experience His abundant and sufficient grace, truthful counsel and forgiving and empowering love. Like the disciples, we too may receive a glimpse and taste of Christ's glory as we pray and worship God.

Thoughts on God's Creation and Personal Healing:

God cares for us in very specific ways. The Psalmist refers to the fingers of God being at work. His creation is both grand and detailed; God is involved at every level.

Earlier in this book I mentioned that an MRI Scan was ordered of my brain. When it was processed, I picked up the film to bring to the Neurologist. I was suffering from something called "Arnold Chiari Malformation", a condition where the lower back portion of my brain skull was slightly small, so my cerebrum was pushing out and down upon my upper spinal cord. The next question was, "Could this be operated upon and fixed?" The answer by Dr. Jackson, the Neurologist, was, "Yes, it can be remedied through brain surgery".

Now most of the time when the words "brain surgery" are presented to someone there is anxiety and fear. For me, having already survived cancer treatments and much more, I was relieved that a solution existed for my condition. Just weeks before I was to have the surgery I went in for another MRI scan of my head. Much to everyone's surprise, something had changed. My brain had shrunk back enough to where it was no longer pressing on my spinal fluid. The old designer's adage, "less is more", was true In my head. I praised God for His grace that had continued to keep me, mold me and heal me. Now, years later, I have no concerns related to the Arnold Chiari Malformation. I am reminded that God has the authority to move and shape us according to His sovereign will and plans. God protects us by His mercy. I have learned not to think too hard and long about those things I can't understand that might crowd my mind with doubt and fear. When we don't give space for God's grace, too often we fill it with the things that make us dizzy, depressed and distraught. Once again, His grace is sufficient, and it gives me the hope and space I need for a lasting peace that surpasses all understanding or circumstances.

In these Psalms a broad picture of God's Kingdom and sovereignty is portrayed and affirmed. *"The earth is the Lord's and everything in it* (Psalm 24:1)." This has great implications for how we view the earth, our bodies, our communities, the land, our homes, what we own, who we know and how we fulfill our responsibilities. The unique position of humanity in God's creation, and our very connection as God's children, is affirmed in God's word: *"What is man that you are mindful of him, the son of man that you care for him? You made him a little lower than the heavenly beings and crowned him with glory and honor"* (Psalm 8:4-5).

We celebrate that we are all made by God and are called to an awareness and faith-filled response under the Sovereignty and Providence of God. This kind of belief is truly possible for all people, from little children to adults. Little children often remind us to be honest and transparent with God and one another. As a pastor, I have enjoyed the interaction of children in teaching situations in which children will interact with me to tell me something revealing. A few parents have been known to squirm or laugh. The simple message of God is that we are to trust in Him like our children need to trust in us.

At a family thanksgiving gathering I was asked to lead a prayer. We had come together for a wedding that would take place the next day near the Gulf Shores of Alabama. In the twilight of the sun's last rays at a beach house, the glow of sunset was warm and calming. The families and friends of the bride and the groom gathered around tables laden with food prepared from many home recipes. One family was Filipino American and the other Caucasian American, each with a heritage from opposite sides of the world. Before praying I commented that the same sun that had just set here was just rising upon the Philippines. In a poetic sense it was a beautiful thought and a powerful image of unity.

The next morning in the quiet stillness of dawn I reconsidered this. Instead of thinking about the sun going around the earth (a very archaic, non-scientific perspective), I thought about how the earth rotates upon an invisible axis, tilted at a slight angle, in an orbit around the sun, within a solar system that is held within an immense galaxy that itself is a speck within the cosmos of the universe. I realized that the wonder of it all is that God's majesty is always bigger than we can at first perceive. Yet I came back to think of the sun's light shining upon the earth. While it is true that the light of the sun is a constant (for however long the sun shall shine), and the continual dawning and rising of the sun is simply our own movement around this constant source of light and energy, the fact remains that it is not only the light of the sun that we behold, we are blessed daily by its rays, warmth and gravitational pull. The sun not only exists, it is working in a powerful way that is both profound and very personal. Therefore, we may conclude that while the sun does not orbit the earth, its light does shine upon us in a circular pattern. The same can be said of God. While God is a constant in glory, power and majesty upon His throne, we behold His glory in creation and experience His power in the light of His goodness that encircles, blesses and affirms our existence. God discloses His existence in a way we can understand, and also in ways that lead us beyond our preliminary assumptions and limited knowledge. With the Lord our God, the great "I am", we have a constant covenant of truth and grace that dynamically changes us through the experience of faith and inspiration from His revelation. When Jesus Christ came to earth to reveal God (the light from which all creation originated from for the universe), a direct encounter came to dawn upon our existence. *"The true light that gives light to every man was coming into the world"* (John 1:9). In Christ we beheld the glory of God in human form; His light still shines within all who believe. His light shall dawn directly in a new day again upon His return. At that time He shall be worshipped without the veil of mercy that currently is in place. When Christ Jesus comes in power and glory He shall issue forth the judgment of God and shall expose all to the light of His Word, His teachings (Torah) and God's righteous and sovereign decree.

Remember Psalm 51:4, "*...my justice will become a light to the nations.*" While this refers to an ongoing light from God's teaching that continues to shine from God's Word, this also is an affirmation both of the Sovereignty of God and the future hope of the Messiah's next coming. God calls us to carry the light of His teaching from the Holy Scriptures as we are citizens of His coming Kingdom. The preparations begin now, and the work of reflecting the light of His presence and revelation is urgent. The culmination and transformation of this work is yet to come. Each of us are called to rely upon God's persistent unchanging nature to be our constant, even though the world itself shall go through ruin and refinement. Ultimately, God's redemption is to transform those of faith and make all things in God's creation new and glorious.

Questions for Class Discussion

1. What are the primary elements of worship that we find in Psalms 8 and 24?

2. Describe the blessings and insights that God has given you in worship.

3. What hope is given to God's people in Psalm 24 about the coming Messiah?

4. How will it be possible for anyone to stand before God in His Holy Temple?

5. In what way does worship prepare us for the coming of Jesus as King?

6. How have you experienced the glory of God in worship or in prayer?

7. What do we teach our children about worship?

In what way could we give them a greater sense of hope through worship?

Closing Idea

When our lives are aligned with true worship of God, then others will desire what we express and will inquire in order to find out what true and genuine worship is all about. Worship is more than words of praise and songs of adoration; true worship extends to every part of life. In Christ we are citizens of God's Heavenly Kingdom, this Kingdom is visible through our lives when we are living faithful and obedient to God's word and Holy Spirit.

The question is not so much "Where is the Kingdom of God?", but "How can we prevail in faith? Being responsive and obedient to Jesus and God's Holy Spirit is essential for fruitfulness and blessing. If you are not living life in view of God's majesty and intimacy, then what are you looking at? Most of us have times when we are short-sighted or blind. To open our hearts and minds to God's surrounding presence will involve a change of perspective. God invites us to be set free by His truth and grace which is given and revealed through His Son. Jesus spoke to a Samaritan woman at Jacob's well about this:

> **John 4:19-24 (NIV)** [19] "Sir," the woman said, "I can see that you are a prophet. [20] Our fathers worshiped on this mountain, but you Jews claim that the place where we must worship is in Jerusalem." [21] Jesus declared, "Believe me, woman, a time is coming when you will worship the Father neither on this mountain nor in Jerusalem. [22] You Samaritans worship what you do not know; we worship what we do know, for salvation is from the Jews. [23] Yet a time is coming and has now come when the true worshipers will worship the Father in spirit and truth, for they are the kind of worshipers the Father seeks. [24] God is spirit, and his worshipers must worship in spirit and in truth."

Jesus disclosed something essential to the "woman at the well", God the Father is looking for those who will worship Him in Spirit and in Truth. She responded in faith and proclamation, bearing witness to Jesus by testifying to her friends and community. Her response to God's revelation in Jesus was personal and worshipful. What we learn from this is that the Kingdom of God is magnified through our response of worship, testimony and creativity. The expression of our faith is a "Prelude" that gives evidence to the work of Christ's revealed glory and ministry of grace.

3

GOD IS MIGHTY AND MERCIFUL

(Psalm 29, 33, and 61; Matthew 18:10-14)

> **Key verse:**
> *The LORD sits enthroned over the flood; the LORD is enthroned as King forever. The LORD gives strength to his people; the LORD blesses his people with peace.* — Psalm 33:10-11

Purpose of study

This chapter's study shall contemplate the nature of God as multifaceted in might and mercy. The goal will be to understand that God's nature and presence is made plain in His revealed Kingdom whereby He reigns through Christ and is sovereign. The people of God are called to trust and give evidence to God's reign. True disciples of Christ are led and empowered to express and experience the mercy of God in service and evangelism. God's might and mercy highlights and rewrites righteousness into our consciences. God graciously authors salvation upon the pages of our souls. Therefore, we will care for the lowly and the lost because our hearts are moved by the redeeming hand of God. This very love of God is transforming us into the likeness of His beloved Son Jesus. Our mindset follows a changed heart. The Kingdom of God is more than a realization or concept; it is a new orientation for the soul set upon the path of God's truth and grace.

Prelude

The might and mercy of God is celebrated throughout the Psalms, and specifically in Psalms 29, 33 and 61. The importance of understanding the height and depth of God's power and love is essential for discovering meaning and purpose in faith and life. Our worship of God needs to reflect awe and humility, wonder and confession, honor and intimacy. The attributes we may ascribe to God include glory and strength, but also unfailing love and all sufficient grace and mercy. Jesus exemplifies the nature of God our Father in the way He humbles the proud and lifts up the lowly.

A young man came to me once seeking to be baptized. He was a bit nervous about being baptized even though he wanted to express his faith and love for God and salvation in Jesus Christ. There were a few things he needed to talk with me about as it pertained to dealing with sin. He wondered if it was possible never to sin again and he also wondered about what changes he might need to make. First of all, we established his understanding of the grace of God and that outward baptism itself does not save a person. Next, we established that he will likely sin again, but that the grace of God in Christ operates to continue to redeem us. Finally, we affirmed the reality that being a Christian involves a response to God's mercy and forgiveness such that we are called to overcome sinful attitudes and behaviors with the help of Jesus daily. I went on to assure him that the Lord would give him strength and help to live as a disciple, to grow as a person, and to enjoy life with the peace that Christ will give to us. He felt he was ready to be baptized, and when the day of baptism came it was a glorious event. When his turn came and I tried to dip him in the water it was difficult to lower him completely because he had a large 'afro" haircut. The air was trapped inside it and so instead of holding him down longer, I simply took my right hand brought a wave of water over his dry hair.

The congregation then sang the chorus of "Nothing But the Blood of Jesus", and when we sang the words "Oh, precious is the flow that makes me white as snow..", in my mind the words were "Oh, precious is the 'fro'...". The young man's face glowed with joy, and we all had a good laugh when I shared this thought with his family. The Kingdom of God is full of bright moments like this when you open your eyes and ears to the leading and voice of God's Holy Spirit.

The Kingdom of God is best seen when people of faith acknowledge and ascribe all blessings as "coming from God", and likewise participate in passing these blessings on to others. Being compassionate and faithful in service to God, extending the kindness and mercy of our Heavenly Father, is at the heart of Jesus (the faithful Son) and His church. Each child is valuable to God, and lost sinners are each loved by God. There is great joy in Heaven for each lost sinner who is saved by grace, this grace being extended by God's people who participate in the saving work of the Kingdom of God.

Once I was called to the hospital to pray with a soul prior to their impending death. Before I entered the patient's room a family member told me that they were concerned for the salvation of their elderly parent. This was based on a conversation where the parent had expressed doubt about Heaven and about God. Another pastor showed up who was closer to the patient. I allowed him to take the lead in initiating the reading of scripture and in the giving of a prayer. I realized that he had not had the benefit of listening to the family's specific concern.   So as the pastor turned the prayer over to me, I simply said to the patient: "Jesus is for real, I can tell you this because He appeared to me and healed me 9 years ago. You may have had your doubts, but it is never too late to trust in God and trust in Jesus. Now is the time for you to let go of your fears and doubts. Now is the time to believe. God is merciful and loving, but you can't be sure of heaven unless you believe and receive Jesus. God is ever present. He wants to come into your heart, but that is up to you. It is up to you to have faith. Jesus is present and ready to save you. If you believe, then just ask him in to your heart and squeeze our hands to let us know that you have received Jesus." The patient, now starting to move (as he had not moved much in the hours before), made every effort to squeeze our hands, open his eyes and move his arms. Holding our hands he used every ounce of effort to communicate something that could only be expressed non-verbally. In a moment like this, faith requires that we trust in God's might and mercy. As the other pastor and I continued in prayer and scripture, I felt led to share a benediction. "The Lord bless you and keep you, the Lord make His face shine upon you and give you peace, now and forevermore." At this, the patient's face beamed with wonder, with eyes that opened wide with faith and awe. What did he behold? What was God doing? An expression of faith and grace was upon his startled face. A gentle peace descended upon him, there was a distinguishable change in his demeanor as his body relaxed, his grip affirmed what he heard and his eyes overflowed with tears. Belief in God's might and mercy is at the very heart of discovering the presence and peace of God and the reality of His Kingdom that is born within.

Scripture Passages (Psalm 29, 33, and 61; Matthew 18:10-14)

Psalm 29

1 Ascribe to the LORD, O mighty ones, ascribe to the LORD glory and strength.
2 Ascribe to the LORD the glory due his name;
worship the LORD in the splendor of his holiness.
3 The voice of the LORD is over the waters; the God of glory thunders,
the LORD thunders over the mighty waters.
4 The voice of the LORD is powerful; the voice of the LORD is majestic.
5 The voice of the LORD breaks the cedars; the LORD breaks in pieces the cedars of Lebanon.
6 He makes Lebanon skip like a calf, Sirion like a young wild ox.
7 The voice of the LORD strikes with flashes of lightning.
8 The voice of the LORD shakes the desert; the LORD shakes the Desert of Kadesh.
9 The voice of the LORD twists the oaks and strips the forests bare.
And in his temple all cry, "Glory!"
10 The LORD sits enthroned over the flood;
 the LORD is enthroned as King forever.
11 The LORD gives strength to his people;
 the LORD blesses his people with peace.

> **I. Proclaiming God's Nature**
>   (Psalm 29:1-4)
>   A. Glory, strength & splendor (1-2)
>   B. Creator, Sustainer, King (3-4)
>
> **II. Proclaiming God's works**
>   (Psalm 29:5-11)
>   A. Humbling the high and mighty (5)
>   B. Renewing strength for all creatures (6)
>   C. Recharging and replenishing the earth (7-8)
>   D. Shaking and pruning the forests (9)
>   E. Cleansing the earth (10)
>   F. Blessing His people with strength and peace (11)

Psalm 33

¹ Sing joyfully to the LORD, you righteous;
it is fitting for the upright to praise him.
² Praise the LORD with the harp;
make music to him on the ten-stringed lyre.
³ Sing to him a new song;
play skillfully, and shout for joy.
⁴ For the word of the LORD is right and true;
he is faithful in all he does.
⁵ The LORD loves righteousness and justice;
the earth is full of his unfailing love.
⁶ By the word of the LORD were the heavens made, their starry host by the breath of his mouth. ⁷ He gathers the waters of the sea into jars ;he puts the deep into storehouses.
⁸ Let all the earth fear the LORD;
let all the people of the world revere him.
⁹ For he spoke, and it came to be;
he commanded, and it stood firm.
¹⁰ The LORD foils the plans of the nations;
he thwarts the purposes of the peoples.
¹¹ But the plans of the LORD stand firm forever, the purposes of his heart through all generations. ¹² Blessed is the nation whose God is the LORD,
the people he chose for his inheritance.
¹³ From heaven the LORD looks down
and sees all mankind; ¹⁴ from his dwelling place he watches all who live on earth--
¹⁵ he who forms the hearts of all,
who considers everything they do.
¹⁶ No king is saved by the size of his army;
no warrior escapes by his great strength.
¹⁷ A horse is a vain hope for deliverance;
despite all its great strength it cannot save.
¹⁸ But the eyes of the LORD are on those who fear him,
on those whose hope is in his unfailing love,
¹⁹ to deliver them from death
and keep them alive in famine.
²⁰ We wait in hope for the LORD;
he is our help and our shield.
²¹ In him our hearts rejoice, for we trust in his holy name.
²² May your unfailing love rest upon us, O LORD,
even as we put our hope in you.

III. Praising God and His Kingdom (Psalm 33)

A. The call to worship (1)
B. The call to make music (2-3)
C. The call to revere God's Word (3-9)

IV. Putting the kingdoms of man in place (Psalm 33: 10-20)

A. Trust in God's plans (10-15)
B. Don't trust in man's plans (16-17)
C. Believe in God's providence (18-19)
D. Rely upon God's unfailing love (20-22)

Psalm 61:1-8

¹ Hear my cry, O God;   listen to my prayer.
² From the ends of the earth I call to you,
 I call as my heart grows faint;
lead me to the rock that is higher than I.
³ For you have been my refuge,
a strong tower against the foe.
⁴ I long to dwell in your tent forever
and take refuge in the shelter of your wings. Selah
⁵ For you have heard my vows, O God;
you have given me the heritage
of those who fear your name.
⁶ Increase the days of the king's life,
 his years for many generations.
⁷ May he be enthroned in God's presence forever;
appoint your love and faithfulness to protect him.
⁸ Then will I ever sing praise to your name
 and fulfill my vows day after day.

> **V. Connecting with God through prayer** (Psalm 61)
>
> A. Crying out in faith (1-3)
> B. Desiring God's manifest presence (4)
> C. Laying our requests before God (5-8)

Matthew 18:10-14

¹⁰ "See that you do not look down on one of these little ones. For I tell you that their angels in heaven always see the face of my Father in heaven.   ¹² "What do you think? If a man owns a hundred sheep, and one of them wanders away, will he not leave the ninety-nine on the hills and go to look for the one that wandered off? ¹³ And if he finds it, I tell you the truth, he is happier about that one sheep than about the ninety-nine that did not wander off. ¹⁴ In the same way your Father in heaven is not willing that any of these little ones should be lost.

> **VI. A new vision and calling for serving God and His Kingdom.** (Matt. 18:10-14)
>
> A. Heaven's equality is humility (10-11)
> B. Heaven's priority is compassion (12-14)

Exploring the Scriptures

These passages from the Psalms and Matthew are oriented around the understanding that God is enthroned in Heaven with sovereign power and authority. This perspective of faith affirms that God's Kingdom is established in Heaven and is also at work in a redemptive sense upon the earth as seen through creation and history. Though man may scheme and plan outside of God's will, ultimately the activity of evil and sinful humanity will not prevail. God has power and authority to allow some things to remain for a while, and then to strategically change things in His own timing. God is also able to deliver and defend His people; through increasing faith His people develop trust in God's providence and protection. Salvation is not just a concept regarding souls being prepared for heaven; it is a historical and continual working of God in human history that has a redemptive design. This was true for Israel in the past, as it will be true for Israel now and into the future. Jewish and Gentile believers throughout the world are invited to faith that Jesus Christ brings all things together under God's saving work and Kingdom design.

Psalm 29 and 33 are enthronement psalms intended to highlight God's rule and power at the New Year festival. Psalm 29 helped to clarify their worldview of God being in control and of their complete reliance upon God. Psalm 33 expressed their joy of worship and praise wherein they discovered God's presence and power. Psalm 61 was a prayer of intercession and petition by King David. Though this prayer/psalm was personal at first, it was later shared publically with the people of Israel in worship and humility before God.

The passage from Matthew highlights Jesus teaching about how the Kingdom of God is designed for the least and lowly as much as for those of learning and status. Jesus also gave them a glimpse of understanding regarding the work of angels for God's Kingdom; they are guardians and protectors who silently and quietly carry out the will of God. Jesus moved from this perspective of angels guarding little children to the compassion of God being like the shepherd whose reach extends to save one lost sheep. The call for joining Jesus in this compassionate venture is clear. The mirror of Christ's cross is lifted up. We are left with the call and challenge to care for individuals who are lost and need to be shown the love and mercy of God in extraordinary ways (even if it means leaving the fold and going out to where there is danger). Connecting Jesus' teaching to the Psalms, which speak of God's power and providence, the Lord is teaching that God will guide and protect us when it comes to reaching out to save the lost and care for those in need. Of course, there will also be times when God allows us to bear the cross for His Kingdom and this too may mean suffering as Jesus did. God takes notice of our willingness to bear pain for the sake of His Kingdom.

Not long ago, someone came in to my office to express their concern about a friend who's very young son was diagnosed with Leukemia. After we prayed about the child (4 years old) and his chemotherapy and prayed for the family in their various needs, God opened our eyes to a few possibilities of service. For indeed God calls us to respond with more than words. With just a week left to go until a large outreach event in late October that we called "Treat of Truth", we wrote a letter to the local newspaper and explained that we were going to raise funds at the event for the child and his family. With our theme, "Faith over Fear", we had prepared a large "Whale maze" and games for children and balloons and goodies for all. A few days before the event, the article and a picture of the child appeared on the front page of the newspaper. Hundreds of people came with their children as support was raised for this family in need. In the midst of the maze, I proclaimed the message of God's love in the warning and call to repentance being in character as the prophet Jonah. My station was in the belly of the whale (big fish), as seaweed was draped all over me as was the slime from a bowl of fresh herring. Here children and parents who had worked their way through the dark tunnels came into a dimly lit room where I shared the story of why I was there. My message went something like this:

> "God loves all people, I should have known that. One day God called me to go to the people in the city of Nineveh to tell them to repent and turn from their wicked ways and be saved. I was afraid and I also did not like the Ninevites because they had been our enemies in Israel. So I disobeyed God and tried to sail on a ship to go far away. Because God loved the people of Nineveh as much as He loved me, God sent a big storm to keep me from running away from my responsibility. When the waves were so big and the wind so strong that we were all thinking that we would drown, I said to the sailors that it was all my fault and they had to throw me overboard. When they did, God sent this big whale to come and swallow me whole. I didn't get chewed up at all, but with

one big gulp I ended up here. God has given me a "time out", and now I know what I must do when I get out. So now, can you help me send a message to the Ninevites, can you tell them that God loves them but wants them to turn away from doing bad things and turn in faith in God and do good things?"

After delivering this message it was interesting to hear peoples' responses, and it seemed as though our attempt to reach our community with the love of God was not falling on deaf ears. The whole evening was a success and everyone who served as volunteers were filled with joy as we shared the love and mercy of God. The child who we were raising funds for that day was at the hospital having chemotherapy, yet his older brother and grandfather came to the church event. The brother remarked: "Wow, they are doing all this for my brother and our family." The grandfather was moved and remarked: "Hey, this is fun and there is something very genuine about this church." In times like this, in practical acts of kindness and compassion, the church can shine brightly. A proper focus on God and His mercy will lead us to respond to people and care for them as Jesus calls and shows us the way.

Bridging into Today

There was a German sculptor named Dannecker who was creating a statue of Christ. He decided that in order to objectively evaluate his work he should ask a young boy what he thought about his sculpture. The child looked at it and said: "That's a great man". Dannecker then set to work for another week and then brought the child back in. The child's face lit up as he proclaimed: "There's Jesus!" Dannecker remembered the Scripture, "Suffer the little children to come unto me, for to such belongs the Kingdom of God." The artist realized that he should not rely upon his own vision, but that he needed to enlarge his vision in humility first, even if it meant seeing through the eyes of a child. Greatness in man's view is not greatness in God's view. Seeing through the eyes of a child helped him to sculpt closer to Christ.

The "greatness of man" can blur our vision of the Kingdom of God. There is a reason why God chooses the lowly and despised of this earth to humble the exalted and strong of this world. God's kingdom is not a matter of physical or military might, but a matter of Spirit, truth, character, morality, peace and love. The more we ascribe to God honor and praise, the more God leads us to experience, understand, and apply His character and nature in our lives. The fact that we are created in His image means that we are already made with this potential. Faith leads us into the participation of God's goodness and into the activation of our potential goodness. God is able to transform us within, thereby liberating us from sinfulness into a state and way of life in which God's light is able to shine; His love then reveals and inspires repentance, reconciliation, justice, righteousness and grace.

The challenge, however, is that the darkness and treachery of evil seeks to lead us astray to think that we are "our own gods". The greatest need of humanity is humility before a mighty and merciful God. Through humility and worship that is genuine and transforming, God forgives us. God lifts us up and gives us the joyful and meaningful responsibilities of a new life born and guided by the Holy Spirit. Through the Holy Spirit we are ignited and empowered to speak of the glory and grace of God. This movement of God through His people brings hope and the reality of salvation to the world. What happened in Israel during tabernacle and temple worship was that the presence of God was manifested powerfully and viscerally. This same moving of God intensified and occurred on the Day of Pentecost for the church. The good news of God's Kingdom, being present and powerful through the Lord and Savior Jesus Christ, leads believers to the highways and byways, to people near and far, to provide hope and rescue in the message and ministry of the Kingdom of God.

In Christ's teaching in Matthew 18:10, one may ask: Who are the "little ones" that Jesus was talking about? Perhaps He means anyone who does not pretend to be larger than or equal to God is a "little one" spiritually. To be a citizen of the Kingdom of God is not a matter of attainment through work, knowledge, effort, cunning, politics, persuasion or power. Indeed, to be a citizen of God's Kingdom is to love, honor, trust and glorify God as our Creator Father. He is head over us all, and sovereign in rule, authority and power. One must become humble in faith to see the Kingdom of God. One must have faith like a child to enter the Kingdom of Heaven.

In Psalm 29, the people praised God through ascribing all glory to God. The response of God to their praise was to grant the people grace, strength and peace. The Lord's voice is described as powerful and is compared to the trembling thunder of desert storms. These storms predictably sweep over the Holy Land from North to South, from Lebanon to Sirion. Lively and intense, the storms were symbolic of Lebanon (like a young calf). These storms grow big and broad as they sweep down from the mountains; they become strong and mighty (like a big ox) into the south.   The winds blow upon God's command and His Spirit is at work upon the face of the earth. While God was described for His awesome work of creation, now He is described as the mover and shaper of His creation.

God spoke and breathed creation into being, and His "Spirit" (Hebrew: "Ruah" which is translated "breath" or "wind") that breathed out the stars and all creation is the same Spirit that breathed life into all creation, Adam and Eve, and all who have followed. Astronomers say that we are created out of the dust of stars. More importantly, the Bible refers to people being given the Spirit of the Living God. We are more than just "Dust in the Wind", if indeed God's grace and love is received for salvation. God's plan is for our deliverance from our mortal bondage to decay and death. God's plan is also for our redemption and salvation from sin and evil and is wrapped up in His unending and enduring love.

God is enthroned. Still, God is also moving in His creation. God is not limited to time and space because He is infinite. Nonetheless, God chooses to manifest Himself into our finite reality. While we are limited to time and space because we are finite, God in Christ gives us unlimited potential as we are born again spiritually. The future of God's children, who shall be resurrected, is a hope that goes beyond our limited imagination. God reigns in heaven and yet works in creation because of His infinite nature, perfect love and enduing power.

Questions for Class Discussion

1. What perspective about life do children express to inspire faith in God?

2. What perspectives and awareness do we gain about God through our shared worship?

3. In what ways does God speak to us in worship and praise?

4. What are a few of the prevailing worldviews of our times? In what ways does a Kingdom of God worldview differ from secular worldviews?

5. How is God working through His angels to protect or preserve us?

6. In what way would you apply the parable of the lost sheep?

    When were you lost or in need? How did God send someone to rescue you?

7. What is the priority of today's church? Is evangelism high on the list?

Closing Idea

When you encourage, talk, listen to, hug, share a smile or play with a child you are living in the priority of God's Kingdom. When you protect and defend children you are preserving and shielding the hope of Christ.

PERSONAL STORY: "Lost"

One night I rushed home from the church to turn on my video recorder, and to watch what was then one of our family's favorite TV show series: "Lost". Already the fifth season of this show, this was to be the first new episode. We finished our prayer at the Bible Study at 8:55pm. I dashed through the back of the church, through the back yard of the parsonage, bounded up the back porch stairs, slid open the back door and raced into the family room to turn on the television. I pushed the correct remote control button to record the show. I was thankful that I had arrived just in time. Just as I was getting into the initial mind stretching beginning of this show, the phone rang. I answered expecting that it would be my wife reminding me to record the episode (she was working at the hospital). Instead, a dear member of our congregation told me of her niece who was brought to the emergency room that day with severe abdominal pains. She told me how they could not determine what was wrong. I told her I could go up just after 10pm, (you know I was still thinking about watching all of "Lost"). But then the Lord convicted my heart to go immediately. "After all", the Lord clarified, "you're watching the show "Lost", now you can be in my own real life episode of Lost." I turned off the TV Cable Box (though at the time I did not know this disabled the recording feature), and I went to the hospital and had a meaningful visit with the niece and her mother.

Before I left my home I prayed for the mother and her daughter at the hospital. When I arrived there she had just fallen asleep after a painful and trying day. I prayed with the mother as she held her sleepy daughter's hand, and then we quietly discussed her fragile condition as she expressed her concern about having the doctor perform any further difficult and trying tests. We prayed that the doctor would be given the wisdom to diagnose the problem. The next morning they determined the problem was the gall bladder, and she would undergo surgery. I prayed with the 12 year old girl and her family. God was at work to provide for a successful surgery. It was a time to give witness to God's grace and intervention. Looking back, I know that the hand of God was at work. I am reminded of how important it is to go out to reach the "lost sheep" wherever they are in need and whenever God calls. God is merciful, and He leads us to extend His mercy. God is mighty, and He inspires us to pray for His mighty working (in healing and intervention). By the way, the next week, I did catch up on the episode I missed. However, it paled in comparison to the real-life drama of being involved in God's Kingdom work. When the series "Lost" came to its final episode, I was left thinking: "Is that all there was to this thing", what a disappointing conclusion. In a way, God was giving me a "reality check". When God's Kingdom comes we will not be disappointed, believers will all be changed, brought in and given a new name. All things will be explained. *"For now we know in part, but then we shall know completely and be completely known"* (I Corinthians 13:12). Now and then we may feel lost in life, but ultimately we are to trust in God's redeeming presence and plan.

GOD IS BUILDING HIS KINGDOM

(Isaiah 62; Revelations 3:11-13)

> **Key verse:**
> ² *The nations will see your righteousness, and all kings your glory; you will be called by a new name that the mouth of the LORD will bestow.* ³ *You will be a crown of splendor in the LORD's hand, a royal diadem in the hand of your God.* ⁴ *No longer will they call you Deserted, or name your land Desolate.* - Isaiah 62:2-3

Purpose of study

The purpose of this chapter's study is to help believers and seekers grasp how God has been preparing the way for the full manifestation of His Kingdom on earth. In considering God's work of building His Kingdom, the reality of both blessing and challenge exist in a paralleled tension. If we were to only consider the blessings without facing the challenges, we would have unrealistic expectations and would become susceptible to frustration and disappointment. If we were to only consider the challenges without the positive reinforcement of the blessings, then we would lose hope and would suffer for lack of having faith, vision and purpose. God calls us to be participants in His Kingdom work. Faithful service to Christ is essential for involvement and fruitful labor. We pray that our vision of God's Kingdom plan will grow clearer with an awareness of how each person's service to Christ matters and becomes a glorification of God and a blessing to others. Blessings and challenges, joy and pain, are coexistent realities during this "in-between time" in which the birth pains of God's Kingdom are experienced. Through it all we must trust God through adversity while the prelude and spiritual preparation process of His Kingdom is underway.

Prelude

God has been preparing all people on earth for the coming of His Kingdom. Since the fall of humanity in the Garden of Eden and the penetrating influence of evil and sin, God has been at work to offer His gift and work of redemption, this being culminated in His personal presence and coming through Jesus the Savior, His Son, our Lord and King, the Messiah. The Old Testament promise of God's Kingdom is fulfilled by Jesus Christ as orchestrated by God the Father/Creator. In Christ we receive new life, a new name and status with God. Also, in Christ, the promise of redemptive fulfillment leads us toward God's Kingdom to come as verified and promised in the power of the resurrection. The Holy Spirit is given to believers for guidance, counsel, discernment, assurance, sanctification and the preparations of God for His gift of eternal life. Believers, by the very work of God within them, are also called to prepare the way and proclaim salvation. This preparation and proclamation is the "prelude" to Christ's second coming. While there is adversity and suffering, believers have a firm hope in Jesus Christ the Savior/King, who shall welcome us into the Holy City of God that He is preparing.

Scripture Passages (Isaiah 62; Revelations 3:11-13)

Isaiah 62:1-12

¹ For Zion's sake I will not keep silent, for Jerusalem's sake I will not remain quiet, till her righteousness shines out like the dawn, her salvation like a blazing torch. ² The nations will see your righteousness, and all kings your glory; you will be called by a new name that the mouth of the LORD will bestow. ³ You will be a crown of splendor in the LORD's hand, a royal diadem in the hand of your God. ⁴ No longer will they call you Deserted, or name your land Desolate. But you will be called Hephzibah, and your land Beulah; for the LORD will take delight in you, and your land will be married. ⁵ As a young man marries a maiden, so will your sons marry you; as a bridegroom rejoices over his bride, so will your God rejoice over you. ⁶ I have posted watchmen on your walls, O Jerusalem; they will never be silent day or night. You who call on the LORD, give yourselves no rest, ⁷ and give him no rest till he establishes Jerusalem and makes her the praise of the earth. ⁸ The LORD has sworn by his right hand and by his mighty arm: "Never again will I give your grain as food for your enemies, and never again will foreigners drink the new wine for which you have toiled; ⁹ but those who harvest it will eat it and praise the LORD, and those who gather the grapes will drink it in the courts of my sanctuary." ¹⁰ Pass through, pass through the gates! Prepare the way for the people. Build up, build up the highway! Remove the stones. Raise a banner for the nations. ¹¹ The LORD has made proclamation to the ends of the earth: "Say to the Daughter of Zion, 'See, your Savior comes! See, his reward is with him, and his recompense accompanies him.'" ¹² They will be called the Holy People, the Redeemed of the LORD; and you will be called Sought After, the City No Longer Deserted.

I. **God Orchestrates His Kingdom Building Plan** (Isaiah 62)
  A. The Future City of God, Zion
    1. Righteousness shining to the world (1-2a)
    2. Salvation for the people of the world (1b)
    3. A new name for a changed city (2b)
    4. God's coming reign in His people
      a. Splendor and beauty in God's care (3)
      b. Satisfaction and abundance (4a)
      c. Delight in God's covenant (4b-5)
  B. The Ongoing Watch and Witness
    1. Watchmen on the walls of Jerusalem (6a)
    2. Witness by serving, Jesus is coming (6b)
    3. Watch by praying, Jesus is establishing God's Kingdom. (7)
  C. The Sure Promise of God (8-9)
    1. The Promise fulfilled in Jesus Christ (8a)
    2. Redemption comes eventually to Israel (8b-9)
  D. Prepare the Way to the City of God
    1. Enter God's promised city by faith (10a)
    2. Prepare the way by removing barriers (10b)
    3. Welcome the nations (10c)
  E. Proclaim the **Coming** of the Savior King (11-12)
    1. The Great Commission of the Gospel
    2. The Great transformation of God's people
      a. "Holy People"
      b. The "Redeemed of the Lord"
      c. "Sought After"
      d. The "City No Longer Deserted"

Revelation 3:11-13

¹¹ I am coming soon. Hold on to what you have, so that no one will take your crown. ¹² Him who overcomes I will make a pillar in the temple of my God. Never again will he leave it. I will write on him the name of my God and the name of the city of my God, the new Jerusalem, which is coming down out of heaven from my God; and I will also write on him my new name. ¹³ He who has an ear, let him hear what the Spirit says to the churches.

II. Jesus Prepares His Church for His Second Coming
(Revelation 3:11-13)
   A. Hold on to Christ for your reward (11)
   B. Remain faithful to stand victorious (12a)
   C. The Promise of Christ to faithful believers: (12b)
     1. He will write the name of God
     2. He will write the name of the city of God
     3. He will write His new name
   D. Listen to the message given by God's Holy Spirit. (13)

Exploring the Scriptures

Isaiah was given words from God ("Yahweh" or "I am that I am" in Hebrew), to speak to His people, and all peoples of the earth, about the eventual establishment of the Kingdom of God on earth. This formative Kingdom is not made by man, but is one in which God invites our participation through preparation. The preparations are similar to those of a wedding and involve physical, mental, relational, emotional and spiritual aspects. The covenant of God with His people has been like that of a groom waiting for His bride to be ready. The coming City of God is like the abode that God prepares for the bride (Israel and the church), and the groom (Jesus Christ). God's coming earthly reign will ultimately transform His people so that we may become pure, holy, and beautiful both inside and out. The faithful shall be made righteous through the completion of God's redemptive grace that accomplishes God's good, pleasing and perfect will. The path of faith in Jesus Christ shall lead God's people into this Holy union, into a spiritual covenant that is righteous and analogous to human/divine matrimony.

Each redeemed person shall receive a new name that identifies them with God the Father, the New Jerusalem, and Jesus Christ the Groom/Messiah. Furthermore, as a personal seal and sign, God's very name is placed upon the redeemed as a vow of love and protection. The Kingdom covenant is personally guaranteed and to be completed by God through Jesus. The Hebrew name for Jesus is "Jeshua" and is reserved as the new name for the fulfilled Savior/Lord of Isaiah 62:2. Some scholars have speculated that when Jesus Christ comes again in power and glory He will have been bestowed by God the Father with yet another name. We do find in Revelation chapter one that Jesus identifies himself as the "Alpha and Omega", "the living one". In Revelation 19, when Jesus leads the host of heaven upon His return, His name is mentioned as "faithful and true". Yet these two descriptive names are subservient to the title that is written upon His robe and thigh: "KING OF KINGS and LORD of LORDS." Finally at the end of the book of Revelation, in chapter 22.16, Jesus affirms His name and identity again: *"I, Jesus, have sent my angel to give you this testimony for the churches. I am the Root and the Offspring of David, and the bright Morning Star."* Revelation 22:16 (NIV) The primary point is that Jesus is to be regarded in light of His role as the Christ and by His identity as the unique and co-eternal Son of the living God. Jesus is Divine Lord and King and His new name in Glory will reflect His fulfilled ministry, role and authority.

In the matter of names, believers will therefore be given a new name when Christ returns in glory, and/or when we are lifted up into glory upon death or rapture. We read in Revelation 2:17 the words of Jesus: *"He who has an ear, let him hear what the Spirit says to the churches. To him who overcomes, I will give some of the hidden manna. I will also give him a white stone with a new name written on it, known only to him who receives it."* This is God's way of personally identifying (naming) and rewarding (blessing) each individual for their faith. This promise provides a measure of comfort and assurance for each child of God. God will no longer think of us by our old name with our list of sins and history of fears and failings. God will give us a new start. In the passage from Revelation 3 we note that Jesus Christ will write the name of God the Father upon His faithful; He will likewise write the new name for the City of God upon believers as well as His very own name. This name writing symbolizes and verifies the ultimate transformation of our souls and the consummation of God's total salvation of His people.

The writing of God and His Son upon the tablets of our souls reveals even more clearly who God is in relationship to us as humanity, what God has planned, the full nature and character of Jesus Christ, and the redeeming work of God's Kingdom that is ongoing and shall be completed. When God's work of salvation and character development have wrought full redemption, God the Father, the Son and Holy Spirit, in artistic unity and joy, shall sign the hearts of His children. Those who are His masterpieces shall be completed and restored in communion so as to be ready to perfectly fulfill their purpose of glorifying God our Heavenly Father/redeemer.

While we go through this re-creative process of transformation we can relate to the Apostle Paul who stated: *Now we see but a poor reflection as in a mirror; then we shall see face to face. Now I know in part; then I shall know fully, even as I am fully known.* (1 Corinthians 13:12 NIV) The admonition of Jesus in this process of redemption and salvation is to listen and be receptive to God the Father by being attentive, available, faithful, obedient, trusting and patient. The Apostle Paul experienced the living Christ who changed his life in one revealing moment of having the mirror of truth convict him and the light of Christ's countenance penetrate his soul's darkness and ignorance. Once a person knows the living Christ their own countenance begins to reflect God's truth and grace, and humility moves their soul toward repentance, inspiration and transformation.

RESPONDING TO GOD'S PROMISE AND HOLINESS:

God's promise to Israel and His promise to the Church are intertwined. God shall fulfill His promise and vow to bring His people into redemptive communion and fellowship through the Christ/Messiah. God's Kingdom is at hand through the creative intersection of His grace and truth in the physical and spiritual realms. There have been people God has called to experience and convey this reality. Isaiah was one who was summoned before God's throne.

Isaiah 6:1-3 (NIV) [1] In the year that King Uzziah died, I saw the Lord seated on a throne, high and exalted, and the train of his robe filled the temple. [2] Above him were seraphs, each with six wings: With two wings they covered their faces, with two they covered their feet, and with two they were flying. [3] And they were calling to one another: "Holy, holy, holy is the LORD Almighty; the whole earth is full of his glory."

Isaiah's response was indicative of one who had experienced an awesome and life-changing encounter before the living God of the universe:

> **Isaiah 6:5 (NIV)** ⁵ "Woe to me!" I cried. "I am ruined! For I am a man of unclean lips, and I live among a people of unclean lips, and my eyes have seen the King, the LORD Almighty."

God's message of truth was accompanied by a ministry of cleansing grace:

> **Isaiah 6:6-7 (NIV)** ⁶ Then one of the seraphs flew to me with a live coal in his hand, which he had taken with tongs from the altar. ⁷ With it he touched my mouth and said, "See, this has touched your lips; your guilt is taken away and your sin atoned for."

The reception of God's grace moved Isaiah to readiness and to participation in proclaiming the Gospel of the Kingdom of God:

> **Isaiah 6:8 (NIV)** ⁸ Then I heard the voice of the Lord saying, "Whom shall I send? And who will go for us?" And I said, "Here am I. Send me!"

The Invitation and the Covenant

The analogy within Scripture for God's Kingdom invitation and covenant is therefore like that of a "marriage covenant". The enthronement of God on earth will include a covenant in which His people are the Bride (the New Israel/ the Body of Christ), and Christ Jesus (Yeshua, the Messiah/God's Son) is the Groom. We are called into this covenant on a myriad of levels. We are called to participate (share in the joy) and invite others (communicate our joy). Within the third and fourth chapters of Revelation we note that the saints are called to hold their crowns (The crowns symbolize the bestowment of God the King placing His gift of grace and salvation upon those who humble themselves to acknowledge and honor Christ's authority). At the time of their Lord's ascent to manifested and complete enthronement, they are then called to let go of their crowns by casting them before the throne of Christ Jesus (an affirmation of how their salvation has been made complete as they honor Christ their victorious and triumphant Lord and Savior). In symbolic and literal terms, the bride is presented to her groom. She is clothed in God's grace and glory. She has gone through extensive preparations so as to be presentable and beautiful. The crown she gives to her groom is her soul that is beaming from a face and countenance that is bright. Her love and devotion is radiant and has been proven and purified.

Considering Isaiah 62:4 and "Hephzibah", she was the wife of Hezekiah the King. She was one who found favor in "her majesty's eyes". So too, does God find "delight" or "favor" in us through Christ's choice to forgive and love us, and our choice to repent and receive His cleansing/transforming love. Regarding the name "Beulah", this was a name given to the land and its people who would be blessed by the marriage of the King and his bride. Beulah means "beautiful". The implication of the covenant between God and His people shall involve a blessing upon the earth. The curse of the fall and of sin shall be reversed. When Jesus comes to establish His Kingdom on earth in its fullness, it will have a profound environmental impact. Not only is this true for God's chosen people, but this shall impact all peoples, all creatures, every aspect of the earth's ecosystems (all protective, preserving and providing processes). Even now, we are called to live according to the principles of God's redemptive covenant for the earth; this is to be our song, a "prelude" of peace and sacred respect.

Bridging into Today

People are looking for something stable and sure to believe in. Global changes in fluctuating economies, fragile and deteriorating ecosystems, a lack of general security because of wars and violence, and the systemic breakdown of families and social support structures make it challenging to find peace and well-being. In the midst of brokenness and sin, the people of God are called to be faithful beacons of God's love, truth and grace. The Body of Christ is called to prepare the way for the eventual return of Jesus Christ the Savior King. Until Christ Jesus comes in power and glory, the church is to be remain strong and vigilant in the teachings and way of righteousness shown through Scripture (particularly in the life revealed personally through Jesus Christ). The joyful and yet difficult responsibility of preaching and living out the gospel of salvation in Christ involves both a witness and work for God's Kingdom. Believers may work together best when they are united in Christ and led by the Holy Spirit. When our vision is clear that God is at work as the reigning King over all things, we are then encouraged and empowered to do great things for God. When our vision is clouded by doubt or fear, we can become discouraged or disabled toward serving God. Jesus called His church to faithfully move forward in active service that prepares the way for God's activity. This is often challenging and overwhelming. People become discouraged as they lose sight of God's eternal and authoritative reign over all creation. We must learn to trust that God is working out His Kingdom plan and it shall involve the transformation of the earth, the heavens, and all who call upon the Lord as Savior and King in repentance, faith and hope.

There are many people who have become disillusioned with the church and its failures. They believe in Christ and are involved in Kingdom work, but they have given up on the church as it exists today. All they see is hypocrisy, passivity and a lack of creative and compassionate conviction. What is to become of the witness of the church? First of all, the truth of the church's brokenness and failing is not to be quickly dismissed or ignored. Honest confession is in order. Yet the church is being broken for a reason, and perhaps God is up to something. God wants the church to learn faith and reliance. God wants the church to relate to and identify with a broken world. His Son Jesus did when He came and associated with sinners and died on the cross. So why should the church be any different? Why would Christians stop picking up the cross of compassion and forgiveness? Why has the church relied upon comfort instead of commitment?   Why have we created church cultures in our own image with their own particular songs and rituals and then neglected or berated those different from "us"? The church has failed on many fronts, not because of God but because of man.   Still, God established the church through Jesus Christ. Though man will fail, Jesus persists in calling, empowering and leading the church to have the strength, encouragement and joy to go out into the fields, the highways and city streets.   The church needs to be renewed as "priests" of the living God, each called to represent Christ within the sanctuary of God's world where many people dwell.

> *As you come to him, the living Stone—rejected by men but chosen by God and precious to him— you also, like living stones, are being built into a spiritual house to be a holy priesthood, offering spiritual sacrifices acceptable to God through Jesus Christ.* (I Peter 2:4-5 NIV).

STORY of "The Czar"

A man walked in off the street and sat down in the class I was teaching at a little inner city church in Flint, Michigan. He was known by the students, and they watched in curiosity to see what my response would be to this man who was at first unassuming, but who would later reveal something very interesting (as apparently he always did). What caught my attention was Ted's belt buckle that had an LED (electronic) moving text display that read: "Ted for Russian Czar of a United Eastern Europe." (Now if that doesn't invite interest and conversation, what else could?) I asked him to explain all this. He went on to tell me how he was rightfully entitled by lineage to be the next Russian Czar and that he believed this would happen someday. I decided to play along with him a bit, so I asked: "Suppose you were asked to come back as the "Czar", then what? What would you do?" Ted was stumped, not sure what his purpose was besides self-fulfillment.

Now Ted could be considered mentally delusional, but in fact his aspirations are more subtly hidden by those of us who call ourselves mentally stable. Who doesn't at times dream of personal glory or at least appreciate being thought of as someone of value and worth? I did challenge Ted after listening to his claims by stating honestly that I felt he had "Illusions of Grandeur", to which he expressed curiosity as to understand what I meant. I then asked him if he knew the impact of his assumptions and aspirations, and whether he was prepared to handle such a role and responsibility. Upon reflection, even with all the knowledge and intellect that Ted had, it turned out that he was quite lost when it came to these questions. He had a difficult time even acknowledging his humility in light of a role that was exalted and overwhelming. While Ted could quote scriptures and understood a few basic concepts of the Christian faith, when it came to a personal relationship with the Living Lord and Savior he admitted that he was not a believer. He could believe that he was destined to be the next Russian Czar, but he could not humble himself before the King of kings, and submit himself to love and serve Jesus Christ. It was as if he was blind to the truth of his need of salvation. Ted was his own advocate, he preached himself to the point of blind ambition.

2 Corinthians 4:4-5 (NIV) [4] The god of this age has blinded the minds of unbelievers, so that they cannot see the light of the gospel of the glory of

Christ, who is the image of God. [5] For we do not preach ourselves, but Jesus Christ as Lord, and ourselves as your servants for Jesus' sake.

GOD IS BUILDING HIS KINGDOM

God is building His Kingdom, even working through His people in this present realm and era. The Great Day of the Lord, the Second Coming of Jesus Christ, is what believers look forward to. Isaiah 62 foretells that Day and the millennial rule of Christ. It begins with the prophet being inspired to speak God's word of promise and hope. God is not going to stop speaking hope to His people about the future coming of His Kingdom. God speaks through Isaiah to engage God's people to prepare a highway for the Lord by removing the rocks and stones that are a hindrance. The purpose of preparation is not so much for the Lord but for the earth's people to come to salvation.

From the words of prophecy, to the fulfillment of prophecy in Jesus ministry, to the witness and work of the church, to the testimony of believers, the dawning of God's Kingdom is preceding the eventual Second Coming of Jesus Christ in power and glory. There is a process whereby God is fulfilling His Kingdom plan. The words of a great hymn "We've a Story to Tell to the Nations" speak of God's process of revelation: "*And the darkness shall turn to dawning, and the dawning to noonday bright. And Christ's great Kingdom shall come to earth, the Kingdom of love and light.*" I thought of this one day as I was driving on an open highway just prior to sunrise. The soft glow of the sun gradually lit and rose upon the eastern horizon, then in time the sun ascended to the center of the sky. Within this illustration of illumination the critical arrival of the sun rising into direct view is what marked a new day. Up until then, everything else was anticipation and preparation for the direct light.

The wonderful news of God's Kingdom, intersecting with us now and coming in time is something that we should not keep still or quiet about. That's what Isaiah was inspired to write and share with the people, and that is why God calls His people to express faith and take responsibility. In the time we are given to watch attentively, we are to be involved in the protection and care of our cities and communities. There is nothing outside of God's power that should keep us from representing Christ and speaking of God's coming Kingdom. The Lord spoke through the prophets of old and works through His anointed advocates and preachers of today to herald His coming. So too, each person should not rest still, or be silent in their witness. The actions and words of a true believer's faith are to reflect and illumine God's grace and truth. Believers are to be evident "signs" that God's Kingdom that is "at hand". Indeed our service to the "least of all" is a service to the "greatest" of all that is coming, Christ Jesus the Lord, the suffering Messiah, the King of Glory. The marriage between God and His people shall be consummated in the completion of God's Kingdom through Christ.

Questions for Class Discussion

1. List the positive and negative aspects of cities (urban environments) in our times.

2. How will the City of God be different according to Isaiah 62?

3. Discuss the beauty of symbolism that God uses when describing His people as being the "Bride" in Isaiah 62.4-5.

   How does this image of Israel in Isaiah compare with how a bride receives a new name through marriage?

4. How are we called to prepare the way for the second coming of Jesus?

   In what ways is this exciting?
   In what ways is this overwhelming?

5. In Revelation 3:11-13 what is Jesus calling for His church to do to prepare for His coming?

6. In what ways has Christ's encouragement helped you through adversity or rejection?

Closing Idea

Seek ways to be available to say to God "Here am I. Send me." Share the good news of Jesus Christ this week by giving a testimony to a stranger. Tell them about what Jesus has done in your life. Make sure you don't dwell upon material blessings or success; be honest about how the Lord is at work to deliver you from sin, sickness, loneliness, bondage to despair, hopelessness, lack of meaning or purposelessness. Confess your struggles and vulnerability. Be willing to represent Jesus through honest sharing.

Knowing Jesus makes all the difference in how you are able to survive and thrive. Tell someone (according to your experience) about how being linked to the Church or having friends with true faith has been a blessing. When you share your faith, talk more about Jesus and God's Holy Spirit than about yourself. While you share your hope with enthusiasm, also give room to listen carefully to what others are struggling with. Listening is how you first discovered God was calling you and listening will be how you will be able to discern how God is at work to call others to faith. Be patient, yet urgent. Look forward to each day as an opportunity to prepare yourself and others for Christ's Kingdom. Live with joyful anticipation for each day that the Lord gives you. Your life song is meant to be heard as a "prelude" that gives glory to Christ prior to His imminent return in glory to the earth.

Selected Reading:

We cannot understand the message and miracles of Jesus unless they are interpreted in the setting of his view of the world and man, and the need for the coming of the Kingdom.

The Old Testament prophets looked forward to the Day of the Lord and a divine visitation to purge the world of evil and sin and to establish God's perfect reign in the earth. We find, then, in the Old Testament a contrast between the present order of things and the redeemed order of the Kingdom of God. The difference between the old and the new orders is described in different terms, with differing degrees of continuity and discontinuity between the two; Amos (9:13-15) describes the Kingdom in very this-worldly terms, but Isaiah sees the new order as new heavens and a new earth (Isa. 65:17).

The idea of a new redeemed order is described in different terms in the literature of late Judaism. Sometimes the Kingdom of God is depicted in very earthly terms, as though the new order meant simply the perfection of the old order, sometimes it involves a radical transformation of the old order so that the new order is described in transformational language. In some later apocalypses, there is first a temporal earthly kingdom, followed by a new transformed eternal order.

The Age to Come and the Kingdom of God are sometimes interchangeable terms. In response to the rich young ruler's request about the way to eternal life, Jesus replied that eternal life is the life of the Age to Come (Mk. 10:30). The Age to Come is always looked at from the viewpoint of God's redemptive purpose for men, not from the viewpoint of the unrighteous. The attaining of "that age," i.e., the Age to Come, is a blessing reserved for God's people. It will be inaugurated by the resurrection from the dead (Lk. 20:35), and is the age when death will be no more. Those who attain to that age will be like the angels in that they will become immortal. Only then will they experience all that it means to be sons of God (Lk. 20:34-36). Resurrection life is therefore eternal life – the life of the Age to Come – the life of the Kingdom of God.

Not only resurrection marks the transition from this age to the coming age; the Parousia of Christ will mark the close of this age (Mt. 24:3). The Son of Man will come with power and great glory and will send his angels to gather the elect together from the four corners of the earth into the Kingdom of God (Mt. 24:30-31).

- George Eldon Ladd. [4]

---

[4] George Eldon Ladd. A Theology of the New Testament, p. 45-47

5

AMBASSADORS OF THE KING

(Matthew 3:1-12; II Corinthians 5:17-21)

> ### Key verse:
> [20] *We are therefore Christ's ambassadors, as though God were making his appeal through us. We implore you on Christ's behalf: Be reconciled to God.* - II Corinthians 5:20 NIV

Purpose of study

The hope of God's Kingdom is realized in the Lordship of Jesus Christ. God calls all people to prepare the way for the ministry of His Son in every aspect of life, this leads believers to prepare the way for His Second Coming. While some will repent and believe the Gospel of the Kingdom, not all people will respond positively. The purpose of this chapter's study is to highlight the ministry of John the Baptist as a model for ministry and evangelism. In addition, the goal of this chapter is to affirm that believers of Jesus Christ need to mature spiritually. Disciples are to become friends and representatives of Christ to this world in which they are called to live in graciously, truthfully and faithfully. To believe in Jesus means that one will become an ambassador for the Kingdom of God.

Prelude

Paul's teaching about ambassadorship in God's Kingdom affirms that service for Christ is life-changing, joyful and meaningful. Once we are reconciled to God, we may then become rightful ambassadors/agents of divinely empowered reconciliation. God's Kingdom is represented and advanced through God making His appeal through us. What an incredible opportunity to experience and extend the grace and glory of God! What an awesome responsibility! The Kingdom we represent calls for all-out commitment and the very best of all we are to offer back to God in gratitude. That's what Jesus modeled and that is to be our aim.

Paul grew to understand this, but how could he inspire the church to do the same? How can we inspire others to catch a vision of serving for God's Kingdom? While John the Baptist inspired many people to repent of their sins and be ready for the coming of the Messiah, he still struggled with the religious leaders who were not open and ready for what God was about to do. How open and ready are we to serve God outside of our comfort zone, outside of our interests, outside of our preconceived notions of service, outside of the scope of people we know, outside of the boundaries of our safe church sanctuaries and homes, outside of our will and into the will of God?

An ambassador is commissioned to go to a foreign place or country where they bring their citizenship so they may represent the country or kingdom they are citizens of. Believers are called to be strong in their faith and identity in Jesus Christ. Jesus' disciples are commissioned to represent the eternal values and truths of God's Kingdom. Within this world where there are many people who live by temporal values and fractured truths (lies), the Christian is an ambassador of God's Kingdom principles, values and integrated truths from Scripture. Yet even more than this, an ambassador for the Kingdom of God is called to represent the King, the Prince of Peace, the Lord. Therefore, it is vitally essential that our relationship with the King is direct and close, genuine and reflective. If not, an ambassador is a fraud who will be held into account for misrepresentation and self-interest. The responsibility for being a good and faithful ambassador for Christ is overwhelming, but it is not impossible.

How then are we called to do this? To where or to whom do we turn for inspiration, example, or for strength? John the Baptist and the Apostle Paul can give us insights; they were used by God in mighty ways. Each lived their lives as a prelude to Christ, as servants who prepared the way for the Lord.

Scripture Passages

Matthew 3:1-12

[1] In those days John the Baptist came, preaching in the Desert of Judea [2] and saying, "Repent, for the kingdom of heaven is near." [3] This is he who was spoken of through the prophet Isaiah:
"A voice of one calling in the desert,
    'Prepare the way for the Lord, make straight paths for him.'"
[4] John's clothes were made of camel's hair, and he had a leather belt around his waist. His food was locusts and wild honey. [5] People went out to him from Jerusalem and all Judea and the whole region of the Jordan. [6] Confessing their sins, they were baptized by him in the Jordan River. [7] But when he saw many of the Pharisees and Sadducees coming to where he was baptizing, he said to them: "You brood of vipers! Who warned you to flee from the coming wrath? [8] Produce fruit in keeping with repentance. [9] And do not think you can say to yourselves, 'We have Abraham as our father.' I tell you that out of these stones God can raise up children for Abraham. [10] The ax is already at the root of the trees, and every tree that does not produce good fruit will be cut down and thrown into the fire.

[11] "I baptize you with water for repentance. But after me will come one who is more powerful than I, whose sandals I am not fit to carry. He will baptize you with the Holy Spirit and with fire. [12] His winnowing fork is in his hand, and he will clear his threshing floor, gathering his wheat into the barn and burning up the chaff with unquenchable fire."

I. **Prepare for God's Kingdom** (Matthew 3:1-12)

A. Preaching repentance (1-2)
B. Preparing to receive the Lord (3)
C. Prophetic warnings (4-11)
  1. A wild and crazy prophet (4)
  2. A compassionate presence (5-6)
  3. An honest confrontation (7-10)
  4. A different baptism (11)
  5. A time of judgment (12)

II Corinthians 5:17-21

[17] Therefore, if anyone is in Christ, he is a new creation; the old has gone, the new has come! [18] All this is from God, who reconciled us to himself through Christ and gave us the ministry of reconciliation: [19] that God was reconciling the world to himself in Christ, not counting men's sins against them. And he has committed to us the message of reconciliation. [20] We are therefore Christ's ambassadors, as though God were making his appeal through us. We implore you on Christ's behalf: Be reconciled to God. [21] God made him who had no sin to be sin for us, so that in him we might become the righteousness of God.

II. Serve in God's Kingdom
   (II Corinthians 5:17-21)
   A. New life in Christ's Kingdom (17)
   B. Share a ministry of reconciliation (18)
   C. Spread the message of forgiveness (19)
   D. Be Ambassadors of God's Kingdom (20)
   E. Trust in Christ as Lord. (21)
      1. For salvation (atonement)
      2. For transformation (righteousness)

Exploring the Scriptures

John the Baptist came as a prophet, anointed and chosen by God to represent His Kingdom and prepare the way for the coming ministry of Jesus Christ. There were those who followed John and congregated daily to hear God's message through him. There were those who came out of great need and desperation for healing and wholeness in their lives. There were those who came looking for purity and forgiveness. There were those who came in skepticism and doubt, and they wanted to watch, observe and find fault. Note that when the Pharisees came they arrived and observed as a group. They could not face John the Baptist individually, face to face. Instead, they stood off and scoffed, much like a gang or a clique that has a false sense of power through agreement to shared faulty assumptions. John's message was revolutionary and clearly challenging for those who were in positions of influence and power. The coming of the Messiah that he was foretelling could spell the collapse of political and religious control for the Pharisees and Sadducees. Still others feared the wrath and power of the Romans, and they saw John the Baptist as a troublemaker, one who might abuse his influence and popularity. John was stirring things up, but not for his personal gain. John the Baptist was a "trouble maker" akin to the prophets of old who had spoken honestly about Israel's sins. In the same spirit, John provided both warning and hope for the generation he lived in.

The most important thing John had to say was *"Repent, for the Kingdom of Heaven is near"* (Mt. 3:2). He repeated this message over and over, and others may have passed this clear and simple message on so that it multiplied in urgency and potency. Like a bell that clearly and loudly tolls, the voice of John the Baptist and his message were inseparable. He came as the fulfiller of the prophet Isaiah, an Elijah of his time, as he prepared the way for the King of Glory. The revelation of the Kingdom of Heaven being "near", or "at hand", stressed the immediacy of God's timing. God's very presence was soon to be made known, the Messiah was in fact in their midst.

The description of John the Baptist is that of a man "gone wild" after God. He was totally committed to God's Kingdom. He lived off the land, relying solely on God, so that he could continue to give an uncompromised and unadulterated message. The food God provided were locusts and honey (this was honey from wild bee hives, not domesticated). Here was a diet that took courage and bravery! His clothing was not made of woven fabric but was made from camel hair and hides; these kept him warm and yet dry. That's important for someone who would regularly be around the water and exposed to extreme temperature changes.

In addition to John's message of preparation, announcing that the *"Kingdom of Heaven was near"*, he was also called to a ministry of extending God's grace through baptism. John preached the truth of God's judgment to those who did not *"produce fruit in keeping with repentance"*. Repentance (turning away from sin and turning toward God) was imperative if persons were to be included within God's Kingdom. John made it clear that the One who was coming after Him would test and determine our spiritual fiber and character. The Savior/King to come would baptize with the Spirit and with fire. The reference to the Spirit affirms the grace of God and the new life that comes through faith in Jesus Christ. The reference to fire has had various interpretations, but is clearly also conveying the matter of purification and refinement. *"With fire"*, for those of faith, affirms the Spirit's role in cleansing, purity and redemption. However, for those who continue to rebel, doubt, or disbelieve in God, the "fire" will mean something quite different, something very definite regarding punishment, Hell and the second death. Souls which are separated from God shall be judged and cut off to be consumed in the fire. We read about the ultimate end of those who do not repent and turn in faith to find life in God: *¹⁴ Then death and Hades were thrown into the lake of fire. The lake of fire is the second death. ¹⁵ If anyone's name was not found written in the book of life, he was thrown into the lake of fire"* Revelation 20:14-15 (NIV).

That's not the kind of fire baptism that John the Baptist wished on anyone, so he warned them all of God's judgment. John's illustration of the threshing floor of grain, where the wheat kernels and chaff are separated through fire, helps us realize that all shall be judged, but not all shall be found true and right with God. The key factor John identifies for salvation is our "fruit". When we have repented of our sin and have faith to believe in the One who has come to be our Savior and Lord, then God will grow good spiritual fruit in our lives. The good fruit authenticates a grace-filled faith. Likewise, the flame of truth and grace received in a believing soul authenticates the Holy Spirit.

Paul's message to the Corinthian church takes up the matter of Spiritual regeneration in Christ, and then instructs us to consider and understand who we are in relationship to God and how we are to live as representatives of God's Kingdom in this world. Paul states this simply: "The old has gone, the new has come!" Personal regeneration involves one's redeemed spiritual condition and a new identity and purpose as a citizen who serves God's Kingdom. In Christ, the risen Lord who makes his home in our hearts, there is a new life given by the Spirit. This new life is not designed to be solitary, it is meant to be lived in and for the greater community of Heaven. The ministry of reconciliation that we are called to represent and bring to others becomes our ultimate life purpose while here on earth. Paul's emphatic plea is that we "implore" people to come to faith in Jesus Christ; this implies passion and love, mercy and hope. Faith in the work of God's Holy Spirit is essential to convince others and express the truth of the Gospel. By faith and obedience, believers are called to behold the transformative power of Christ's revealed Word, life, death and resurrection. *"God made him who had no sin to be sin for us, so that in him we might become the righteousness of God"* II Cor. 5:21. God gives a joyful and meaningful responsibility to believers to participate in the reconciling work of His Kingdom, to share the word of unconditional love, forgiveness and new life in Christ. The work of God's righteousness is that of His Holy Spirit leading people into holy living (discerned, distinct and different from the wisdom of the world). We are called to trust Jesus and follow His example of righteousness. The people of God are called to become reliant and resourceful. God's Holy Spirit leads and empowers their steps and service.

Bridging into Today

People often wonder about what God is doing. From our human point of view we observe that things are not going so well. Doubters find it difficult to trust that the reign of God exists and is in their midst. In our fallen condition we struggle to believe in something that requires faith and hope beyond our immediate senses or experiences. The first step of faith is to repent of our sinfulness, ignorance and pride so as to ask Christ into our hearts. Repentance, however, involves more than the initial confession of our sins. An ongoing surrender and commitment to change is necessary and vital. Therefore, we need assistance, accountability and strength to grow and bear fruit for God. This is why Christ began the Church. Jesus followed the wisdom of His Father for fellowship. God has designed the Church, the Body of Christ, to provide this support and to give resources for combined strength. Furthermore, believers in the church are called to be ambassadors of reconciliation both outside of the church and inside of the church. Spiritual passion and purpose are fused together when people's lives are changed through true faith and submission to Jesus Christ. When we serve Him by caring for others we find our calling, we grow in developing lasting fruit in lasting relationships, and we represent the Kingdom of God faithfully in and through the context of community.

Questions for Class Discussion

1. Why is confession and repentance necessary for change to happen?

How do we see this in our times?

2. How has repentance and faith brought change or healing for you?

3. What meaning does baptism have through water, Spirit and fire?

4. Think of ways that people have been reconciled to one another after a conflict or misunderstanding; how is this similar to, or different from, reconciliation with God?

5. How is God calling you to be an ambassador of reconciliation for His Kingdom this day or week?

Closing Idea

Prepare for the Kingdom of God first through humble prayer. The Lord will cleanse you within your inner being for the sake of service out into the world. To live life as a "Prelude" for the Kingdom of God requires keeping one's heart and mind "in tune" with Christ and the leading of God's Holy Spirit. How can we stay in tune if we don't give our Lord time to adjust our tone, attitude, pitch or direction? Prayer involves ongoing tuning, adjustment, and openness to the leading of the Spirit; prayer is therefore essential for serving and glorifying God.

PERSONAL STORY: A Prayer of Mercy

My wife Marilyn is an excellent nurse. She has a wonderful witness to Christ and serves as an ambassador for God's Kingdom through her patient care. One night, some of the nurses down the hall were helping a patient who would soon die. The woman was in her 80's and was now at the stage of shallow breathing. One of the nurses had read the 23rd Psalm for her and had prayed with her. Marilyn came in and also held the dying woman's frail hand. Then, being led by God's Holy Spirit, she spoke to her saying: "Jesus loves you. Your sins are forgiven." The woman who had been restless and struggling with each breath then released the burden that was holding her back. She needed to hear words of grace in order to let go and trust in God's ministry of grace. In that moment of peaceful release into the arms of the Almighty, she embraced the gift of God's mercy. Marilyn was the ambassador of the message of sweet salvation.

There are times that the message of forgiveness must be clearly stated or demonstrated. Jesus taught us to pray saying, "Forgive us our trespasses (sins) as we forgive those that trespass (sin) against us." That is what we need for salvation, and that is what gives us peace through reconciliation with God. Forgiveness is the message of the cross, and it is to be the message of God's Kingdom in Christ. When we can be ambassadors of Christ, sharing the message and ministry of forgiveness, then we are being faithful to the work of God's Kingdom.

Selected Reading:

The Word of God is very clear: we begin to understand the Church and its mission as we see the Church as part of God's plan and purpose for the whole creation.

Not Just "Plan B" - But what is God's master plan? Simply this: that God may glorify himself by uniting all things under Christ." "God's plan is to unite and reconcile all things in Christ so that men can again serve their maker." The key idea is clearly that of reconciliation. God's plan is for the restoration of His creation, for overcoming, in glorious fulfillment, the damage done to persons and nature through the Fall. God's design for the reconciliation of all things in Christ reaffirms His original intention at creation now adjusted to the realities of the presence of sin in the world. But this is to speak humanly, from our underside view of reality; we must not suppose that God's cosmic plan for reconciliation is "Plan B," a second-best, back-up plan that God thought up because He failed at creation. For God's eternal plan predates both the Fall and the creation; it existed in the mind of God "before the creation of the world" (Eph. 1:4).

This plan includes not only the reconciliation of people to God, but the reconciliation of "all things in heaven and on earth" (Eph. 1:10). Or, as Paul puts it in Colossians 1:20, it is God's intention through Christ "to reconcile to himself all things, whether things on earth or things in heaven, by making peace through His blood, shed on the cross." Central to this plan is the reconciliation of persons to God through the blood of Jesus Christ.

- Howard Snyder. (46-47)[5]

---

[5] Howard Snyder. "The Community of the King" 46-47.

6

THE KINGDOM OF GOD IS NEAR

(Matthew 4:8-17; Psalm 84)

> **Key verse:**
> *From that time on Jesus began to preach, "Repent, for the kingdom of heaven is near."* - Matthew 4:17 NIV

Purpose of study

This chapter's study will focus on the aspect of how God's Kingdom is in our midst through the ministry of Jesus Christ. Jesus is ever so near as God has ordained Him to be the redemptive advocate and consummate friend. Jesus fulfilled the role of Savior by overcoming temptation as a human being and befriending us through incarnate presence and compassion. At the same time He also affirmed His Divinity as the Son of God through His faithfulness and devotion to His Heavenly Father. Jesus came preaching repentance, just as John the Baptist had. The difference was that Jesus had direct authority as the Savior/Messiah. Christ Jesus is vested with true transforming power. God the Father gave this ministry and authority to His Son for our salvation and has interwoven the work of His Holy Spirit into the hearts of all who will believe and receive Jesus as Savior. Let's investigate the connection of Jesus' presence and the words of the Psalmist who longed to be where God dwelt. May we also consider the faith of Jesus in His Father, and His Father's faith in Him, even while He was being tested and tempted by the devil. Consider how we too are tested and tried, tempted and tempered by the adversary through adversity. Trusting that God is near and available to guide and help us, even when we find it difficult to see this, is the key to discovering that the Kingdom of God develops through our faith and the Lord's ministry of truth and grace.

Prelude

The Psalmist, who was the director of music, had a kingdom heart and a kingdom priority for service. He didn't mind whatever level of service God called him to, as long as he could do God's will and dwell in God's presence. In the fullness of time, Jesus came to humbly serve as the Son of God. Yet often he referred to Himself as the "son of man". Jesus was revealing that His role as our Savior and Lord was also to become our Servant-King. The last of the devil's temptations aimed to challenge Jesus' call of humble service. The devil tried to tempt Jesus to take a shortcut to kingship; our Lord did not flinch, but stood His ground in faithfulness to trust His Father God in the fullness of time.

What does this mean for us? We are called to repent of our sin and be faithful to God. Disciples are to reprioritize their devotion and energies. In Christ, we are welcomed to abide in the shadow of our Lord and God, we are called to "seek first the Kingdom of God", and in Christ we may find direction to overcome diversions and temptation. Furthermore, we are called to be servants who seek to do the will of God above our own personal agenda and selfish advancement. We learn from Jesus who fulfilled God's Kingdom plan. Just as He did not forsake the cross and its shame, we also take up our crosses and bear the shame of unpopularity, misunderstanding, hate, prejudice and injustice. Perseverance is possible because we believe in the power of God's forgiving/redeeming love. Salvation is not for the faint of heart, and discipleship involves laying down our lives, trusting in God and submitting to His ultimate Kingly authority and power manifested through Jesus Christ.

Scripture Passages

Matthew 4:8-17

⁸ Again, the devil took him to a very high mountain and showed him all the kingdoms of the world and their splendor. ⁹ "All this I will give you," he said, "if you will bow down and worship me." ¹⁰ Jesus said to him, "Away from me, Satan! For it is written: 'Worship the Lord your God, and serve him only.' " ¹¹ Then the devil left him, and angels came and attended him. ¹² When Jesus heard that John had been put in prison, he returned to Galilee. ¹³ Leaving Nazareth, he went and lived in Capernaum, which was by the lake in the area of Zebulun and Naphtali-- ¹⁴ to fulfill what was said through the prophet Isaiah:
¹⁵ "Land of Zebulun and land of Naphtali, the way to the sea, along the Jordan, Galilee of the Gentiles-- ¹⁶ the people living in darkness have seen a great light; on those living in the land of the shadow of death a light has dawned."

¹⁷ From that time on Jesus began to preach, "Repent, for the kingdom of heaven is near."

I. Jesus faces the devil (Matthew 4:8-11)
   A. The devil's reign in humanity (8)
   B. The devil's temptation to Jesus (9)
   C. Jesus rejects the devil's offer (10)
   D. Angels minister to Jesus (11)

II. Jesus begins His ministry (Matt. 4:12-17)
   A. Placement of ministry: Galilee (12-16)
   B. Preaching repentance and hope (17)

Psalm 84

For the director of music. According to *gittith*. Of the Sons of Korah. A psalm.

¹ How lovely is your dwelling place, O LORD Almighty! ² My soul yearns, even faints, for the courts of the LORD; my heart and my flesh cry out for the living God.
³ Even the sparrow has found a home, and the swallow a nest for herself, where she may have her young-- a place near your altar, O LORD Almighty, my King and my God.
⁴ Blessed are those who dwell in your house; they are ever praising you. Selah
⁵ Blessed are those whose strength is in you, who have set their hearts on pilgrimage.
⁶ As they pass through the Valley of

III. We need Jesus to be our Lord and King (Psalm 84)
   A. Our need for knowing the Living God (1-2)
   B. Our need for God's Kingdom (3-4)
   C. Our need for God's grace and strength (5-7)
   D. Our need for God's protection (8-9)
   E. Our need for serving in God's Kingdom (10)
   F. Our need for the Lord's protection and provision (11)
   G. Our need for trusting God (12)

Baca, they make it a place of springs; the autumn rains also cover it with pools.
⁷ They go from strength to strength, till each appears before God in Zion.
⁸ Hear my prayer, O LORD God Almighty; listen to me, O God of Jacob. Selah
⁹ Look upon our shield, O God; look with favor on your anointed one.
¹⁰ Better is one day in your courts than a thousand elsewhere;
I would rather be a doorkeeper in the house of my God than dwell in the tents of the wicked. ¹¹ For the LORD God is a sun and shield; the LORD bestows favor and honor; no good thing does he withhold from those whose walk is blameless.
¹² O LORD Almighty, blessed is the man who trusts in you.

Exploring the Scriptures

Jesus came to establish the Kingdom of God. This was to begin within the lives of people who would repent and believe the good news of salvation. Jesus came to dethrone the prince of this world, the prince of darkness, Satan. Later in Jesus' ministry, He referred to the importance of His coming death and resurrection: *³¹ Now is the time for judgment on this world; now the prince of this world will be driven out. ³² But I, when I am lifted up from the earth, will draw all men to myself."* John 12:31-32 (NIV) From this passage we see that humility came before honor for Jesus. His sacrifice was necessary for our participation in God's Kingdom. For without His atonement and victory we are not able to inherit eternal life. Yet because of His love that forsook self, and considered our lost condition, we are drawn to receive God's gift of grace and new life in Christ. We are called to turn away from sin and selfishness, from the kingdoms of man, from the pride of our ways. We are called to trust and follow Jesus because He is the way, the truth and the life. Jesus is the life of righteousness with God.

Here in this passage we see the strength of Jesus' conviction to do the will of God His Father. If Jesus had given into the devil's temptation, Jesus would have broken the first of the Ten Commandments "Thou shall have no other god before me" Deuteronomy 5:7. The temptation of the devil to Adam and Eve was that they could become like God by eating the forbidden fruit. The temptation of the devil to Jesus was that Jesus could become a king immediately if He would just bow down and worship him. The comparison is that the devil masks the truth; in neither case was the temptation accurate or its claims true. Adam and Eve were made in the image of God, and yet they were still children of God developmentally and quite dependent on God. Jesus was already the One and Only Son of God, the Messiah King. Because of this He did not need to prove Himself or act hastily to promote God's Kingdom agenda. He did not have to assume His Kingly role prior to assuming His servant role. Certainly the Kingdom of God was His priority, but it was not to be realized through His own show of force or through compliance to the devil's farce. The Kingdom of God comes to transform people spiritually through peaceful persuasion and pervasive truth and grace. Jesus' response to the devil's temptation of "going solo" is to act in concert with the leading of God the Father so as to be in harmony with the work of the Holy Spirit.

    For us, the Holy Spirit is received by surrender to Jesus Christ, and through His Lordship we are transferred from the kingdom of darkness into the Kingdom of God's love and light. Jesus was baptized by John prior to His temptation in the wilderness in order to "fulfill all righteousness" (Matthew 3:15). The intent of Jesus was to righteously handle the test He would face in the wilderness. This was a prelude to the ultimate test: Would the Son of God actually humble Himself, even to a cross? The death and resurrection that Jesus foretold to John in His baptism would surely strike a lethal blow to Satan. If the devil could convince Jesus to take a short cut, a route that could bypass the work of God's Holy Spirit for changing humanity, then God's work of salvation would be thwarted by the "author of lies". The temptation in the wilderness for Jesus reveals this spiritual struggle, but Jesus is up for the challenge through a time of fasting and prayerful preparation. Satan is trying to divide the Trinity, seeking to pry Jesus away from trusting His Father and believing in the work of God's Holy Spirit for the transformation of humanity. The devil does not deny Jesus' role as being the Savior, but instead tries to make Jesus look at His role apart from His relationship with God the Father and the Holy Spirit. Jesus overcomes the trial and temptation by saying, "Away from me Satan, for It is written: 'Worship the Lord God, and serve Him only.'" Jesus was not going to assert His own Lordship as being above His Father's, and He was also not going to deny the work of His Father's Holy Spirit.

    Throughout His life Jesus reveals that for the sake of God's Kingdom the Holy Spirit is an essential part of God's team. The Holy Spirit is actively working to transform the hearts and souls of those who would repent and believe. By trusting in Jesus, and receiving the gift of God's grace in the Holy Spirit through faith, our repentance affirms the call of God to follow the example and leading of the Savior/King who laid His life down for us. Likewise, by the strength of the Holy Spirit, we too can overcome temptation and serve God obediently and faithfully.

John the Baptist was concerned about whether or not Jesus was the true Messiah because he expected Jesus to powerfully overthrow the principalities and powers of darkness that were evident in Roman rule and Jewish power structures. Jesus assured John the Baptist that He was the Messiah by quoting an important passage from the prophet Isaiah.

[1] Nevertheless, there will be no more gloom for those who were in distress. In the past he humbled the land of Zebulun and the land of Naphtali, but in the future he will honor Galilee of the Gentiles, by the way of the sea, along the Jordan-- [2] The people walking in darkness have seen a great light; on those living in the land of the shadow of death a light has dawned. (Isaiah 9:1-2 NIV)

The coming of the Messiah in this passage is like that of a gentle dawning, not like a thunderous surprise of quick and immediate judgment of which John the Baptist and many others had hoped for. Jesus came to reveal God the Father and introduce the Holy Spirit, and through this revelation people were given the opportunity to repent and believe. The dawning of the new age Jesus initiated first calls for repentance, humility, patience, prayer and perseverance.

Psalm 84 is a wonderful prayer of reliance upon God. Jesus reflected a similar attitude in His ministry, and He calls believers to follow His lead. We note that in Psalm 84 the author had discovered a very personal revelation of God as he focused faithfully upon God in worship. In the dwelling place of God he describes the joy of being in God's presence and the security of a relationship of faith. The Psalmist senses that there is an anointed One to come who will be our shield and protector, One who will lead us from temptation into triumph over the tempter.

Jesus is the anointed One. He justifies us through His shed blood on the cross. When we rely upon ourselves we have no lasting defense against evil, but when we rely upon Christ Jesus as Lord and Savior, we have a sure defender and redeemer. In Christ Jesus, we are brought into intimate and transformative communion with God our Heavenly Father. In Christ Jesus, we are given the Holy Spirit to be our counselor, comforter and security. In Christ Jesus, we have one who helps us fight spiritual battles with honor, courage and dignity. In Christ Jesus, affirmation is given from God the Father in a voice that speaks above the waters "This is my beloved Son in whom I am well pleased, listen to Him." In Christ Jesus, validation is given through the descending dove (a visual sign of God's Holy Spirit and manifest peace). God the Father affirms the sweet communion that exists in the Trinity, an unshakable harmony of love, truth and grace. Jesus Christ is the Messiah, the Savior, the Son of God, the rightful heir to God's throne. His Kingdom has come, God's will is being done, the world will never be the same, and the devil's days are numbered.

Bridging into Today

Currently the devil has a temporary reign over many people's hearts and minds. The scheme of the devil is to maintain power and control over people's desires and priorities, and to lead people astray to believe lies and practice disobedience from the ways and will of God. The devil can never dethrone God because he is an imposter, but many people have been fooled to believe the devil's philosophy of selfishness and pride. Political leaders abuse their authority, business leaders accept big bonuses for extravagant lifestyles, television and movie celebrities justify their extra marital affairs, a poor man rationalizes that robbery is necessary to feed his family, athletes cheat by using steroids, and economies collapse because of reliance upon credit cards and false security.

The devil has humanity on the run; people are trying to survive even though they are tragically traveling in the wrong direction. Without faith in God, and without knowing and trusting the Savior Jesus Christ, people are blind to the fact that sin is sweeping much of humanity downward upon a path that is leading toward destruction and hell. Jesus came to conquer sin and death, to defeat the devil and bring us victory. Through His death for our sins on the cross of Calvary, Jesus forgave us and accomplished a work of redeeming love. Through Christ's shed blood, God paid the ransom of sin's captivity. By faith in Jesus, we are justified before God by Christ's perfect redeeming love. We must trust in God's work of salvation made perfect through Jesus.

We learn from the Psalmist that our worship can prepare us for meeting God on His terms. When we open our hearts and minds to trust the living God, and are willing to serve as He leads, then we will know true contentment and joy. Jesus exemplified worship and service in His life and through His sacrifice. Likewise, worshipping and serving God are the two key elements of healthy Christians and churches. Repentance and humility before a loving and Holy God will turn our lives around toward the path that leads to eternal life and participation in God's Kingdom.

Questions for Class Discussion

1. In what ways do we struggle with the devil tempting us?

2. Why is repentance difficult?

3. What does Jesus teach us about reliance upon God?

4. What do we learn about trusting and loving God from the Psalmist?

5. How has God ministered to you with an intangible reward for your faith and trust in Him?

Closing Idea

What would happen if repentance was a daily act of picking up our cross? The discipline of seeing our service in light of God's Kingdom being present, in our midst, can help us see life from a new perspective. Perhaps the dove of God's Spirit is revealing God's grace and favor to people of faith in more ways than we might at first be aware of. Think of the simple things God provides for life, like a heartbeat, our ongoing breath, the provision of daily bread, the light of the sun and the complexity and beauty of nature and framework of the creation that surrounds and sustains us. The devil dares us to doubt God's provision and protection. The Holy Spirit calls us to trust and believe our Savior/King, to personally have faith in God's anointed One, Jesus the Christ.

The work of God's Kingdom is not for the faint of heart. The call of Christ is not going to be popular or pleasing to those who are unwilling to repent of sinful ways. However, the reward of faith and obedience to God the Father yields the greatest good and the finest fruits of God's Spirit. Those who live their lives as a prelude of God's truth and grace in Jesus Christ will not be disappointed; they shall be rewarded in the fullness of time upon Christ's return in glory.

Selected Reading:

In a day like this, wonderful yet fearful, men are asking questions. What does it all mean? Where are we going? What is the meaning and the goal of human history? Men are concerned today not only about the individual and the destiny of His soul but also about the meaning of history itself. Does mankind have a destiny? Or do we jerk across the stage of time like wooden puppets, only to have the stage, the actors, and the theatre itself destroyed by fire, leaving only a pile of ashes and the smell of smoke?

In ancient times, poets and seers longed for an ideal society. Hesiod dreamed of a lost Golden Age in the distant past but saw no brightness in the present, constant care for the morrow, and no hope for the future. Plato pictured an ideal state organized on philosophical principles; but he himself realized that his plan was too idealistic to be realized. Virgil sang of one who would deliver the world from its sufferings and by whom "the great line of the ages begins anew."

The Hebrew-Christian faith expresses its hope in terms of the Kingdom of God. This Biblical hope is not in the same category as the dreams of the Greek poets but is at the very heart of revealed religion. The Biblical idea of the Kingdom of God is deeply rooted in the Old Testament and is grounded in the confidence that there is one eternal, living God who has revealed Himself to men and who has a purpose for the human race which He has chosen to accomplish through Israel. The Biblical hope is therefore a religious hope; it is an essential element in the revealed will and the redemptive work of the living God. - George Eldon Ladd [6]

---

[6] George EldonLadd, "The Gospel of the Kingdom" p. 13-14.

7

SEEK A KINGDOM OF RIGHTEOUSNESS

(Matthew 5:17-20; Psalm 72)

> Key verse:
> *"Do not think that I have come to abolish the Law or the Prophets; I have not come to abolish them but to fulfill them..."*
> (Matthew 5:17)

Purpose of Encounter Study

This chapter's study will look at how Jesus clarified the connection between the purpose of God's laws and the importance of prophetic fulfillment. Jesus came to satisfy and fulfill both of these aspects of God's revelation through His ministry. Jesus is the living Word of God, the incarnate answer of God to satisfy our seeking. Christ is the High Priest who reconciles our corrupted hearts and cleanses us with perfect love. The aim of this chapter is to help people understand more clearly why we need Jesus Christ to be our King (Lord) and Savior.

While understanding is the beginning of wisdom, it is also vital that we apply what we are taught by God the way of integrity. Righteousness is not simply an attribute of God; it is the basis for God's Kingdom, the embodiment of justice, mercy, grace and holiness. Righteousness is a pure and holy gift and pathway for believers; it is received and grown through faith. God's grace and goodness are poured out into the hearts and lives of believers. God's transforming work leads us in the path of righteousness, into the way of Christ, into the work of a Kingdom that is above the ways of man. The incarnation, teachings, acts of kindness and healings of compassion of Jesus reveal the nature of God's plan of righteousness.

Prelude

Have you ever known of someone who repeatedly objected to the importance of seeking righteousness? If you asked this person to come to church or a Bible Study, did they give you odd looks and then tell you about why they have no need for the church? Did they tell you how busy their lives are or how some church messed up their lives? People dodge the issue of seeking righteousness by blaming the church or a few errant Christians. Some do so based on wanting to avoid change because they have fallen into the pattern of rationalizing their sinful ways. Others avoid righteousness because they don't understand the importance of it, they have substituted many other temporary things for the eternal matters of the soul. Still others have not tasted in the goodness and grace of God and the only kind of righteousness they are familiar with is legalistic or manipulative. Then there are those who rationalize their current passive and weak spiritual condition by misinterpreting the Scripture passage "all have sinned and fallen short of the glory of God" (Romans 3:23) to mean that righteousness (of any sort) is impossible to achieve. When such faulty logic is used it assumes that because we do fall short of God's glory there is no point in trying to seek after the righteousness we long for and spiritually need.

What is the answer? A closer look at the Scripture text from Romans 3:21-23 reveals that Jesus alone is the one who can administer the work of God's gift of grace that brings righteousness. Jesus did not come to abolish the law, He came to fulfill its righteous requirements. This is how He proved His worthiness to be our Savior. Jesus came as prophesied; God's Son was sent to fulfill His identity and role as Priest and King, the Savior/Messiah. By faith, we may receive Jesus Christ as God's greatest gift. In so doing and believing, we receive the blessing of His perfect love that fills our hearts and minds. The transforming work of Christ reconciles us so that we may become "righteous" by grace for God's eternal Kingdom. Through the path of discipleship we are transformed. The work of God's righteousness involves a marriage of our faith with Christ's work of salvation; the endowment of God is the blessing of receiving and being filled with His Holy Spirit.

Romans 3:21-23 reveals the following about the new covenant of God's Kingdom being manifested through grace that fulfills God's law of justification:

> *^{21} But now a righteousness from God, apart from law, has been made known, to which the Law and the Prophets testify. ^{22} This righteousness from God comes through faith in Jesus Christ to all who believe. There is no difference, ^{23} for all have sinned and fall short of the glory of God, ^{24} and are justified freely by his grace through the redemption that came by Christ Jesus.*

Jesus fulfills the law and prophets by bringing about a new covenant that satisfies the requirements of the old covenant. This new covenant respects the old, but it is set apart in that it is based upon a new outpouring of God's redeeming grace in Christ Jesus the Messiah. Each covenant respects the importance of faith, but the new covenant relies upon the justification of God that was freely given through Jesus Christ and His sacrifice on the cross. Entry into God's Kingdom is not a matter of human will, but of God's gracious response to our humility and faith. God grants entry for all who seek first His Kingdom and His righteousness. Seeking continues throughout life and is the key for growing into the wisdom and ways of God and His Kingdom.

Scripture Passages

Matthew 5:17-20

[17] "Do not think that I have come to abolish the Law or the Prophets; I have not come to abolish them but to fulfill them. [18] I tell you the truth, until heaven and earth disappear, not the smallest letter, not the least stroke of a pen, will by any means disappear from the Law until everything is accomplished. [19] Anyone who breaks one of the least of these commandments and teaches others to do the same will be called least in the kingdom of heaven, but whoever practices and teaches these commands will be called great in the kingdom of heaven. [20] For I tell you that unless your righteousness surpasses that of the Pharisees and the teachers of the law, you will certainly not enter the kingdom of heaven.
Matthew 5:17-20 (NIV)

> I. Seek First the Kingdom of God (Matthew 5:17-20)
> A. Believe in Jesus (17)
>   1. He fulfills the requirements of the law
>   2. He fulfills God's word of promise
> B. Rely upon Jesus (18)
> C. Follow Jesus (19-20)
>   1. Serve His Kingdom faithfully
>   2. Seek the reward of Christ's respect
>   3. Rely upon His surpassing truth and grace.

Psalm 72

Of Solomon. (Psalm 72 A Prayer for King David's Son by King David)
[1] Endow the king with your justice, O God, the royal son with your righteousness. [2] He will judge your people in righteousness, your afflicted ones with justice. [3] The mountains will bring prosperity to the people, the hills the fruit of righteousness. [4] He will defend the afflicted among the people and save the children of the needy; he will crush the oppressor. [5] He will endure as long as the sun, as long as the moon, through all generations. [6] He will be like rain falling on a mown field, like showers watering the earth. [7] In his days the righteous will flourish; prosperity will abound till the moon is no more. [8] He will rule from sea to sea and from the River to the ends of the earth. [9] The desert tribes will bow before him and his enemies will lick the dust. [10] The kings of Tarshish and of distant shores will bring tribute to him; the kings of Sheba and Seba will present him gifts. [11] All kings will bow down to him and all nations will serve him. [12] For he will deliver the needy who cry out, the afflicted who have no one to help. [13] He will take pity on the weak and the needy and save the needy from death. [14] He will rescue them from oppression and violence, for precious is their blood in his sight. [15] Long may he live! May gold from Sheba be given him. May people ever pray for him and bless him all day long. [16] Let grain abound throughout the land; on the tops of the hills may it sway. Let its fruit flourish like Lebanon; let it thrive like the grass of the field.
[17] May his name endure forever; may it continue as long as the sun. All nations will be blessed through him, and they will call him blessed.

> II. Pray for the Growth of God's Kingdom Psalm 72: 1-17
> (*A big vision of hope beyond Solomon*)
> A. Justice and righteousness (1-2)
> B. Restoration and deliverance (3-4)
> C. Preservation and Prosperity (5-7)
> D. Sovereignty and majesty (8-11)
> E. Compassion and salvation (12-14)
> F. Honor and blessing (15-17)

¹⁸ Praise be to the LORD God, the God of Israel, who alone does marvelous deeds.
¹⁹ Praise be to his glorious name forever; may the whole earth be filled with his glory. Amen and Amen.
²⁰ This concludes the prayers of David son of Jesse.

III. Praise to God our King
Psalm 72:18-20
A. God's deeds are glorious (18)
B. God's name is glorious (19a)
C. God's Kingdom is glorious (19b)

Exploring the Scriptures

The Sermon on the Mount in Matthew chapter five summarizes the ministry and Gospel message of Jesus Christ. His sermon on that lovely spot overlooking the blue waters of Galilee could be considered the inaugural address for proclaiming the values and principles of the Kingdom of God. His first words were *"Blessed are the poor in spirit, for theirs is the kingdom of heaven."* Matthew 5:3 (NIV). Jesus began with words of humility for humanity. While Jesus was addressing the crowd at hand, He was also proclaiming to all mankind the Kingdom and ministry that He came to set forth. We observe in this first beatitude the basic criteria for entry into God's Kingdom; one begins with an awareness of spiritual need. A repentant confession of the poverty of one's soul is essential. Jesus did not preach anything that He would not personally model or exemplify. He would soon humble Himself in the form of a servant, even submitting Himself to live in poverty in the desert where He was tempted by Satan. Throughout His life He chose service over self, love over pride and compassion over arrogance. While He could have manipulated crowds and disciples, He gave them freedom to follow and serve.

Over and over again Jesus chose humility and was obedient to His Heavenly Father. He was eventually put on trial by a human court and was rejected by His own people. Through Christ's purity and contrition, God the Father could show Himself best in sacrificial love. In this respect, Jesus' humility was very different from our own need for humility. What differs in us is that we are rebellious, sinful and needy. Our condition as fallen humanity is the reason why humility is necessary before a righteous and Holy God. Jesus was the perfect Son of God, and He was also a flawless human being. He had no personal need for humility. Our need for humility is imperative; His humility was His choice so as to redeem us. Jesus humbled Himself in order to bless us who are "poor of spirit" (Matt. 5:1) with the riches of God's grace (2 Cor. 8:9).

Jesus, in Matthew 5:17-20, was correcting two false assumptions that people were making about His ministry. (1) Just because He was showing God's grace and mercy through preaching repentance and healing people did not mean that He came to negate the Law; and (2) just because He was not bringing the Kingdom of God in through a big sweep of powerful political and physical might did not mean that He was not fulfilling the words of the prophets for a Messiah. Jesus was accomplishing the work of God's Kingdom, but it entailed a process of salvation that involved God's work of justification and sanctification within those who will believe and obey the word of God.

Historically, the church has struggled with pride and selfish ambition. This is not the way of Jesus or of God's Kingdom. While there are still churches that are led by a remnant of pastors/leaders faithful to God's Word, there is contention from those who defy the authority of the Scriptures by asking their pastors/leaders to lower standards on matters of doctrine, character, service and ordination. Churches are compromised when their pastors, leaders and members emphasize charisma and Spiritual Gifts but neglect discipline, training, support and accountability. The point is not that leaders in the church (pastors, deacons, elders, teachers, trustees, etc.) have to be perfect, but there must be a desire and resolve to please God before pleasing man. Disciples of Christ are to be sincere, honest, humble and available to God. The matter of "seeking first the Kingdom of God and His righteousness" has been sadly neglected. It is better for a church to have a few Christ-centered people leading than have full boards with a lack of maturity and wisdom. It is better for a church to be faithful than to be popular, and to be making a few good disciples than attracting a sea of shallow-deep attendees.

The way to have a righteousness that surpasses that of the Pharisees and Scribes is to have faith in the righteous "Lamb of God" who takes away the sins of the world (recall John the Baptist in John 1:29). Jesus is the Word of God, and He embodied the righteousness of God as the incarnate and beloved Son of God. Jesus was sent to be our Savior/King, our High Priest from Heaven to reconcile us to God our Father. The religions of man may attempt righteousness and purity, but redemption is a gift from God's throne of grace. Jesus was given authority to defeat sin and death. He has the authority to grant forgiveness and new life born of the Holy Spirit. Only in Christ, and through the new life of God's Holy Spirit that believers receive, is a person made righteous and acceptable before God's judgment seat.

The hope of God's eventual Kingdom on earth is contained within Psalm 72 in a wonderful prayer by King David for his son Solomon and his future as the next king of Israel. While David's hope and vision is much bigger than what his son will accomplish. David gives an inspiring prayer that must likewise be interpreted as having its final fulfillment in the coming of God's personal reign on earth through Jesus Christ. The hope of David is realized in Jesus Christ, not Solomon. The manifestation of God's Kingdom on earth will involve a reign of justice and righteousness, a restoration of God's presence in worship, a renewal of the earth, a reverence of God and His sovereignty, a respect of people toward God and one another, a responsiveness of God to redeem His children, and a spirit of praise and adoration of God among His people.

Bridging into Today

While Jesus came in humility, He shall one day come in power and glory to fulfill both God's promises. The hopes and dreams that He inspires within us shall become realized. Jesus evidenced the nature of God's Kingdom through His life as He gave us a taste of His future millennial reign upon this earth. Until then, we look to Jesus as personal Lord and Savior; we grow in faith as we serve His Kingdom. His reign is working its way into the hearts and lives of all who believe. The Kingdom of God is a reality that we may humbly grow to understand, participate in, appreciate and be blessed by. Citizenship in God's Kingdom is granted by grace through faith in Jesus Christ.

The first matter of faith, therefore, is confession that leads to repentance. From this repentance our lives turn around in orientation and direction. Our devotion and service is reoriented from self and worldly pursuits toward the Kingdom of God. Hunger and thirst for righteousness is satisfied and quenched in Jesus Christ. He resides within the heart and reigns upon the throne of the soul through honor and worship. Genuine worship is not simply affection for the Lord but service in His name. Worship is externalized and carried forth into mission through words and songs that arise from our work out in the harvest fields. Worship is to be non-stop, a life of giving ultimate worth to Christ our King. What a joyful, purposeful, calling!

Questions for Class Discussion

1. Why do people in general have a desire for what is just, right and true?

   What does this say about our God-created nature as contrasted with our fallen and sinful nature?

2. In what ways did Jesus evidence God's truthfulness and righteousness?

3. In what ways did Jesus fulfill prophecy in Psalm 72, and in what ways has He yet to fulfill this prophecy?

4. Why is humility important when it comes to faith?

5. What hope do we have of Christ's future reign according to Psalm 72?

Closing Idea

Imagine what you would feel and what you would do if you were to be alive when Jesus comes again. The thought of beholding Jesus incites various kinds of reactions and responses.   For believers the response is not always inspiration and hope, sometimes even people of faith contend with a sense of being overwhelmed and unprepared. This is actually an honest feeling when one considers the need for greater faith, the realization of uncompleted work, the concern for people who have not received salvation, and the need to humbly accept that it is by "grace alone" that we are saved. Concern, however, will be replaced by the comfort of the Holy Spirit. The tears we shed will be dried by the loving hand of the Heavenly Father. The hurts we harbor and the scars we suffer will be healed in the power of the resurrected Christ who shall give us a new body and life fit for the eternal Kingdom of Heaven.

Selected Reading

"Matthew's Jesus issues His greatest instructions in the Sermon on the Mount, at the start of His ministry. Matthew has organized the sermon's material with great care. He frames the bulk of it with two attacks on those who could so easily mislead his readers. As a preface to His instruction on the Law, He turns as well to a person or type who is the "least." It has long been wondered if He has Paul's self-description in mind."

- Robert Griffith Jones [7]

---

[7] Robert Griffith Jones – "The Gospel According to Paul" pp. 260-261

8

PLEASE GOD IN SECRET SERVICE

(Matthew 6:1-4; II Corinthians 5:9-10)

> ### Key verse:
> 10 *For we must all appear before the judgment seat of Christ, that each one may receive what is due him for the things done while in the body, whether good or bad.* - 2 Corinthians 5:10 (NIV)

Purpose of study

We have already affirmed that the Kingdom of God is to be served with humility and sacrifice. Honor will come to those who faithfully and unselfishly give of and use their abilities, talents, resources and spiritual gifts. The point of this chapter's study is to underscore the importance of what motivates our actions. Genuine service for God is expressed through unselfish actions that arise naturally in response to people's needs and God's internal prompting. May we pray to grow to serve for the sake of doing the right thing and not for the approval and praise of others.

Prelude

Someone once defined "character" as "what someone does when no one is looking".[8] Jesus refers to such unseen secret service for His Kingdom as being exemplary and genuine, arising from a Spirit-led character. God wants to reward us for good service; the whole question of reward revolves around who you are striving to please. If your service is to please God by doing the right thing, especially when others don't know or see it, or even don't understand, then you are truly near to the heart and pulse of the Kingdom of God. If your service is to please others and receive their praise, then you have already been rewarded in a different and temporal sense. Such rewards depend upon the whims of human approval and popularity. God has something much better for us if we make it our goal to please Him through faithful service in Jesus' name.

Scripture Passages

Matthew 6:1-4

[1] "Be careful not to do your 'acts of righteousness' before men, to be seen by them. If you do, you will have no reward from your Father in heaven. [2] "So when you give to the needy, do not announce it with trumpets, as the hypocrites do in the synagogues and on the streets, to be honored by men. I tell you the truth, they have received their reward in full. [3] But when you give to the needy, do not let your left hand know what your right hand is doing, [4] so that your giving may be in secret. Then your Father, who sees what is done in secret, will reward you.

I. Be Careful in Your Service (Matthew 6:1-4)
  A. Check your motivation (1-2)
   1. Don't justify yourself before people (1a)
   2. Don't think your reward is from man (1b)
   3. Be modest before people (2a)
   4. Be humble and faithful to God (2b)
  B. Check your actions (3)
   1. Be active in giving
   2. Be discrete in charity
  C. Check your results (4)
   1. Before God our Father
   2. According to His Grace and Truth

---

[8] H. Jackson Browne, "Life's Little Instruction Book" Thomas Nelson, 2000.

2 Corinthians 5:9-10

⁹ So we make it our goal to please him, whether we are at home in the body or away from it. ¹⁰ For we must all appear before the judgment seat of Christ, that each one may receive what is due him for the things done while in the body, whether good or bad.

II. Aim to Please God
   (II Corinthians 5:9)
   A. The ultimate goal
   B. God's eternal Kingdom priority

III. Prepare to Appear Before Christ (II Cor. 5:10)
   A. Christ require our appearance
   B. Christ judges our lives
   C. Christ rewards us fairly

Exploring the Scriptures

In these passages the backdrop is the judgment of believers before God. While some passages deal with the judgment that will come to all humanity regarding salvation, one's ultimate destination of heaven or hell, these passages deal with the variation of reward given to those who shall enter God's Heavenly Kingdom. Since we shall be held into account, our lives should change toward positive participation in God's Kingdom. Our work involves helping those around us who have various needs, but our purpose and vision is toward pleasing God and affirming His unseen awareness. God knows everything and is the comprehensive observer who appreciates, corrects, judges and rewards the actions and words that come from our hearts. With this in mind, Jesus calls His disciples to be careful in how they serve. If they were expecting to be praised by people, then they might be doing things for the wrong reasons.

"Acts of righteousness" would describe what the Pharisees did using the status and stage of their religious office so that the general populace would think that they were holy and righteous. In fact, holiness and righteousness cannot be faked before God. People may not always be discerning and can be fooled by displays of religious expression or humanitarian aid. Clearly, God knows the heart and motivation of all people.

Jesus challenged His followers to check their motivation and purify their intent by being humble, discrete and modest. In one instance, Jesus stood by watching people as they gave their money at the temple (Mark 12:41-44). Some Jews made a big display of their giving. They would throw their coin offerings into big open brass (tuba-like) receptacles. If people brought in large sums to throw in these openings it made a loud and obvious noise for everyone to hear. On the other hand, the widow giving her mite was quiet and unassuming and she is the one whom Jesus commended. The kind of giving Jesus calls for is selfless, discrete and sacrificial. Such giving comes mainly as a matter of service to God, an expression of devotion and faith. Quantitative measurements of faith miss the quality of goodness and grace.

Paul's second letter to the Corinthians gives us a parallel message from a man who knew first hand that you cannot fool God by doing self-righteous things. Paul had thought he was doing the will of God by persecuting the church, but when Jesus came to him in blinding light, with a call upon His life, Paul was properly humbled. In the light of God's righteousness, in the midst of the glory and grace of Jesus, with consideration of his own failed attempt of righteousness, Paul was ready to repent in order to serve God correctly. Paul grew to serve according to the very transforming truth of Jesus Christ. Jesus led Paul through a path of reconstructive humility. The judgment seat that Paul refers to in his second letter to the Corinthians (9:5) is applicable for all believers; Jesus sits at the seat of grace and truth as our Lord and Savior King. When we obey His leading we fulfill the work of God's righteousness. We too can then shine the light of faith, hope and love in order to glorify God our Heavenly Father.

Bridging into Today

Believers will all come before Jesus in Heaven or at Christ's enthronement on earth so that their refinement and reward shall be given to them personally. This means that our Lord will look us in the eye, cleanse us completely by the light of judgment in His truth and grace, and then give us the rewards of His grace, praise and blessing (far beyond what anyone could ever deserve). What we do not display to honor good deeds in this life may indeed be paraded by God in the life to come. Our salvation is not contingent upon us achieving goodness (for in the light of God we are all sinners in need of grace and forgiveness). Goodness or righteousness is possible only through faith in Jesus Christ. Faith in Jesus involves confession of our sin and a true repentance that receives the grace of God. We experience a cleansing release through surrendering all to Jesus Christ and God our Father. When this surrender takes place there is a moment of conversion that involves a spiritual exchange. Jesus takes our sins away and gives us the Holy Spirit. This is the only way that we may be born again, redeemed and purified so that our righteousness becomes greater than that of the "Pharisees".

Once a person has received the saving grace of God through faith in Jesus Christ there is still an ongoing work of holiness from God. Through His Holy Spirit, God is guiding, empowering and refining believers. Our act of righteousness involves continued steps on a journey of faith and obedience. This is different from the old covenant of the law in that believers now have the Lord Jesus as their Savior and High Priest. Through faith in Jesus we are reckoned righteous before God, and through Him the character of a believer is transformed.

All around the world there are diverse ways that people express their belief or denial of God. There are those who seek to grasp a right standing with God based upon living up to a standard of righteousness that they define for themselves. Such a belief assumes that man may achieve righteousness before God independently. This common approach is a denial of our sinful and corrupted nature that exists because of Adam and Eve's fall. There are also advocates and practitioners of faithlessness and atheism who go out of their way to live in rebellion to the precepts of God's truth; they deny the witness of God's Spirit speaking to their own consciences. The assumption made is that God is irrelevant or uninvolved. The variance of error with people's approaches to God's Kingdom can therefore range from those who believe that God's Kingdom can be established without repentance and faith in Jesus Christ to those who completely miss or deny the reality of God's Kingdom through various forms of escape, avoidance and utter defiance.

One pastor was leading a Bible study at a mental health care facility when one of the participants stated firmly that they did not believe in God. This person explained that while he had survived a horrible accident, he had also tried to find God during his recovery but had not found success. The pastor asked the man how he had searched for God. The man told him that he looked at the light around his hospital room and did not feel anything was there but the light alone. The pastor asked him if he had prayed. "No, I didn't think that prayer would make a difference." "Did you read the Bible?" "No", said the man, "I can't be sure because I doubt it is inspired from God." Have you talked with anyone about this? "No", said the man, "not until now." At this the pastor expressed the truth of God's revelation in creation, the reliability of God's Word in Scripture, God's work of grace in preserving the man's life and the love of God for him revealed through Jesus Christ. When presented with a message of mercy and the evidence of God's truth and grace in Jesus (with emphasis on the work of Jesus on the cross), the man went from being defiant and depressed to being open and thankful as he joined the pastor and others in prayer. The pastor helped represent Christ and God's Kingdom.

What can you do to reach people for Christ and His Kingdom? The first thing that disciples of Jesus can do is have faith to trust and believe in Jesus being present and ready to reveal Himself. This will help believers to stand tall and strong in order to affirm our Lord's presence and fulfill Jesus' command to share the gospel of salvation. One prepares their heart to fulfill Christ's call by responding personally to His invitation to come and follow Him. We do this by first repenting (turning away from our old life and sin) and believing (turning toward Jesus and His leading) as we are changed through the power of God's saving grace.

From a surrendered life in Jesus, believers are called to love God to the point of risking the venture of sharing faith gracefully and truthfully with others. Believers are moved to joyfully and sacrificially make disciples, going into the entire world with the faith, hope and love God has given them. This journey will not always be easy, immediately fruitful, or without temporary setbacks and long term challenges. What believers can be sure of is that they are not without the help of Jesus, the host of Heaven and the Holy Spirit. God shall indeed enter into our struggle with sufficient grace and abundant encouragement. The Lord directly guides and strengthens us. From the crucible of adversity a work of God's Kingdom is birthed. Faith gives way to God's transforming Spirit through the presence of the living Lord and Savior. Jesus Christ brings hope and healing for the souls of mankind; the good news of the Gospel is that God's Kingdom is at work.

Questions for Class Discussion

1. When you watch the news, or various types of competitions, how does the media place a high level of scrutiny on those in the public eye? What are some examples?

2. How does our standard of righteousness vary according to who we are thinking about or talking to? Should such variances of moral standards exist?

3. What standard of righteousness has God set forth for us?

4. Why did the disciples doubt their ability to be as righteous as the Pharisees?

5. What did Jesus do to make it possible for us to be righteous before God?

6. In what ways is Jesus still at work bringing righteousness into your life today?

Closing Idea

Think of your laundry washing machine at home. When you wash your clothes, is it possible to get them perfectly clean? Is your water perfectly pure to start with? What softening system helps you make your water more effective and pure? Also, are there are various detergents that help you achieve a greater clean than you would otherwise have? When it comes to the soul, God has used the cleansing agent of Jesus' blood and righteousness in order to provide for our forgiveness and soul's spiritual cleansing. When Jesus comes He will complete the good work of salvation. At that time, we will come before His cleansing throne, and He shall wash us as white as snow in the light of His presence. Until then, any time spent in His presence through prayer, serving and being in His Word will have a cleansing and renewing effect.

Selected Reading

The Church therefore is not the Kingdom of God; God's Kingdom creates the Church and works in the world through the Church. Men cannot therefore build the Kingdom of God, but they can preach it and proclaim it; they can receive it or reject it. The Kingdom of God which in the Old Testament dispensation was manifested in Israel is now working in the world through the Church.

There is therefore but one people of God. This is not to say that the Old Testament saints belonged to the Church and that we must speak of the Church of the Old Testament. Acts 7:28 does indeed speak of the "church in the wilderness"; but the word here does not bear its New Testament connotation but designates only the "congregation" in the wilderness. The Church properly speaking had its birthday on the Day of Pentecost, for the Church is composed of all of those who by one Spirit have been baptized into one body (I Cor. 12:13), and this baptizing work of the Spirit began on the day of Pentecost.

While we must therefore speak of Israel and the Church, we must speak of only one people of God. This is vividly clear in Paul's illustration of the olive tree in Romans 11. There is one olive tree; it is the people of God. In the Old Testament era, the branches of the tree were Israel. However, because of unbelief, some of the natural branches were broken off and no longer belong to the tree (v.16). We know from verse 5 that not all of the branches were broken off, for "there is a remnant, chose by grace." Some Jews accepted the Messiah and His message of the Gospel of the Kingdom. We must remember that the earliest Church consisted of Jewish believers; but they came into the Church not because they were Jewish but because they were believers.

- George Eldon Ladd [9]

---

[9] George Eldon Ladd, "The Gospel of the Kingdom" p.118

9

TREASURE THE KINGDOM OF GOD

(Matthew 6:19-24; Psalm 62)

> ### Key verse:
> *For where your treasure is, there your heart will be also.*
> – Matthew 6:21

Purpose of study

This chapter's study will affirm the ultimate value of God's Kingdom for personal and corporate devotion, loyalty and purposeful service. The Kingdom of God is the most important matter in our lives. Therefore, it is essential that we grow in our love, understanding and worship of Christ, the Holy Spirit and our Heavenly Father. Anything that competes with God for our allegiance must be recognized and placed under subjection to our Heavenly Father's Kingdom. The priority is faith and obedience to our Lord and Savior. Nothing is of greater value than to pursue a personal faith relationship with God in Christ Jesus.

Prelude

I knew a friend who preached a sermon called "The Right Stuff". For an illustration he talked about his own family's process of preparing to move, and of all the stuff his family had accumulated. His children were all grown up and now he and his wife were about to move from the East coast to the West coast where he was called to serve. He confessed that he was overwhelmed by all the useless stuff they didn't really need. There were certain things they would bring, and many things they would not bring. He concluded that all they really needed was faith in God so they could go forth to serve Jesus Christ unhindered by things.

Admittedly, most people will agree that they have too much of the wrong stuff. However, it's not just material possessions that we must consider. We must also include meaningless activities, prideful or pessimistic attitudes, complicated issues in relationships, overextended commitments, competing priorities, and way too much media stimulus. Furthermore, there are those things that we worry about, or leave at loose ends. In it all we often neglect to regularly go to God in prayer for wisdom and guidance, knowledge and understanding, peace and inspiration. When all things are considered, is it any wonder or surprise that our focus in life is often not upon God and His Kingdom. The remedy is Jesus Christ, and He is only a prayer away.

Recent economic concerns in our world, combined with wars and terrorism, should alert us to the fleeting nature of wealth or security that is offered by our fractured human institutions. If one has placed their treasure in stock markets, they come to realize how fickle the markets of man are. If one has hoped for salvation from government, they come to realize how finite the authority is of those who are elected or appointed. The pervasive reality is that what we have attained is temporal, or what we formulate or institute is corruptible. We are left with nagging questions about what life is all about, or to whom we are to give our devotion, commitment and value to. Jesus called people to exchange the vain values of the world for a new life where we embrace the eternal and redemptive values of God's Kingdom. The following passages from Matthew 6 and Psalm 62 are messages that call us to re-evaluate our purpose and priority in life. Jesus calls us to take on the values and priority of God's Kingdom above the materialism and consumerism that plague our world.

Scripture Passages

Matthew 6:19-24

¹⁹ "Do not store up for yourselves treasures on earth, where moth and rust destroy, and where thieves break in and steal. ²⁰ But store up for yourselves treasures in heaven, where moth and rust do not destroy, and where thieves do not break in and steal. ²¹ For where your treasure is, there your heart will be also. ²² "The eye is the lamp of the body. If your eyes are good, your whole body will be full of light. ²³ But if your eyes are bad, your whole body will be full of darkness. If then the light within you is darkness, how great is that darkness! ²⁴ "No one can serve two masters. Either he will hate the one and love the other, or he will be devoted to the one and despise the other. You cannot serve both God and Money.

I. What is Your Heart's Treasure? (Matt. 6:19-24)
  A. Problems with earthly treasures: 19-20
    1. Dust
    2. Rust
    3. or Bust
  B. Problems with displaced affection (21)
    1. Where are you looking? (22-23)
    2. Who are you serving? (24)

Psalm 62

¹ My soul finds rest in God alone; my salvation comes from him. ² He alone is my rock and my salvation; he is my fortress, I will never be shaken. ³ How long will you assault a man? Would all of you throw him down-- this leaning wall, this tottering fence? ⁴ They fully intend to topple him from his lofty place; they take delight in lies. With their mouths they bless, but in their hearts they curse. Selah
⁵ Find rest, O my soul, in God alone; my hope comes from him. ⁶ He alone is my rock and my salvation; he is my fortress, I will not be shaken. ⁷ My salvation and my honor depend on God ; he is my mighty rock, my refuge. ⁸ Trust in him at all times, O people; pour out your hearts to him, for God is our refuge. Selah
⁹ Low born men are but a breath, the highborn are but a lie; if weighed on a balance, they are nothing; together they are only a breath. ¹⁰ Do not trust in extortion or take pride in stolen goods; though your riches increase, do not set your heart on them. ¹¹ One thing God has spoken, two things have I heard:

II. Do You Know the Rock of Salvation? (Psalm 62)
  A. The soul that cannot be shaken. (1-2)
  B. The schemes of man will fail (3-4)
  C. Salvation comes from God alone (5-7)
  D. Safety is found in God (8)
  E. Set your heart on God's Kingdom (9-10)
  F. Serve for the sake of God's reward (11-12)

that you, O God, are strong, ^{12} and that you, O Lord, are loving.
Surely you will reward each person   according to what he has done.
Psalms 62:1-12 (NIV)

Exploring the Scriptures

Jesus challenged those listening that day upon a rocky hillside above the blue waters of the Sea of Galilee when He preached this "Sermon on the Mount." What was their priority in life? Whose Kingdom were they going to serve? Would it be God's Kingdom, or their imagined constructed kingdoms? The challenge of Jesus is personal and pointed as we consider His words. His teachings move the listener to reflect and respond on a deeper spiritual level. Where is your heart's affection and devotion? Is it for God, or is it simply for self and for temporal pursuits and things that will not last? Jesus was calling for faith and commitment from His disciples, and for repentance and decision for all who listened. Jesus called people to live a more purposeful life, the life of serving and participating in God's Kingdom.

The disciple's level of commitment had to increase for them to continue to grow and be focused in their service to God. Jesus knew that their hearts were still divided between the pursuits of this fallen world and the eternal priorities and values of God. Though the disciples were willing, they would need to focus upon Him as Lord and Savior. If they did so their souls would continue to be filled with light from heaven, if they did not continue to follow they would revert to darkness. Their eyes were like the lamp to the body in that, as they followed and trusted Jesus, He would reveal the light of the knowledge of God. Furthermore, this light brings hope, purpose, wisdom and truth as it pertains to God and His Kingdom. Following Jesus is a walk in the light of God, and our focus upon Him is vital for life, knowledge, hope and heavenly direction.

Jesus then referred to those whose eyes are dark, who do not follow Him. Believers can experience spiritual darkness that can limit their focus and make them question their destiny. Jesus gives hope and vision by clarifying that the key issue is a matter of who you serve. In Christ, the light of God has been revealed and the life of God's Spirit is given. Outside of Christ, there is darkness which leads to spiritual death. Therefore, keep following and trusting Jesus through the tough times of persecution, temptation and adversity.

One of the illustrations Jesus used to illustrate His point about priorities related to how people use money or power. To the problem, Jesus directly states: "No one can serve two masters" (Matthew 6:24); one will ultimately become authoritative over your life. Money ("Mammon") symbolized power or influence. Some scholars note that "Mammon" was a term that referred to one's political and financial wealth or influence. Jesus' challenge is that we should not idolize such power, nor abuse such influence. Jesus is not against people having wealth or resources, but He does call for His disciples to place their priority on God's Kingdom and of following His lead. This involves letting go of our wealth and possessions for the sake of doing the will of God and not building or storing for the sake of self-sufficiency or a lack of security.

Psalm 62 was written by King David in the midst of a rebellion by one of his sons, Absalom. The heart of Absalom was oriented toward abusing his position of royalty, and he wanted to do anything he could to become the next king, even if that meant killing his brothers and eventually having his father killed in battle. David loved his sons, yet ultimately he treasured the things of God over (and sometimes against) what his family strived for. David placed his hope and treasure in God, and sought God's intervention to salvage hope for future generations. In the midst of stormy times, David affirmed that their stability was in God who is the Rock of Salvation. Absalom tried to topple his father's kingdom, but it did not work. Absalom tried to steal the affection of the people through favors and bribery, but the truth of his insubordination and insurrection came out. David had to face the reality that his own family was a mess, but that God's true family of faith represented the redemptive community that he ultimately was called to serve.

The themes of David's life, as reflected in the Psalms, help us to realize that while he was at times emotionally shaken by trying turns of events, David knew the Lord God as his rock of salvation. David had learned through failure and the abuse of power that the schemes of man will fail. His safety and protection came from the Lord, who was establishing a bigger Kingdom beyond his own frail and fragmented royal family line. In the end, David affirms that it is the very love of God that we must rely upon. God expresses His love for us by rewarding us according to what we have done with our lives in service for His Kingdom.

Bridging into Today

To follow Jesus one must change the direction of their desire. Otherwise, people will be encumbered by sin or hindered from following and serving wholeheartedly. The writer of the letter to the Hebrews was inspired to compare the journey of discipleship to that of a race.

> Therefore, since we are surrounded by such a great cloud of witnesses, let us throw off everything that hinders and the sin that so easily entangles, and let us run with perseverance the race marked out for us.
> Let us fix our eyes on Jesus, the author and perfecter of our faith, who for the joy set before him endured the cross, scorning its shame, and sat down at the right hand of the throne of God. - Hebrews 12:1-2 (NIV)

Faith commitment in life is not just willingness, but involves the real cost and consequence of obedience and action. These costs may include what we give up and how we may be misunderstood, but the benefit and blessing that comes through faith and participation in God's Kingdom is priceless peace and abundant grace. When our heart is right for God, then God will show us what to do to follow and serve in faith. God knows our needs and shall provide for them, yet God is also calling us to be careful about what we obtain, who we are to trust and how we are to serve. For example, problems with finances often stem from living beyond our means or from trying to keep up with a materialistic norm. Is there a living human being who is exempt from desiring things that promise much but ultimately will rust, bust, or turn to dust? Money is not eternal, neither are the stocks people follow and investments found in the Wall Street Journal. Eternity and sufficiency are found in God and His Kingdom through Christ. His reign shall last forever. God has a strategy to occupy this world through His people; believers are the redeemed of His grace and truth. God's people are to be salt and light to flavor and light the world as a prelude to God's Kingdom to come. Christians are "elected" or "set apart" as witnesses within society of God's greater Kingdom.

King David learned (through the consequences of his own mistakes and poor choices) that the future of his Kingdom in Israel would not be preserved through his own sons. David's sons argued, conspired, competed, and even killed one another for the throne. Immorality and indecency were things that

David became aware of within his own family, and so he turned his ultimate hope and trust to God. He looked forward to the coming of God's own established Kingdom on earth. David placed his ultimate affection and hope toward the Lord his God who alone reigns in righteousness. So too, believers today are called to learn from their mistakes and grow into service for Christ and His Kingdom. We are refined by the working of God's truth and mercy, righteousness and grace. Believers are called to reflect the love of God to the world as a witness of God's Kingdom that is both a present reality within the soul and a coming reality that is promised in Christ's powerful return in glory. Accountability is a reality now, throughout life, and then again in the ultimate judgment before the throne of God. The decisions we make and the priorities that influence us reveal a great deal about what motivates us. Jesus taught, *"Where your heart is, there will your treasure be also"* (Matthew 6:21). When one's priority is the Kingdom of God and His righteousness, then everything else will be in the right perspective. God is faithful and does not leave His children without help, direction, provision and protection. Jesus calls people to joyfully participate in a Kingdom that has no end; in Christ there is a Kingdom that is blessed within God's covenant of grace and truth.

A beloved Christian scholar, William Barclay, wrote of how the Jewish view of the Kingdom of God was "forward looking".[10] Barclay sites the vision God gave the prophets, how God's mercy was preached and offered even when the people had failed as a nation. God's steadfast love and saving work shall not ultimately be deterred. Despite their own failed attempts as a nation, God gave the Jews hope in the Lord's own coming Kingdom. The prophet Amos was inspired to speak about God's Kingdom to come (Amos 9:13-15).

> [13] "The days are coming," declares the LORD, "when the reaper will be overtaken by the plowman and the planter by the one treading grapes. New wine will drip from the mountains and flow from all the hills. [14] I will bring back my exiled people Israel; they will rebuild the ruined cities and live in them. They will plant vineyards and drink their wine; they will make gardens and eat their fruit. [15] I will plant Israel in their own land, never again to be uprooted from the land I have given them," says the LORD your God. (Amos 9:13-15 NIV)

---

[10] Barclay, William. The King and the Kingdom. P.98 -121. Westminster Press, 1968 Philadelphia

William Barclay identified with this passage from Amos as He witnessed the partial fulfillment of these ancient words in the re-establishment of Israel as a nation that began after the suffering of the Jews in World War Two. From Israel's re-establishment in 1948, God has continued to fulfill this initial promise given to His people. The vision is not yet complete, however, and the prophetic hope of God's Kingdom transforming the world is still to be manifest in God's personal and direct reign and rule. Looking forward is essential. Unless we have a vision of God's Kingdom to come in Christ, we would end up settling for what man (or an Anti-Christ) might try to accomplish through corrupted efforts that miss the mark of God's will and sovereignty. No society, culture, race, political or governmental party, nation or government will be able to establish a society that will come close to what God has planned and promised in Scripture. Does this mean that we give up and think that we should do nothing but wait for God's Kingdom to come? Does this mean that accountability and representation is vain and should not be administered? Of course the answer to these questions is "NO". Jesus called for His disciples to be both forward- looking and present and accounted for. The Kingdom of God is not simply a long term hope for Christ's second coming, the Kingdom of God consists of present service for believers to faithfully use their talents, care for the sick, visit people in prison, minister to those who suffer, hurt, or are in grief.

The Kingdom is more than a Divine dream of future transformation; the Kingdom of God is a present reality within the hearts of believers. The Holy Spirit of God inspires understanding of this truth and assures us of God's might and mercy. The Holy Spirit of God is given into our hearts from God's throne. The anointing of God's Spirit empowers believers to serve and shine so as to make the Kingdom of God a present reality. Before David Livingstone knew how and where he would serve as a missionary he was asked where he wanted to go. To the mission society in England he responded: "I am ready to go anywhere, as long as it is forward".[11]

---

[11] David Livingstone, 1856 returned from African Missions, spoke these words to Christians in Scotland, his homeland, regarding the need to be available to God's call. He went on the reach people in remote parts of the African continent. He died while kneeling in prayer at his bed. When people came to bring his body back to England, the tribesmen had cut out his heart. They said, "You may have his body, but his heart belongs to Africa."

How many times do we miss the moment of opportunity that God is giving us because we fail to move forward? Sometimes we allow the unfamiliar to make us feel uncomfortable or anxious. Sometimes we allow fear to hinder our faith. Often we go back in our affections to a time past, we revisit the "golden days" of our childhood and reminisce. While this can be instructive for learning and understanding, and can help us appreciate blessings; we must still move forward because God is calling us to learn from our mistakes and improve upon our successes. God has a Kingdom purpose in mind as we serve and follow Jesus Christ. His Kingdom has no end, and it shall replace the flawed kingdoms of this earth. If we "seek first the Kingdom of God and His righteousness" then we can be assured of moving forward in step with God's Word and Holy Spirit.

May it be that we never confuse human progressiveness with God's vision of promise for a Kingdom of righteousness and justice. Progressiveness in human standards has often elevated man's importance and independence as being greater than God's will and revealed hope. Philosophers will say that "man is the measure of all things"[12] and some believe in the "ascent of mankind".[13] These views were popular in the Renaissance and then again in the last half of the 20th century. Now, however, with cities beset by ruin and economies beset by collapse, governments growing more inept and corrupt, and with a growing concern about hope for justice and equality in society, there is valid doubt about mankind (in itself) having lasting hope for long term transformation or survival. One may choose to think like many "Post-moderns" that everything is relative and broken and that no purpose exists for our human condition other than self-definition and personal actualization. One may also choose faith in God's revelation in Scripture and see the existing "lost" condition of humanity as a partial rendering of life as it exists prior to the coming of God's Kingdom in Christ. Truly moving forward is impossible without a firm ground of truth and grace, and this is found in covenant with God through faith and service to God's Heavenly Kingdom through faith and allegiance to the Lord Jesus Christ. Believers may now live in alignment to the priorities and values of God's Kingdom. Believers may now abide in communion with the King of Glory. Believers may now serve their King through faith and good works. Believers may now abide as citizens of the Kingdom of

---

[12] Protagoras, Greek Philosopher. 490 B.C., *Antilogiae* and *Truth*
[13] Bronowski, Jacob. "The Ascent of Man" 1974   BBC film series, later in book 1976

God in their way of life, while still looking forward to the coming manifestation of God's Kingdom in Christ Jesus the coming Lord. The vision is near and at hand of God's transformative and coming powerful reign. This hope is not simply a wish, it is founded upon the revelation God has given in History through Jesus (the Word made flesh) and through the deposit of God's Holy Spirit given to all who truly repent and believe.

Questions for Class Discussion

1. How are the priorities of our lives in need of adjustment?

2. What would Jesus say to us about where we have misplaced our hearts?

3. How is David's dilemma about his sons and the kingship similar to the problems in politics today?

4. How does following Jesus change our values, principles and allegiances?

Closing Idea

Write down how you use your time. How many hours of your week are wasted? How much of your time is well invested? What changes do you need to make? Being a faithful Christian is challenging. There are many competing interests for people's time and resources. Jesus gave His disciples the instruction to be "in the world" but "not of the world" (John 17:15-19). Living with this tension is what Jesus calls us to do. The Lord has given us potential to gain wisdom and character if we remain faithful in our service for His Kingdom by following His teaching and being filled and directed by God's Holy Spirit.

Selected Reading

The mystery of the Kingdom is this: The Kingdom of God is here but not with irresistible power. The Kingdom of God has come, but it is not like a stone grinding an image to powder. It is not now destroying wickedness. On the contrary, it is like a man sowing seed. It does not force itself upon men. Some, like good soil, receive it; but there are many others who do not receive it. Some hear the word of the Kingdom but it never enters their heart. They hear the Gospel of the Kingdom but they do not understand the truth which they hear. Satan comes and snatches away the seed. There is no root, there is no life.

Others are shallow. They hear the Word of the Kingdom; they seem to receive it; they make a response. There is the semblance of life, but there is no depth. Perhaps the intellect or the emotions have been stirred but the will has not been moved. There is no real life. When trouble arises, when they find that the reception of the Gospel of the Kingdom does not deliver them from evil; indeed, when they meet persecution and evil for the very reason that they have received the message of the Kingdom, they wither and die because there is no life. Their profession is spurious.

Still others are like the thorny ground. They seem to receive the word of the Kingdom, they appear to believe and to evidence life. But they are not prepared to accept the humble form of God's Kingdom. The care of the age, the love of riches, the ambition, the ostentation, the pressure of conformity to This Age in which they still live choke the Word and it becomes unfruitful.

This is the mystery of the Kingdom: that the Kingdom of God has come among men and yet men can reject it. The Kingdom will not experience uniform success. Not all will receive it. This was a staggering thing to one who knew only the Old Testament. When God's Kingdom comes it will come with power. Who can resist it? Who can withstand it? But precisely this is the mystery of the Kingdom. The Kingdom is here, but it can be rejected. One day God will indeed manifest His mighty power to purge the earth of wickedness, sin and evil; but not now. God's Kingdom is working among men, but God will not compel them to bow before it. They must receive it; the response must come from a willing heart and a submissive will.

God is still dealing with us in this same way. God will not drive you into His Kingdom. It is not the business of those who are called to the ministry of the Word to speak with authoritarian compulsion. We speak as emissaries of God, but we plead and do not demand, we persuade and do not drive. We implore men to open their hearts that the Word of His Kingdom may have its fruitage in their lives. But man can reject it. They can spurn the Gospel of the Kingdom. They can scorn the preacher of the Word; and he is helpless.

George Eldon Ladd. "The Gospel of the Kingdom". (56-57)

10
JUDGMENT IN GOD'S KINGDOM

(Matthew 7:1-12; 20:1-16 and Psalm 67)

> ### Key verse:
> *¹² So in everything, do to others what you would have them do to you, for this sums up the Law and the Prophets. - Matthew 7:12*

Purpose of study

The Kingdom of God is not something people can create or legislate. However, God calls people to joyfully humble themselves in order to participate according to His grace, truth and will. People are called to work from the foundation of Christ-centered faith. Believers are to hold fast to the truth that the Kingdom of God is established firmly in Heaven and is increasingly at work in this realm we experience. Within those who have faith, God is at work to reveal His redeeming and transforming power.

The purpose of this study is to see how the judgment of God plays an important role in how we live. Furthermore, the judgment of God can lead us to repentance and reconciliation, confession and transforming accountability. The practical aspect of this study is that we will seek God's wisdom and understanding as it pertains to our relationships. May it be that we learn to be discerning practitioners of God's wisdom and word. Otherwise, we end up placing ourselves in a position of misjudging or misinterpreting others. In fact, in everything we should practice the "Golden Rule" of Matthew 7:12. *"So in everything, do to others what you would have them do to you, for this sums up the Law and the Prophets."*

Prelude

Jesus warned His disciples not to judge others. This was very important to the Lord because He saw the abusive side to how people use prejudice, greed, envy, political interest, social injustice and hypocrisy to put others down. Jesus also saw how people misjudge others due to ignorance and false assumptions. The Kingdom of God is to be served with humility, not pride. The work of sharing the Gospel of the Kingdom is to be done in the way of humility, truth and grace that Jesus showed us. This means that we will take time to understand and be patient to be understood. We are to seek God's revelation to improve our interaction with one another. Indeed, we are called to be discerning and wise, but this does not come naturally. We need God to be our guiding and merciful judge. We must seek our Lord's wisdom past our initial assumptions, misjudgments and miscalculations. God shall justly guide us if we honestly desire His counsel and direction. God calls people to pursue a dialogue of respect and understanding with one another.

Eventually God shall hold us all in the balance of truth, and the judgments of mankind shall be revealed for their inaccuracies and ignorance. Personally, our judgments are important, but without God's help and counsel we will make grave errors and cause great havoc. Jesus is the wise Lord and King who leads us into truth and grace. Jesus teaches us how to approach God with honest humility and others with kindness, truthfulness, forgiveness and peace. Unless a person understands the role of Jesus the Christ, the Suffering Servant Savior, they will not have the life and peace that God intends or the salvation and redemption that God offers.

Scripture Passages

Matthew 7:1-12 (NIV)

¹ "Do not judge, or you too will be judged. ² For in the same way you judge others, you will be judged, and with the measure you use, it will be measured to you. ³ "Why do you look at the speck of sawdust in your brother's eye and pay no attention to the plank in your own eye? ⁴ How can you say to your brother, 'Let me take the speck out of your eye,' when all the time there is a plank in your own eye? ⁵ You hypocrite, first take the plank out of your own eye, and then you will see clearly to remove the speck from your brother's eye. ⁶ "Do not give dogs what is sacred; do not throw your pearls to pigs. If you do, they may trample them under their feet, and then turn and tear you to pieces.

⁷ "Ask and it will be given to you; seek and you will find; knock and the door will be opened to you. ⁸ For everyone who asks receives; he who seeks finds; and to him who knocks, the door will be opened. ⁹ "Which of you, if his son asks for bread, will give him a stone? ¹⁰ Or if he asks for a fish, will give him a snake? ¹¹ If you, then, though you are evil, know how to give good gifts to your children, how much more will your Father in heaven give good gifts to those who ask him! ¹² So in everything, do to others what you would have them do to you, for this sums up the Law and the Prophets.

> I. Be Humble and Wise (Matthew 7:1-6)
>   A. Do not misjudge people (1-2)
>   B. Do not misjudge yourself (3-5)
>   C. Do not lack discernment (6)
>
> II. Be Actively Seeking God (7-12)
>   A. A.S.K. (7-8)
>   B. Receive (9-11)
>   C. Bless (12)

Matthew 20:1-16 (NIV)

¹ "For the kingdom of heaven is like a landowner who went out early in the morning to hire men to work in his vineyard. ² He agreed to pay them a denarius for the day and sent them into his vineyard. ³ "About the third hour he went out and saw others standing in the marketplace doing nothing. ⁴ He told them, 'You also go and work in my vineyard, and I will pay you whatever is right.' ⁵ So they

> III. Be Involved in God's Kingdom (Mt.20:1-16)
>   A. Respond to the work (1-7)
>   B. Receive your reward (8-12)
>   C. Respect God's generosity (13-16)

went. "He went out again about the sixth hour and the ninth hour and did the same thing. ⁶ About the eleventh hour he went out and found still others standing around. He asked them, 'Why have you been standing here all day long doing nothing?'

⁷ "'Because no one has hired us,' they answered. "He said to them, 'You also go and work in my vineyard.' ⁸ "When evening came, the owner of the vineyard said to his foreman, 'Call the workers and pay them their wages, beginning with the last ones hired and going on to the first.'

⁹ "The workers who were hired about the eleventh hour came and each received a denarius. ¹⁰ So when those came who were hired first, they expected to receive more. But each one of them also received a denarius. ¹¹ When they received it, they began to grumble against the landowner. ¹² 'These men who were hired last worked only one hour,' they said, 'and you have made them equal to us who have borne the burden of the work and the heat of the day.'

¹³ "But he answered one of them, 'Friend, I am not being unfair to you. Didn't you agree to work for a denarius? ¹⁴ Take your pay and go. I want to give the man who was hired last the same as I gave you. ¹⁵ Don't I have the right to do what I want with my own money? Or are you envious because I am generous?' ¹⁶ "So the last will be first, and the first will be last."

Matt 20:1-16 (NIV)

Psalm 67:1-7 (NIV)

For the director of music. With stringed instruments. A psalm. A song.

IV. Honor God's Wisdom and Grace (Psalm 67:1-7)
A. The face of God. (1)
B. The way of salvation (2)
C. Praise and joy (3-5)
D. Harvest of Blessing (6-7)

¹ May God be gracious to us and bless us and make his face shine upon us,
Selah
² that your ways may be known on earth, your salvation among all nations.
³ May the peoples praise you, O God; may all the peoples praise you.
⁴ May the nations be glad and sing for joy, for you rule the peoples justly
and guide the nations of the earth. Selah
⁵ May the peoples praise you, O God; may all the peoples praise you.
⁶ Then the land will yield its harvest, and God, our God, will bless us.
⁷ God will bless us, and all the ends of the earth will fear him.

Exploring the Scriptures

Many times Jesus observed how people misjudged one another. Religious leaders were often hypocritical in that they were not repentant of their own failings and faults. Those following their leaders lacked respect. Humility and honesty by Pharisees and Scribes was largely absent. In this passage from the Sermon on the Mount, Jesus held up a high standard of righteousness, one that surpassed that of the Scribes and Pharisees. In His teaching, and in His life's ministry, Jesus held up a mirror of God's righteousness. When each person comes before Christ Jesus, God's Son who reflects the perfect image of God's righteousness, each will be confronted to acknowledge their own sins and shortcomings in comparison. Jesus clearly stated how important it is that we do not take the place of God as it pertains to ultimate judgment. To take the place of God in judgment is to assume superiority. Even with the revelation God has provided in the Scriptures, in Jesus, through creation and through the Church; our judgment is still impaired by sin. The issue is not only discernment; people must recognize their limitation to judge.

The judgment and wisdom we need for life must be fully reliant upon God and His truth. To know God's truth and wisdom will lead us to become discerning and understanding. For this to occur we must first ask God for wisdom and faith, direction and insight. Asking that is humble and unselfish shall lead to God's disclosure and our understanding. Seeking that is earnest and open is the gateway toward God. The Lord helps us to find His truth for direction and discernment in decisions. Knocking that is open and intentional shall lead us to discover God's revelation of knowledge and wisdom for service in His Kingdom. The wonderful blessing from God is that as we grow in our wisdom and awareness we also become more humble and liberated from pride and sinfulness. Instead of judging others we grow to bless and love others and not judge or curse them. We see our common human frailty in light of God's grace, kindness, provision and protection.

In Psalm 67 the people of Israel exhibited this kind of humility as they awaited the coming of God's Kingdom and the manifestation of God's grace, judgment and glory. God reveals His face to us in ways that we may not at first recognize. Such was true in the prophets and in John the Baptist. Such was true in completeness and brightness of truth and grace in Jesus Christ. God's will is to bless us. His design is that our praise shall prepare our hearts for His work of salvation. The realization of God's judgment expedites the heart's need for saving grace and forgiveness. A time is coming when the harvest of the land will produce more than the seasonal crops; a greater harvest of God's Kingdom is at hand. God will personally come through Jesus to judge, purify and bless those who are reconciled to Him. God's direct reign on earth will begin with the great and awesome Day of the Lord. *"Every knee shall bow and every tongue shall confess that Jesus Christ is Lord"* (Philippians 2:10).

In Matthew 20, the message is that God has great work for people to become involved in now for the sake of His Kingdom. God has a vineyard and believers are invited to come and participate in the work. Being a part of God's Kingdom work is a privilege. Who is in a position of judging what is fair when it comes to God's generous ways of rewarding those who become involved? The reward for all who believe and follow Jesus, who labor in the vineyard, is salvation. No one should begrudge God for generously and mercifully bestowing this gift and opportunity to others. When people come to saving faith later in life, and have only served Christ briefly, we must not consider that they are less worthy. All of us are invited to be recipients of God's undeserved grace and saving unconditional love. For those who respond in faith early on, they experience the blessed joy of fulfilling a lifelong call to be involved in God's Kingdom. Ultimately, God is the one who calls the shots and judges the hearts and lives of humanity. God is generous and fair in the ways of His Kingdom.

Bridging into Today

Christians have been guilty of judging or misjudging others while not being honest about their own shortcomings and sin. Jesus calls for believers to be wise and discerning, but not to abuse the gift of God's grace and love. When it comes to the way we relate to one another, God is watching us. When it comes to how we try to compare ourselves to the work of others, God calls us to simply serve and have joy in our work without being affected too much by what others are doing or are not doing. With the Parable of God's Kingdom being like that of a vineyard, with workers coming in to do the work for the same salary (no matter if they started in the morning or afternoon), long term believers can relate to those who came in the morning and complained that those who came later received the same amount. Jesus explained that the owner of the vineyard was justified in paying them all the same total, as this was his prerogative to decide. Likewise, in the final judgment of God's Kingdom, the reward of salvation will be given to all who believed and participated by faith in serving God. The joy of serving earlier is worth far more than the reward we receive at the end. In the final judgment, believers shall receive the same gift of grace in the resurrection and glory of Christ and His Kingdom. God will take care of all other matters of reward and justice by His authority. We should simply be thankful for the opportunity presented by our Savior to be welcomed into citizenship and invited to serve on His behalf in His vineyard.

When we allow envy or jealousy to take over we are in essence saying that we know better than God or those to whom God has given responsibility. Judging can often lead to hypocrisy, and comparisons can often lead to resentment and unnecessary conflict. The body of Christ will be healthiest when we ask for God's wisdom, seek God's counsel, and knock upon the door of God's revealing truth. The people of God are called to participate in a Kingdom where God is generous and kind. When we approach involvement in God's Kingdom in a non-competitive way it will allow us to serve with joy and humility. That is the kind of witness the world needs to see today. Steve Green once stated: "No one wants to see the church in disarray like a ship of squabbling sailors."[14] Instead, our witness of unity with respect for the truth and grace that unites us is far more compelling. This unity is not produced by cheap grace, nor is it unbiblical or compromised truth; otherwise unity is simply fabricated and unspiritual. True unity is in line with God's revealed word in the Bible while being in fidelity with the example and teaching of God's Son and the leading of God's Holy Spirit. Judgment and decision-making are matters of prayer and humility, not pride or arrogance.

---

[14] Steve Green speaking at the Pastor's Promise Keeper gathering, Atlanta, GA 1995.

Questions for Class Discussion

1. What is at the root of most interpersonal conflict?

2. How can misjudgment affect trust in relationships?

3. Where do we see Christians making the mistake of competing with one another?

4. How can worship give us the right perspective for our service in God's Kingdom?

5. Think of a situation where you were misjudged. How was it resolved or not resolved?

Closing Idea

Think of a specific person you may need to talk with in the next few days who you don't understand too well or who you may need to seek reconciliation with. Pray for God to lead you that you may find understanding and/or healing. Jesus lived to forgive that we might receive God's grace in order to be forgiven and live to forgive. The Kingdom of God is bigger than our differences of perspective or expressions of the Christian faith. The Kingdom of God is not built through people seeking dissension but through the working of God that brings transformation through understanding, distinction, clarity, healing, grace and truth. God's Word is perfectly sufficient to guide and lead us in all matters of defining and practicing faith. God's Holy Spirit will guide believers toward righteousness and peace. Ultimately, Jesus is Lord and King. God has given Him authority to judge the hearts and deeds of mankind. The first step toward reconciliation with God and others is to come before Jesus in humility and prayer. When we present our requests before Christ we gain the assurance of divine justice and mercy. Life is meant to be lived with the very perspective of Christ being enthroned over our lives and inter-relationships.

Selected Reading

> The overwhelming preoccupation in the parables, despite their various accretions after Jesus' time, is a message about a coming Kingdom which will overwhelm all the normal expectations of Israel and take its establishment figures by surprise. People must be watchful for this final event, which is inevitably going to catch them unawares: so both the wise and the foolish virgins snatch a nap before the bridegroom arrives, but the wise virgins have provided ample oil for their lamps of celebration, still burning when they need to wake up.
>
> Much celebration and joy run through these stories, which tell of feasts and wedding banquets, yet also custom, common sense and even natural justice are at times ruthlessly ignored: laborers in a vineyard who have done a full day's work are told to stop complaining when they get the same wage as latecomers who only put in an hour. The coming Kingdom will make up its own rules. The later Church found this an uncomfortable message as it settled down to make sense of people's everyday lives.[15]   - Dairmaid MacCullough

---

[15] Dairmaid MacCulloug "Christianity: The First Three Thousand Years" (87-88)

11

THE GREAT MERCY OF THE KING

(Matthew 8:1-17; Psalm 57)

> ### Key verse:
> *¹ Have mercy on me, O God, have mercy on me, for in you my soul takes refuge. I will take refuge in the shadow of your wings until the disaster has passed. ² I cry out to God Most High, to God, who fulfills [his purpose] for me.* - Psalm 57:1-2 NIV

Purpose of study

God responds mightily to people in need through His mercy. The goal of this chapter is to affirm God's ministry of mercy as it involves our call to respond to one another's concerns and needs. Biblically and practically, when God's mercy is received it should also translate into mercy shared to others. Our Lord and Savior, who was both Servant and Lord, shows us that God's Kingdom is best expressed through acts of mercy. People are called to follow Christ's example of compassionate service and unselfishness. The Kingdom of God is so infused with mercy that there are some who might think of God to be unfairly generous in His kindness. Yet when one considers the magnitude of sin and the great need for forgiveness, the cross of Christ is the perfect revelation of God's unconditional love. God met the requirement for the righteous atonement of our sin by His abundant grace. Through the work of Jesus on the cross, God satisfies His justice through the righteous and merciful act of His Son. The Lord and King sacrificed everything for us.

Prelude

Have you ever met someone who would do just about anything to help others in need? They go the extra mile, give generously, or remove the coat off their back to help warm someone who feels cold and unprotected. Mercy is an admirable trait because it appeals to something deep within us. Kindness inspires God's nature within us. Mercy is divinely inspired, a response to the leading of God's Spirit that empowers grace to prevail and forgiveness to be primary. Still, time and energy are required to help others patiently and sacrificially. Mercy is not always a common human response. In fact, it runs counter to the fallen human tendencies of personal interest, self-justification and competition.

Jesus did not shirk away from His responsibility to address people in need as the Son of God. He helped anyone who came and asked. At times, Jesus even helped those who did not directly come to ask for help. Some were along the path of life, others were brought to Him. Either way, faith and humility were essential factors leading to God's mercy being extended. People don't normally want to admit their weakness or vulnerability. We often want others to think we have it "all-together", or that we are self-reliant. In reality, a time eventually comes for all people when illness, danger, brokenness, bankruptcy, barriers, failures, or stress are overwhelming. To acknowledge this is being honest about our limitations. If we think that we will always be able to manage without the help of others, then we live in denial of our humanity and of God's offer of mercy. Granted, there are a few individuals who seem to go unscathed by trouble or trials; looking deeper one discovers there is a chasm of great need.

The humble that came to Jesus had nothing to hide. They were transparent about their needs. In trust they demonstrated faith in His healing power. They believed He was more than a mere man. They believed He was sent from God. They desired His mercy, asked for His intervention and received the ministry of His mercy as it was needed.

Scripture Passages:
Matthew 8:1-17

¹ When he came down from the mountainside, large crowds followed him. ² A man with leprosy came and knelt before him and said, "Lord, if you are willing, you can make me clean." ³ Jesus reached out his hand and touched the man. "I am willing," he said. "Be clean!" Immediately he was cured of his leprosy. ⁴ Then Jesus said to him, "See that you don't tell anyone. But go, show yourself to the priest and offer the gift Moses commanded, as a testimony to them." ⁵ When Jesus had entered Capernaum, a centurion came to him, asking for help. ⁶ "Lord," he said, "my servant lies at home paralyzed and in terrible suffering." ⁷ Jesus said to him, "I will go and heal him." ⁸ The centurion replied, "Lord, I do not deserve to have you come under my roof. But just say the word, and my servant will be healed. ⁹ For I myself am a man under authority, with soldiers under me. I tell this one, 'Go,' and he goes; and that one, 'Come,' and he comes. I say to my servant, 'Do this,' and he does it." ¹⁰ When Jesus heard this, he was astonished and said to those following him, "I tell you the truth, I have not found anyone in Israel with such great faith. ¹¹ I say to you that many will come from the east and the west, and will take their places at the feast with Abraham, Isaac and Jacob in the kingdom of heaven. ¹² But the subjects of the kingdom will be thrown outside, into the darkness, where there will be weeping and gnashing of teeth." ¹³ Then Jesus said to the centurion, "Go! It will be done just as you believed it would." And his servant was healed at that very hour. ¹⁴ When Jesus came into Peter's house, he saw Peter's mother-in-law lying in bed with a fever. ¹⁵ He touched her hand and the fever left her, and she got up and began to wait on him. ¹⁶ When evening came, many who were demon-possessed were brought to him, and he drove out the spirits with a word and healed all the sick. ¹⁷ This was to fulfill what was spoken through the prophet Isaiah: "He took up our infirmities and carried our diseases." **Matthew 8:1-17**

I. Mercy to Strangers (Matt. 8:1-4)
  A. The outcasts came to Jesus (1)
  B. Outcasts believed in Jesus (2)
  C. Jesus ministered to their needs (3)
  D. Jesus called for obedience (4)

II. Mercy to Foreigners (5-13)
  A. The Roman Centurion came to Jesus (5-6)
  B. Jesus was willing to help (7)
  C. The Centurion believed in Jesus' authority (8-9)
  D. Jesus was astonished by his faith (10)
  E. Jesus judges the faithlessness of Israel (11-12)
  F. Jesus heals the Centurion's servant. (13)

III. Mercy to Friends/Family (14-15)
  A. Peter's mother in law had a fever (14)
  B. Jesus touched her and healed her (15a)
  C. She responded in grateful service (15b)

IV. Mercy to the Sick Soul & Mind (16a)

V. Mercy to the Sick Body (16b)

VI. Jesus Fulfilled God's Promises (17)
  A. Jesus removes sickness
  B. Jesus carries us through disease

Psalm 57:1-11

For the director of music. (To the tune of) "Do Not Destroy." Of David. A miktam. When he had fled from Saul into the cave. (Psalm 57:1-11)

¹ Have mercy on me, O God, have mercy on me, for in you my soul takes refuge. I will take refuge in the shadow of your wings   until the disaster has passed.
² I cry out to God Most High, to God, who fulfills [his purpose] for me.
³ He sends from heaven and saves me, rebuking those who hotly pursue me;

Selah

God sends his love and his faithfulness.
⁴ I am in the midst of lions; I lie among ravenous beasts-- men whose teeth are spears and arrows, whose tongues are sharp swords.
⁵ Be exalted, O God, above the heavens; let your glory be over all the earth.
⁶ They spread a net for my feet— I was bowed down in distress. They dug a pit in my path-- but they have fallen into it themselves. Selah
⁷ My heart is steadfast, O God, my heart is steadfast;   I will sing and make music.
⁸ Awake, my soul!   Awake, harp and lyre! I will awaken the dawn.
⁹ I will praise you, O Lord, among the nations;   I will sing of you among the peoples.
¹⁰ For great is your love, reaching to the heavens; your faithfulness reaches to the skies.
¹¹ Be exalted, O God, above the heavens; let your glory be over all the earth.

> VII. Take Refuge in the Mercy of God (Psalm 57)
> A. Cry out for God's mercy (1-2)
> B. Trust in God's love and faithfulness (3)
> C. Trust in God's protection in danger (4)
> D. Exalt God and give Him glory (5)
> E. Rely upon God's justice (6)
> F. Praise God for His greatness (7-10)
> G. Exalt God to glorify His Kingdom (11)

Exploring the Scriptures

Mercy was shown by Jesus to a wide variety of people. The order in which people came to Jesus in our passage from Matthew 8:1-17 is interesting. Jesus healed the leper, someone whom everyone considered an outcast, a health risk. The leper bowed before him, not wanting to get too close. Jesus took the initiative to touch and heal the leper. Jesus revealed His sovereignty over infection and disease. The next person Jesus healed was the Centurion's servant, a foreigner. The faith of the Centurion was such that he believed that all Jesus had to do was say the word and his servant would be healed. This Roman soldier didn't have to see the miracle to believe it would happen through Jesus' authority. Jesus was so moved that He loudly declared that He was astonished to His own doubting disciples. Jesus began to reflect upon a future time of God's grace being extended to the Gentiles and of God's judgment coming upon unbelieving Jews. Christ indicated that some Israelites, who were intended to be covenant participants in the Kingdom of God, would lose their inheritance because of their lack of faith in Him as the Messiah/Savior.

Jesus ministered through an intensive healing campaign. Matthew 8 records a portion of the ministry life of Jesus. The Lord healed Peter's mother-in-law, and in this gracious and thoughtful action the Savior forever reinforces the importance that must be given to extended family. Jesus sets up a medical clinic in the mother-in-law's home. Soon, just about all the mentally ill, spiritually possessed, and physically diseased people in the area come knocking at the door looking for healing and deliverance. Jesus compassionately healed people as a matter of humanitarian service to glorify His Father in Heaven. Jesus' ministry and presence signified that the Kingdom of God was at hand. The working of God's Kingdom had begun and much more was yet to come. Jesus was able to heal through His very Word of life. Since He was the Word of God made flesh, He had authority to deliver people from bondage and even carry people's diseases away. Ultimately, upon the cross, the greatest of diseases, sin, was defeated by Jesus as He bore our burdens and forgave our sins in a way that was perfect and all encompassing.

Moving over to Psalm 57, we hear David's cry for God's mercy. He found relief and strength in the Lord's presence. God ministers to David with steadfast love. David is relieved, renewed in his faith and encouraged to face his foes. David at this time was not yet king, and he did not desire to be king as long as Saul was. Saul was paranoid and internally conflicted. He resented David's popularity and was envious of David's accomplishments and gifts. Saul was a man divided in his heart between love for David and jealousy for David's charisma. Instead of being grateful for David's loyalty and humility, he could not overcome the demons of his own insecurity.

David writes Psalm 57 in the midst of being pursued and hunted by Saul's men. David had experienced the mercy of God throughout his life, but in this Psalm we see the pattern of an honest plea for help followed by recalling God's sovereignty. David praises God in the midst of his trials. David ultimately acknowledges the primary authority of God as our King. While he remains respectful of the authority given to Saul, David places his trust in God's mercy and might. David's distress is real, and so will be the answer to his prayers as God will step in to protect and defend him. Waiting for this required faith, and it helped David to look back over his life to see how God had been faithful and present. When one is faced with danger and confusion, we must consider God's previous protection and provision.

Bridging into Today

Jesus is still at work as the merciful Savior. When we turn in faith to Him we will not be disappointed. Jesus touches our hearts with redeeming love. Through faith in Jesus God fills our souls with the life-giving infusion of His Holy Spirit. Our minds are then directed to the transforming work of God's truth and grace.

Modern medical science has developed a means by which anti-bodies may be produced in the lab and may then be given to those who are lacking them. The infusion of immunoglobulin G is something that this author knows about first hand. Having survived cancer, I have dealt with the side effect of a compromised immune system. Thankfully, the infusions of anti-bodies boost my immunity. When people believe in Jesus, the Lord infuses their lives with the Holy Spirit to strengthen and protect them from the presence and contagion of sin. Caution and good habits will combine with God's grace to protect His people, and responsibility is still given to individuals to protect themselves and others from the disease of sin. The sinful world will still impact believers, this cannot be completely avoided, but the ultimate consequence of spiritual death must be avoided and treated.

Jesus responds to us as we seek Him, as we reach out in faith to Him. Jesus cares for the untouchables, the outcasts, the stranger, the foreigner, the friend and the mother-in-law. Jesus casts out demons and carries us through illness and disease. Jesus is still Lord and Savior, so it should come as no surprise that He is establishing His Kingdom in our midst. Jesus is calling believers to participate in acts of healing and reconciliation. Jesus works through people who prayerfully show their concern and care. One practical administration of God's grace is the development of medical knowledge, skill and care. Mercy is a ministry that Jesus began and invites us to receive and share freely. In fact, mercy is like manna, new and fresh every day. Mercy is the healing balm of Christian's mission. It's not that believers are to condone sin; instead they are called to care for and love sinners while not compromising biblical values. Ultimately, every person is accountable before God. Therefore, when one's patience is stretched by trials, persecution or injustice, we must place our trust in God's sovereign justice, providence, mercy and protection.

David experienced the faithfulness of God to administer mercy and protection. We too are to trust in the Lord our God through difficult and trying times, through persecution or danger. There is nothing that can separate us from God's love when we place our faith in the Lord Jesus Christ. David teaches us to rely upon the strong and mighty hand of God. So too, we are called to believe that God is present and available at any given moment. God is quicker than quicksand, faster than a speeding bullet, more powerful than any mass or force of nature.

Loneliness, however, is a powerful reality that exposes our need for relationships. In quiet and still moments, when we feel the void of others, we may discover the presence of God and abide close within the "shadow of His wings" (Ps. 57:1). God will attend to us in many ways. Sometimes He sends us His Holy Spirit to touch our hearts and minds. Other times God speaks to us through His awesome creation, reminding us of His provision and power. In a very tangible and personal way, God will speak to us through others and will provide friends and support. Rescue from danger is in God's providence. Still, the most powerful and personal revelation of God is His Son Jesus Christ. Jesus is not limited to time and place. Believers discover the truth of His promise, and fulfill the purpose He gave us, when we believe and act upon His words of authority, hope and commission:

Matthew 28:18-20 (NIV)
[18] Then Jesus came to them and said, "All authority in heaven and on earth has been given to me. [19] Therefore go and make disciples of all nations, baptizing them in the name of the Father and of the Son and of the Holy Spirit, [20] and teaching them to obey everything I have commanded you. **And surely I am with you always, to the very end of the age."**

Questions for Class Discussion

1. How has God been merciful to you this week?

2. Who besides God has shown you the most mercy in your life?

3. When do you find it most difficult to be merciful?

4. How well does the church show mercy in practical ways?

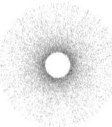
Closing Idea
Make it a goal this week to show mercy in some tangible way each day. When the day is over pray for the person(s) you showed mercy to, then think of how others were merciful to you. Take time to thank God for people who are your friends. Also, thank God for people who are difficult to get along with. Pray that God gives you wisdom and patience to know how to handle those who may be envious or jealous of you. If you have any envy or jealousy for people who have something you wish you had or blessings you don't have, ask for God to give you a Spirit of peace and contentment. Do not harbor any grudges or grievances. Ask God to infuse your heart with mercy and kindness, even to the most challenging of relationships. God works best when we receive and show radical grace.

12

THE GREAT FORGIVENESS OF THE KING

(Matthew 9:1-8; 18:21-35; Psalm 32)

> ### Key verse:
> *1 Blessed is he whose transgressions are forgiven, whose sins are covered. 2 Blessed is the man whose sin the LORD does not count against him and in whose spirit is no deceit.* – Psalm 32:1-2

Purpose of study

God's desire is for people to be reclaimed into a right relationship with Him and with one another. Forgiveness is both a gift and act of God that we are called to receive by faith. Likewise, forgiveness received should lead to a change in how we treat others. The purpose of this chapter's study is twofold: To highlight the ministry of forgiveness that God has initiated through Jesus Christ, and to inspire the sharing of forgiveness between persons for healing and wholeness.

Prelude

Being apologetic or sorry for something implies that one feels guilt or remorse. Why would people even feel this way if there was not a sense of right and wrong that accompanies the decisions, actions, feelings and expressions of our lives? Going way back to Genesis, we were created in the image of God for communion with God and one another. When anything breaks, hinders, or pollutes our relationship with God, our relationships with one another, or even negatively affects one's personal integrity, then it is "sin". Evil has wrought sin, which has produced brokenness and strife. Graciously, God has provided a means for healing, a way to be forgiven and to forgive. While the law's purpose is to guide us in righteousness, it also leads us to accountability and repentance. God desires to restore our relationships and renew our souls when we repent of sin, then ask for and receive true forgiveness. Such forgiveness liberates us into the joy of cleansing renewal. Vital relationships are made new through God's unconditional redeeming love. True forgiveness is contagious; it is passed on through loving words and actions.

Scripture Passages:

Matthew 9:1-8

¹ Jesus stepped into a boat, crossed over and came to his own town. ² Some men brought to him a paralytic, lying on a mat. When Jesus saw their faith, he said to the paralytic, "Take heart, son; your sins are forgiven." ³ At this, some of the teachers of the law said to themselves, "This fellow is blaspheming!"

⁴ Knowing their thoughts, Jesus said, "Why do you entertain evil thoughts in your hearts? ⁵ Which is easier: to say, 'Your sins are forgiven,' or to say, 'Get up and walk'? ⁶ But so that you may know that the Son of Man has authority on earth to forgive sins...." Then he said to the paralytic, "Get up, take your mat and go home." ⁷ And the man got up and went home. ⁸ When the crowd saw this, they were filled with awe; and they praised God, who had given such authority to men.

I. God's Ministry of Forgiveness (Matthew 9:1-8)
  A. Forgiveness starts at home (1)
  B. Forgiveness involves friends who have faith (2a)
  C. Forgiveness is what we really need (2b)
  D. Forgiveness is from God's Son (3)
  E. Forgiveness overcomes evil with good (4-6)
    1. Evil must be confronted
    2. Jesus has authority to forgive and heal
    3. Restoration by grace
  F. Forgiveness is healing to the body (7)
  G. Forgiveness brings hope to a community (8)

Matthew 18:21-35

²¹ Then Peter came to Jesus and asked, "Lord, how many times shall I forgive my brother when he sins against me? Up to seven times?"

² Jesus answered, "I tell you, not seven times, but seventy-seven times.

²³ "Therefore, the kingdom of heaven is like a king who wanted to settle accounts with his servants. ²⁴ As he began the settlement, a man who owed him ten thousand talents was brought to him. ²⁵ Since he was not able to pay, the master ordered that he and his wife and his children and all that he had be sold to repay the debt. ²⁶ "The servant fell on his knees before him. 'Be patient with me,' he begged, 'and I will pay back everything.' ²⁷ The servant's master took pity on him, canceled the debt and let him go.

²⁸ "But when that servant went out, he found one of his fellow servants who owed him a hundred denarii. He grabbed him and began to choke him. 'Pay back what you owe me!' he demanded. ²⁹ "His fellow servant fell to his knees and begged him, 'Be patient with me, and I will pay you back.' ³⁰ "But he refused. Instead, he went off and had the man thrown into prison until he could pay the debt. ³¹ When the other servants saw what had happened, they were greatly distressed and went and told their master everything that had happened.

³² "Then the master called the servant in. 'You wicked servant,' he said, 'I canceled all that debt of yours because you begged me to. ³³ Shouldn't you have had mercy on your fellow servant just as I had on you?' ³⁴ In anger his master turned him over to the jailers to be tortured, until he should pay back all he owed.

³⁵ "This is how my heavenly Father will treat each of you unless you forgive your brother from your heart." **Matthew 18:21-35 (NIV)**

II. Man's Ministry of Forgiveness (Matt. 18:21-35)
A. Bearing with others to forgive (21)
B. Believing in God to forgive others (22)
C. Be changed by gratitude to forgive (23-35)
   1. God's Gift of Grace (23-27)
   2. Man's lack of gratitude (28-30)
   3. God's just indignation (31-34)
   4. Man's need for compassion (35)

Psalm 32

Of David. A *maskil.*

¹ Blessed is he whose transgressions are forgiven, whose sins are covered.
² Blessed is the man whose sin the LORD does not count against him and in whose spirit is no deceit.
³ When I kept silent, my bones wasted away through my groaning all day long.
⁴ For day and night your hand was heavy upon me; my strength was sapped as in the heat of summer. Selah
⁵ Then I acknowledged my sin to you and did not cover up my iniquity. I said, "I will confess my transgressions to the LORD"-- and you forgave the guilt of my sin. Selah
⁶ Therefore let everyone who is godly pray to you while you may be found; surely when the mighty waters rise, they will not reach him.
⁷ You are my hiding place; you will protect me from trouble
    and surround me with songs of deliverance. Selah
⁸ I will instruct you and teach you in the way you should go;
    I will counsel you and watch over you.
⁹ Do not be like the horse or the mule, which have no understanding but must be controlled by bit and bridle or they will not come to you.
¹⁰ Many are the woes of the wicked, but the LORD's unfailing love
    surrounds the man who trusts in him.
¹¹ Rejoice in the LORD and be glad, you righteous; sing, all you who are upright in heart!

> III. The Blessings of Repentance and Grace (Psalm 32)
>   A. The Blessing of being forgiven. (1-2)
>   B. The importance of confession (3-5)
>   C. The faithfulness of God's deliverance (6-7)
>   D. The wisdom of God's ways (8-9)
>   E. The strength of God's unfailing love (10)
>   F. The joy of restored righteousness (11)

Exploring the Scriptures

    Capernaum was a thriving urban center on the Sea of Galilee. This was a very diverse community with fishing and commercial vitality; it also was the headquarters for a large Roman army garrison. The influence of Greek and Roman architecture was seen in the buildings, homes, markets and public places. It is interesting to note that Jesus called this city "home". While he had grown up mostly in Nazareth, Capernaum was His chosen base of operation. Why? Perhaps it was the fact that Jesus could envision the work of God's Kingdom to the whole earth from the vantage point of Capernaum's multicultural flavor. Perhaps Jesus was fascinated by this densely populated, diverse and vibrant, place. There was one thing that held true about Capernaum; Jesus could minister more freely there compared to Jerusalem. While on-looking religious leaders from the local synagogue could watch and criticize Jesus, the Lord had fewer hindrances to teach, preach and move about. Jesus was actively meeting people's needs with the manifested grace and mercy of God. Specifically, in Matthew 9, Jesus identified forgiveness as the greatest of needs for which He came to address. Jesus said to the man who was crippled, "Your sins are forgiven". The on-looking religious leaders were savvy and theologically accurate to be thinking in their minds that only God has the ability to forgive. Amazingly, Jesus knew their thoughts; Jesus addressed them with authority by intently making eye contact and by confronting them verbally. No mere man could know their inner thoughts and deepest doubts. Jesus knew if people believed in Him or not. Jesus knew if the spark of faith was present or absent. Through the windows of their souls, their eyes, He could see when they were scoffing Him and when they disbelieved His authority and power to forgive sins. As Jesus went on to heal the crippled man as Savior and Beloved Son; here we witness both Christ's power to forgive the soul and His authority to heal the body. Jesus, however, prioritized forgiveness; it was truly why He came. The cross would become the ultimate expression of Christ's ministry of forgiveness; His ministry on the cross of Calvary brought a critical pivotal turn to God's work of reconciliation and redemption.

Later that day in Capernaum, after leaving Peter's home, Jesus was followed by a large crowd. While Jesus taught them as He walked along the shore of the Sea of Galilee, Jesus had a specific person in mind to reach. In Mark 2:14 we observe how Jesus went directly to Levi (Matthew), the very one who would write the great gospel account that highlights the ministry of Christ and the Kingdom of God. Jesus is concerned for the masses, but His ministry of salvation personally calls individuals to repentance and new life. Salvation is the invitation and reception of God's intimate care for people, God respects the will of our souls and works to inspire and nurture individual faith. Jesus revealed the intimate knowledge of God for the potential of one man (Levi) and

God's plan of using Him for the work of His Kingdom. Jesus desires to reach each of us so we may discover our potential in God's Kingdom service.

Imagine Levi (Matthew) sitting at his tax booth, watching the Savior make His way directly to him. He had heard of Jesus and had perhaps even heard Him speak in the Synagogue, but now the Christ was coming specifically and purposefully to him. Levi was tired of being ridiculed by fellow Jews for being a representative of Rome as a tax collector. Fishermen would sell their catch to buyers on the shore. Immediately, at the nearby tax booth, they would have to pay taxes on their income. Peter and Andrew may have wondered (as fisherman) what Jesus saw in Levi. Yet, Levi hears the voice of the Master, "Come and Follow Me". Levi does not have to think twice about this invitation. He immediately left his booth and a secure, income producing, job (though it was a job in which people despised what he did and who he represented). Levi followed Jesus and that night threw a party for all his friends to come celebrate His decision and meet Jesus. The party was loud enough to attract attention and the teachers of the law watched Jesus with scorn. Instead of approaching Jesus directly they went to His disciples with criticism, thinking they could derail their confidence in Jesus. After all, how could the "Christ" associate with tax collectors and sinners? These "party poopers" were sure that they could create confusion in the hearts of the disciples. Jesus knew the divisive plan of the teachers of the law. He came out from the party to confront the cowardice of the religious "stiffs" to clarify His ministry to the disciples. *"On hearing this, Jesus said to them, "It is not the healthy who need a doctor, but the sick. I have not come to call the righteous, but sinners."* Mark 2:17 (NIV)

Moving on in Jesus' ministry, in Matthew 18, we find Jesus teaching through a parable that spoke of humanity's overall stubbornness to truly repent and change. The prompting of this parable came as Peter was curious about how many times he should forgive someone. Peter anticipates that Jesus will be generous, so he suggests seven times, which is more than the Pharisees would acknowledge (which was normally three times). Jesus surpasses this and reveals the depth of forgiveness we are called to receive and share, "seventy times seven". Our Lord then uses an extreme example of forgiveness. Jesus' weaves a parable that sounds like a modern day financial scandal. A King catches a trusted civil servant with the crimes of fraud and embezzlement. He is brought to justice, is found guilty and is presented before the King for his sentence. Upon pleading for mercy and forgiveness, surprisingly, the King grants him mercy through the dismissal of his debt and the opportunity to start anew. Although this man has been forgiven for so much, alas, he afterward goes to a man who owes him just a small amount of money and has him thrown in prison for not paying up. Word gets back to the King. The man is brought into account before the King once more, this time his crime is recalled for judgment because of the man's lack of mercy toward a debtor. Jesus points out that "one who was forgiven much is expected to forgive freely as he had been forgiven". Because the man had not apprehended or appreciated how blessed he was in being forgiven, the penalty of his previous sin comes back upon him. The lesson of grace is meant to be absorbed so that we will change the way we live and relate to others. Forgiveness is to be the new mode of operation for a repentant believer.

In Psalm 32 we hear the words of a broken king David; we listen to plumb deep emotions within this timeless story of God's grace and forgiveness. Here we see a penetrating self-portrait of David's repentant heart. He is a man who has learned the lesson of how damaging sin can be. Even more, David has experienced the power of God's forgiveness. What led to his fall from following God's ways and His need for forgiveness? David had lost his moral compass and was not being obedient to His responsibilities as King. During a war when he was supposed to be out with the army in battle, instead he was taking his ease upon the rooftop of his palace in Jerusalem. From his lofty balcony David beheld the beautiful Bathsheba sunbathing, David allowed lust to enter his heart. He desired this woman so much that he decided to have her husband Uriah killed in battle so he could take her to be his wife. While the thought was evil, sin entered David's heart as he conspired (instead of confessing his thoughts) and followed through to have Uriah killed. The prophet Nathan was told by God what David did, and so he confronted the king. Nathan told David that he would suffer from the consequences of his sin.

Not until David's first child with Bathsheba died, and a confrontation by the prophet Nathan, was David willing to admit his sin. The full weight of his conscience and the ugliness of his evil actions tore him up within. David repented of his sin as he was keenly aware of how much he needed to be forgiven. God forgave David and renewed His covenant with David's seed and the people of Israel. The consequence of his poor judgment and sin would continue in violence and palace intrigue. Eventually, the people of Israel and their kingdom would be divided into Northern and Southern kingdoms (Israel in the North and Judah in the South). Nevertheless, God's Kingdom plan was still unfolding within human history, but not in a way that people could at first understand. The coming of Jesus Christ, born in the city of David, represented a fresh start of God's grace and truth that the world so needed. David had allowed pride and power to lead him to think that he could have anything he wanted. God showed David that righteousness is far more important that selfish ambition or pleasure. David knew he did not deserve the forgiveness of God, but the Lord was kind and loving to reconcile David back to Himself. Jesus exhibited the very grace of God the Father as He called sinners to repentance and invited fishermen and tax collectors to come and follow Him.

Bridging into Today

Jesus cares about people's needs today. The most important concern of Jesus is to glorify God through our salvation. His primary reason for coming was to reclaim us to God by forgiving our sins and teaching us how to live for God's Kingdom. If we believe in Him and receive the ministry of His forgiveness, we will not only be cleansed within, but we shall be restored to a right relationship with God. We are all modern day "prodigal" sons and daughters; Jesus pictured His Heavenly Father's longing for our repentance and reconciliation. God the Father runs to us when we humble ourselves in faith and come to Him. God wants to embrace us in His love, but we must be willing to leave the life of sin behind us and come to receive the saving gift of grace, and the robe of righteousness in Christ, that God is ready to place upon us. Forgiveness is what must be received for one to be reconciled ("made right"). This precedes the receipt and powerful working of the gift of new life in the Spirit of God. Jesus makes this change possible through His substitutionary death and redeeming resurrection; in Christ we are "born again". When one has been forgiven through Jesus Christ, it should lead the will of a person to then live so as to forgive and love others. The reception of God's grace leads people to pursue righteousness and holiness. Accountability is therefore both encouraging and essential in the new covenant of grace and truth that we share as God's people.

Nathan was led to confront David. His objective was not to destroy the king he served, but to follow God's plan to humble him to repentance. David's honest confession and detailed feelings of brokenness are accurate descriptions of the effect of sin. There are times when the appropriate response to our guilt and shame will be sadness and grief. Moments of confession are a time to be honest before God and others for the sake of recognizing our need for God's ministry of forgiveness, inner healing and restoration.

Jesus cared more for reaching individuals with an invitation of forgiveness, hope and discipleship than he did for manipulating crowds to his advantage or personal glory. Jesus came to express the love of God the Father to lost and sinful human beings. Ultimately, in choosing the cross in the Garden of Gethsemane, Jesus demonstrated that "humility comes before honor". Unselfishness also preceded the miracle of God's redeeming grace that is bestowed through sacrifice, pardon and ransom being made.

The load of emotional burden from un-forgiveness is heavy. As a pastor and chaplain I have heard many stories of pain and brokenness. I have walked with people through uncertainty, grief, loss, suffering and frustration. My own valleys have been filled with tests, trials and heaviness. Central to the concern, when people do not forgive the sin of others, or themselves, it can break people apart and it can destroy people from within. When people do horrendous things, even small acts of cruelty and unkindness, it breaks the heart of God. Jesus wept over Jerusalem as He considered the magnitude of sin. Jesus could see from the all-knowing perspective and compassion of God His Father. This stirred His heart with resolve to go to the cross. Only Jesus as God's Son could forgive us perfectly. The "Christ" came first to serve, not to be served. The Good Shepherd laid down His life for lost humanity. Jesus alone fulfills the prophecy of Isaiah as the "Christ", the promised "Suffering Servant":

Isaiah 53:4-12 (KJV)
[4] Surely he hath borne our griefs, and carried our sorrows: yet we did esteem him stricken, smitten of God, and afflicted. [5] But he *was* wounded for our transgressions, *he was* bruised for our iniquities: the chastisement of our peace *was* upon him; and with his stripes we are healed. [6] All we like sheep have gone astray; we have turned every one to his own way; and the LORD hath laid on him the iniquity of us all. [7] He was oppressed, and he was afflicted, yet he opened not his mouth: he is brought as a lamb to the slaughter, and as a sheep before her shearers is dumb, so he openeth not his mouth. [8] He was taken from prison and from judgment: and who shall declare his generation? for he was cut off out of the land of the living: for the transgression of my people was he stricken. [9] And he made his grave with the wicked, and with the rich in his death; because he had done no violence, neither *was any*

deceit in his mouth.

¹⁰ Yet it pleased the LORD to bruise him; he hath put *him* to grief: when thou shalt make his soul an offering for sin, he shall see *his* seed, he shall prolong *his* days, and the pleasure of the LORD shall prosper in his hand.

¹¹ He shall see of the travail of his soul, *and* shall be satisfied: by his knowledge shall my righteous servant justify many; for he shall bear their iniquities.

¹² Therefore will I divide him *a portion* with the great, and he shall divide the spoil with the strong; because he hath poured out his soul unto death: and he was numbered with the transgressors; and he bare the sin of many, and made intercession for the transgressors.

In response to Jesus, and to God the Father's appeal through His beloved Son, we may either declare Jesus to be truly Lord and Savior or we may dismiss all that God had previously revealed about Him and remain unconvinced (even with the mountain of evidence pointing toward God's revealed love in Christ on the cross of Calvary). Denial is epidemic among humanity when it comes to the Jesus' sacrifice for us, we don't want to admit either our need or our willingness to forgive others. Until we do accept forgiveness, and live following Jesus daily by picking up the cross of forgiving others, we will be distant from God's heart of mercy and from Christ's throne of saving grace.

Questions for Class Discussion

1. Why is it so hard to forgive people?

2. Jesus told Peter to forgive 490 times, how might this relate to the process of letting go?

3. Who do you relate to in the Parable in Matthew 18? Why?

4. When someone close to us commits a sin, how can we apply the approach of the prophet Nathan as he confronted David?

Closing Idea

Whenever you start to think of someone who has been unkind or mean; ask God to help you with forgiveness. Stop and consider what Jesus modeled. Seek to forgive repeatedly and habitually. You will probably lose count before you reach 490 moments of forgiveness. Reconciliation and healing involves time and a deliberate process. Quite often the process of forgiveness in our minds and hearts calls for us to let go of recollection, pain, resentment, fear or pride. Forgiving is a venture in faith that involves inner healing and increasing release into God's sovereign ministry of truth and grace. Forgiveness is possible, but it must be received and shared as a gift, not as a commodity. To live as a "Prelude", giving witness to God, believers are to become forgiving and gracious. As James said: "Be quick to listen, slow to speak and slow to anger" (James 1:19).

13

SERVICE IN THE NAME OF THE KING

(Matthew 10:1-42; Psalm 145)

> **Key verse:**
> ¹ *He called his twelve disciples to him and gave them authority to drive out evil spirits and to heal every disease and sickness. ..*
> ⁷ *As you go, preach this message: 'The kingdom of heaven is near.'*
> - Matthew. 10:1. 7 NIV

Purpose of study

Jesus called the original 12 disciples to specifically be a part of His ministry team. Jesus inaugurated a renewed covenant requiring faith and obedience like that of Abraham and his descendants. Jesus continues to call us today to join the work of His Kingdom, to join Him in cultivating and harvesting God's vineyard. This ministry involves acts of kindness, prayers of healing and sharing the Gospel of God's Kingdom. Believers follow Jesus by proclaiming salvation from sin and death. There is new life born of God's Spirit that leads to eternal life and citizenship in God's eternal Kingdom through faith in Christ Jesus.

The purpose of this chapter's study will be to embrace and respond to Jesus' call in our lives. The Kingdom of God is a present reality whenever people humble themselves and pray, turn from their wicked ways and serve Christ Jesus for the sake of bringing healing, truthfulness, mercy and wholeness to the land and its people.

Prelude

This passage from Matthew chapter 10 reveals how personal and direct Jesus was in His ministry. Here, the disciples are each named. To be a follower of Jesus Christ you cannot remain anonymous. There is a commitment and an association with the Master that one must make. The original disciples' names are verified and put on record by Matthew. Israel had its twelve tribes; Jesus had His twelve key disciples. While there were others besides the named twelve, these are named in order to affirm the accountability they would have to the Lord in their unique calling as heralds, helpers and healers for God's Kingdom in Christ. Jesus would impart His teaching and responsibility to them. Jesus gave them the authority to heal the sick, cast out demons, feed the poor, and tell people the good news of God's Kingdom that was "at hand". Repentance and new life burst forth in glorious bloom as people began to trust and believe in Jesus. People even believed in the witness of His disciples. God's Son demonstrated the compassion and mercy of the Heavenly Father in acts of service and love. The disciples grew in faith and wisdom as they followed Jesus. Their growth in service to Christ would not come without suffering or sacrifice. Jesus did not try to "sugar-coat" the cost of discipleship to make it seem simple or without danger. In fact, He said,

Matthew 10:37-39 (NIV)
[37] "Anyone who loves his father or mother more than me is not worthy of me; anyone who loves his son or daughter more than me is not worthy of me; [38] and anyone who does not take his cross and follow me is not worthy of me. [39] Whoever finds his life will lose it, and whoever loses his life for my sake will find it.

We too are called to participate in God's work of redemption in human history. Service in Jesus' name will inevitably involve encountering resistance from the forces of evil. These forces have inhabited the persons and systems of humanity such that oppression, suffering, injustice and brokenness continue to wreak havoc and mayhem. Principalities and powers, then and now, have maintained a grip on the administration of resources, land, and opportunities such that God's intent has been corrupted with human greed and prejudice. The call of Christ for His disciples, for the Church, is to be salt and light that gives flavor and revelation to the principles of God's Heavenly Kingdom. To live according to a Christian worldview involves more than mere Sunday attendance in the local church or mere ascent to Christian values. Believers are to be "doers of the Word". Service is the signature affirming that your name is written down as a committed follower of Jesus. Service likewise reveals Christ's signature in your life. One's actions and attitudes reveal God's gentle or radical sculpting in your life; the shape is noticed in care and service.

One more important note; God's Kingdom did not at first commence with Jesus' incarnation; it was inaugurated on earth prior to Jesus with those whom the Lord called starting with Adam, leading to Noah, Abraham, Jacob and all who helped form, found and preserve the whole nation and people "Israel". The name "Israel" means "those who prevail with God".[16] The name was given to Jacob after he had wrestled with the Lord: *^{28} Then the man said, "Your name will no longer be Jacob, but Israel, because you have struggled with God and with men and have overcome"* **Genesis 32:28 (NIV)**.

The significance of this for today is that Israel includes all who will openly struggle with the claims of salvation and redemption as revealed by God in both Old and New Testaments. God calls us to wrestle with Him long enough to believe and obey, trust and serve for His Kingdom. God's people shall prevail as they place their ultimate worth in the Lord their God, who is worthy of all honor, glory and praise. The man who wrestled with Jacob is not specifically named, though one might draw from Jacob's description a possible manifestation of Christ appearing to him. *So Jacob called the place Peniel, saying, "It is because I saw God face to face, and yet my life was spared"* **Genesis 32:30 (NIV)**.

Ever since then the people of Israel have had an understanding that God calls us to seek personal encounters: face to face we may actually wrestle with the One who can train us to overcome our sinfulness and shortcomings. God uses those times when we are in solitude to pray and be spiritually, physically, mentally and emotionally trained. This is God's way of making believers strong for life's battles. Wrestling with God is therefore good for us, as God often

---

[16] A Dictionary of the Holy Bible, William Wilberforce Rand, 1859. American Tract Society.

initiates the encounter when we make our selves available. God approaches us personally and intimately. Jesus came at a level we can could begin to understand. The challenge to developing spiritual disciplines is therefore at the heart of discovering that all of life is sacred and to be devoted to God. Worship is both a way of life and involves special places and times that are set aside to seek the face of God personally and corporately. Together, in adoration, thanksgiving, prayer, petition and praise we prevail with the help and strength of the Lord who is personally training believers in righteousness.

Given the bigger historical context of God's Kingdom, we look to Psalm 145 for inspiration. Here the author pens beautiful words of exaltation. Praise was sung by the Jews in the face of worship before the King of Glory, the One True and Holy God, Yahweh. The theme is the proclamation of God's Kingdom. The emphasis of Jesus ministry also started with proclamation and was then accompanied by actions and miracles. Jesus demonstrated the mercy and love of God, beginning with the Jews and extending to the Gentiles. Jesus realized that people were wrestling with the ministry and message of the Gospel of God's Kingdom that He embodied. Therefore, Jesus trained His disciples to likewise engage in the work of the Kingdom as He gave them authority to represent Him and contend for the hearts of men.

Scripture Passages

Matthew 10:1-42

> **I. Kingdom Service is a Personal Commitment (Matthew 10:1-42)**
> A. Jesus calls His disciples (1)
> B. Jesus empowers His disciples (1)
> C. Jesus names His disciples (2-4)

[1] He called his twelve disciples to him and gave them authority to drive out evil spirits and to heal every disease and sickness. [2] These are the names of the twelve apostles: first, Simon (who is called Peter) and his brother Andrew; James son of Zebedee, and his brother John; [3] Philip and Bartholomew; Thomas and Matthew the tax collector; James son of Alphaeus, and Thaddaeus; [4] Simon the Zealot and Judas Iscariot, who betrayed him.

[5] These twelve Jesus sent out with the following instructions: "Do not go among the Gentiles or enter any town of the Samaritans. [6] Go rather to the lost sheep of Israel. [7] As you go, preach this message: 'The kingdom of heaven is near.' [8] Heal the sick, raise the dead, cleanse those who have leprosy, drive out demons. Freely you have received, freely give. [9] Do not take along any gold or silver or copper in your belts; [10] take no bag

for the journey, or extra tunic, or sandals or a staff; for the worker is worth his keep. ¹¹ "Whatever town or village you enter, search for some worthy person there and stay at his house until you leave. ¹² As you enter the home, give it your greeting. ¹³ If the home is deserving, let your peace rest on it; if it is not, let your peace return to you. ¹⁴ If anyone will not welcome you or listen to your words, shake the dust off your feet when you leave that home or town. ¹⁵ I tell you the truth, it will be more bearable for Sodom and Gomorrah on the day of judgment than for that town. ¹⁶ I am sending you out like sheep among wolves. Therefore be as shrewd as snakes and as innocent as doves. ¹⁷ "Be on your guard against men; they will hand you over to the local councils and flog you in their synagogues. ¹⁸ On my account you will be brought before governors and kings as witnesses to them and to the Gentiles. ¹⁹ But when they arrest you, do not worry about what to say or how to say it. At that time you will be given what to say, ²⁰ for it will not be you speaking, but the Spirit of your Father speaking through you. ²¹ "Brother will betray brother to death, and a father his child; children will rebel against their parents and have them put to death. ²² All men will hate you because of me, but he who stands firm to the end will be saved. ²³ When you are persecuted in one place, flee to another. I tell you the truth, you will not finish going through the cities of Israel before the Son of Man comes. ²⁴ "A student is not above his teacher, nor a servant above his master. ²⁵ It is enough for the student to be like his teacher, and the servant like his master. If the head of the house has been called Beelzebub, how much more the members of his household! ²⁶ "So do not be afraid of them. There is nothing concealed that will not be disclosed, or hidden that will not be made known. ²⁷ What I tell you in the dark, speak in the daylight; what is whispered in your ear, proclaim from the roofs. ²⁸ Do not be afraid of those who kill the body but cannot kill the soul. Rather, be afraid of the One who can destroy both soul and body in hell. ²⁹ Are not two sparrows sold for a penny ? Yet not one of them will fall to the ground apart from the will of your Father. ³⁰ And even the very hairs of your head are all numbered. ³¹ So don't be afraid; you are worth more than many sparrows. ³² "Whoever acknowledges me before men, I will also

> **I. Kingdom Service is a Personal Commitment (cont.)**
> (Matthew 10:1-42)
> D. Jesus instructs His disciples (5-42)
>   1. Focus: Where and who. (5-6)
>   2. Message: Nearness of God's Kingdom (7)
>   3. Ministry: Participate in God's healing and redemptive work (8)
>   4. Means: God will provide (9-10)
>   5. Contact: Search for a person (11-15)
>   6. Survival: Be wise (16)
>   7. Adversity: Be courageous (17)
>   8. Opportunity: Be bold (18-20)
>   9. Rejection: Be faithful (21-22)
>   10. Persecution: Be quick (23)
> E. Jesus Encourages His Disciples
>   1. To Trust His Leading (24-25a)
>   2. To Trust His Authority over evil (25b- 26)
>   3. To Trust His Message (27)
>   4. To Trust His Salvation (28-31)
>   5. To Trust His Promises (32)
> F. Jesus Warns His Disciples
>   1. Not to disown Him (33)
>   2. Not to be cowardly (34-36)
>   3. Not to forsake loyalty (37)
>   4. Not to lose faith (38-41)
>   5. Not to lose compassion (42)

acknowledge him before my Father in heaven. ³³ But whoever disowns me before men, I will disown him before my Father in heaven. ³⁴ "Do not suppose that I have come to bring peace to the earth. I did not come to bring peace, but a sword. ³⁵ For I have come to turn "'a man against his father, a daughter against her mother, a daughter-in-law against her mother-in-law-- ³⁶ a man's enemies will be the members of his own household.' ³⁷ "Anyone who loves his father or mother more than me is not worthy of me; anyone who loves his son or daughter more than me is not worthy of me; ³⁸ and anyone who does not take his cross and follow me is not worthy of me. ³⁹ Whoever finds his life will lose it, and whoever loses his life for my sake will find it. ⁴⁰ "He who receives you receives me, and he who receives me receives the one who sent me. ⁴¹ Anyone who receives a prophet because he is a prophet will receive a prophet's reward, and anyone who receives a righteous man because he is a righteous man will receive a righteous man's reward. ⁴² And if anyone gives even a cup of cold water to one of these little ones because he is my disciple, I tell you the truth, he will certainly not lose his reward." **Matthew 10:1-42 (NIV)**

Psalm 145

¹ I will exalt you, my God the King; I will praise your name for ever and ever.
² Every day I will praise you and extol your name for ever and ever.
³ Great is the LORD and most worthy of praise; his greatness no one can fathom.
⁴ One generation will commend your works to another; they will tell of your mighty acts. ⁵ They will speak of the glorious splendor of your majesty, and I will meditate on your wonderful works. ⁶ They will tell of the power of your awesome works, and I will proclaim your great deeds. ⁷ They will celebrate your abundant goodness and joyfully sing of your righteousness. ⁸ The LORD is gracious and compassionate, slow to anger and rich in love. ⁹ The LORD is good to all; he has compassion on all he has made. ¹⁰ All you have made will praise you, O LORD; your saints will extol you.
¹¹ They will tell of the glory of your kingdom and speak of your might,
¹² so that all men may know of your mighty acts and the glorious splendor of your kingdom. ¹³ Your kingdom is an everlasting kingdom, and your dominion endures through all generations.
   The LORD is faithful to all his promises and loving toward all he has made.
¹⁴ The LORD upholds all those who fall and lifts up all who are bowed down.
¹⁵ The eyes of all look to you, and you give them their food at the proper time.
¹⁶ You open your hand and satisfy the desires of every living thing.
¹⁷ The LORD is righteous in all his ways and loving toward all he has made.
¹⁸ The LORD is near to all who call on him, to all who call on him in truth.
¹⁹ He fulfills the desires of those who fear him; he hears their cry and saves them.
²⁰ The LORD watches over all who love him, but all the wicked he will destroy.
²¹ My mouth will speak in praise of the LORD. Let every creature praise his holy name for ever and ever. **Psalms 145:1-21 (NIV)**

> **II. Kingdom Service Involves Public Worship (Psalm 145)**
> A. God's Name is praised (1-3)
> B. God's Acts are remembered (4-6)
> C. God's Attributes are recalled (7-9)
> D. God's Kingdom is glorified (10-13)
> E. Glorify the LORD (14-21)

Exploring the Scriptures

These passages reflect the depth of commitment God calls His people to in His Kingdom's service. Following and serving Jesus Christ is not easy. Nonetheless, by God's grace our efforts and faithfulness shall have an eternal impact as we represent Christ. The reward we seek and experience becomes the joy we discover as God's Kingdom is manifested through people coming to faith in Christ. Together, believers receive God's grace and truth in Christ and consequently grow in the gift and work of salvation. This calling forth of the twelve disciples represented a new level of participation and risk. Jesus would empower and equip His disciples with an imperative Kingdom mission. At times the work would be overwhelming and the results were to be quite different than what many would consider to be "successful" in worldly standards. How were they going to make it evident to their people that the Kingdom of God was at hand? How were they going to share the message of the Gospel of salvation? Jesus prepared them for what they were up against; He warned them that they would run into rejection, persecution and adversity. Even so, the ministry of Jesus was effective and powerful. The disciples were inspired and persuaded to go with Him into the unknown.

Jesus taught them what God the Father had taught Him so that His disciples would eventually develop a tremendous faith. God would fulfill His purposes through the beginning ministry of these first disciples, imperfect as they were. Jesus strongly shaped their understanding through His instruction, as He would likewise strongly shape their character as they went forth to serve. Jesus expressed His concern for the loyalty and faithfulness of His disciples. Therefore, while the overall work of God's Kingdom is exciting; to be a faithful and fruitful disciple requires careful training and spiritual maturity. Even so, the Lord told them to "go" and "do" the work of the Kingdom. When believers represent Him to others by accepting the reality of spiritual battle, there will be people who shall be saved and made right with God. The faithful witness of God's prevailing people, starting with the disciples and the early church, is evidence of God's providence, a prelude to His coming Kingdom.

Psalm 145 balances the elements of God's strength and beauty in worship. God's name is revered. Historical highlights are recounted about how God's hand had been at work to preserve and guide the people of Israel. Through it all, God had always provided. God's goodness is magnified in the light of His grace and compassion, as well as through His Truth and Holiness. A wonderful element of rhythm develops within the Psalm from the worship leader to the response of the people of God who participate in the wonder and joy of trusting, serving and praising God. A dynamic tension is at work between the people in their trials and the hope God gives them to endure. God is faithful to fulfill His promises. God will uphold, even lift up, all who are bowed down in worship. God desires that His people open their eyes and discover His provision, protection and salvation. God is not far from us; He sees into our eyes to know the sins and problems we struggle with. God also knows the potential of our faith and His saving grace. Israel prevailed then through many challenges. Today, people of faith also prevail through reliance upon the mercy and strength of God.

Bridging into Today

In today's world it has become increasingly difficult to be a distinctive and faithful follower of Jesus Christ. There are many who will say "Lord, Lord", but not many who will genuinely follow Him. Worshipping God requires that we prevail against the current of popular culture and the false gods and idols of society. Worship and service in Christ involves discipleship that at times resembles learning how to wrestle or battle. Paul himself gave training advice:

> [10] Finally, my brethren, be strong in the Lord, and in the power of his might.
> [11] Put on the whole armour of God, that ye may be able to stand against the wiles of the devil. [12] For we wrestle not against flesh and blood, but against principalities, against powers, against the rulers of the darkness of this world, against spiritual wickedness in high *places*. [13] Wherefore take unto you the whole armour of God, that ye may be able to withstand in the evil day, and having done all, to stand.
> **Ephesians 6:10-13 (KJV)**

Those who do follow Jesus in any time of history will portray a resemblance of the Master. Disciples will always in some way be imperfect. Nonetheless, God uses disciples of Jesus to proclaim His Kingdom in word and deed. God calls people personally by name today as He did then. You and I may learn from Jesus' discipleship training and apply it to personal mentoring, small group support, teaching and preaching, compassionate outreach and corporate worship. We may join Jacob in the Lord's training and learn from the Master how to handle spiritual battles.

The words of the Psalmist help us to see that the act of worship is one of the key means by which God strengthens and trains us. Worship is likewise the expression of what we have learned in contending for our faith; it is a means by which God allows us to work out, witness and reveal His love and truth to the world. Certainly the church and its members are imperfect; however, they are in the midst of being trained, refined, filled and transformed. The church's spiritual regimen in righteousness is essential for it to survive and thrive upon this journey of serving and praising God. Christ came to approach us face to face. He continues to call, make and send His disciples out to spread the Gospel and to prevail in life over sin and death.

Many people will make excuses for not following Jesus with devotion into service. Nonetheless, it is important that fellow believers do not judge too critically how others are serving as we must recognize that the Lord Jesus sits in that position of authority and shall hold all people into account. More important than any comparison that we might be tempted to make with others is the need to develop a heart to serve. Discipleship training involves desire, availability and attentiveness. Our calling is to be more focused upon our faith and trust in Christ Jesus than to be dependent upon our gifts and talents. When Jesus called the disciples, the on-looking Pharisees must have wondered: "What is Jesus thinking of in calling common fisherman, a few daydreamers, a tax collector and a few sinners?" The Pharisees had their followers, and they were the best and brightest from among the tribes and towns. One can almost imagine the Pharisees scoffing at Jesus' selection (much like a little league baseball coach scoffs at the selection of another coach for his team). Still, Jesus looked into their hearts to see the brilliance of His Father's creativity in each one of them. Jesus looks into our hearts and minds and can see great potential. The key element of discipleship is willingness, a determination to follow and get out there and work. Jesus saw disciples who were ready for adventure. Today He still calls those who are ready for the great adventure of loving others in real and practical ways (in His name) for the sake of God's Kingdom.

Questions for Class Discussion

1. What makes commitment to Jesus Christ both joyful and challenging?

2. In serving Christ, how have you grown to rely upon His strength?

3. Share examples and stories of how service for Christ has involved "picking up your cross".

4. What role does worship have in bearing a faithful witness to the world?

Closing Idea and Story

Take a piece of paper with a pencil/pen and chart your walk with Christ as a disciple in a way where ups and downs indicate your spiritual condition upon a line going from left to right (This is called making a journey map). Could you say that it is always possible for believers to be moving upward in their faith? How does God use the highs or lows in the journey? Are there any points in the journey map when you wrestled more with God than at other times? What did you learn through those wrestling (training) times with the Lord?

Life experiences that are hard to explain or deal with can be a matter of training for righteousness. These may include unanswered questions, the scars of the past or personal stress points that are tender or weak. When Jacob wrestled with the Lord he was surprised when the Lord pressed on his hip at a "weak spot". Sometimes we are not aware of our "weak spots" and we need a good coach to show us where training is necessary. Take some time to talk with God about your struggles, let Him help to firm you up in His spiritual training in those areas where you are weak. Acknowledge that the Lord will come near to you. He even looks us eye to eye, going hand to hand so as to train and strengthen our faith.

Recall those times when you (or someone close to you) had to battle illness or disease. How did God help you through such times? As a cancer survivor, I have learned the purpose of God within adversity. The Lord has taught me reliance and given me inner strength. Since my immune system is compromised, each time I contract a cold, flu or infection I fight a battle. The spiritual conditioning that takes place in wrestling disease can never be taken lightly. In a recent battle with a severe cold I felt the Lord help me overcome the "cloud" of confusion that can accompany nights of severe coughing and drainage. At one point I thought I might lose my mind, even seeing a shadowy figure in my mind coming toward me. In prayer, I called out to Jesus and soon felt the strength He gave me to endure in faith. While standing at my bathroom sink with my eyes closed, I had a vision of Jesus sitting down on a tree stump. He was calling me to also sit down and talk with him face to face, man to man. He looked a bit like a hiker, with boots, flannel shirt and beige cargo shorts. I sat down on the humble ceramic throne and prayed. He was there to give me strength, wisdom and support; I felt His nearness and encouragement.

The next night, as I continued to have a sleepless struggle, the battle with the cold was filled with the presence of the Lord. He helped me to envision that He was with me on a journey up through a series of mountains. When I thought I could not take any more, He gave me rest. Then, as the climb continued, I was able to endure more of the cold's symptoms because I kept my heart fixed on the Lord. I was able to rely upon the promise He gave me to prevail. The next day I was tired but the Lord gave me further rest and strength, even so that I could continue to recover with His strength. The journey of life is not meant to be traveled alone; the Lord wants to be our guide and coach. He will lead us in the path of righteousness until we reach the shore of His Kingdom. Upon coming to the summit of the Lord, all our wrestling will be replaced by the full embrace of Heaven as we see our Savior's face and He opens His arms to receive us.

14

THE KING WHO SUFFERED

(Matthew 21:33-46; Psalm 22)

> ### Key verse:
> *38 "But when the tenants saw the son, they said to each other, 'This is the heir. Come, let's kill him and take his inheritance.' 39 So they took him and threw him out of the vineyard and killed him.*
> - Matthew 21:38-39

Purpose of study

Jesus would suffer for our salvation and redemption. He is the Son of God, the Prince of Peace, the Lord and King. He gave His life willingly, obediently, sacrificially to save us. Through His perfect offering, giving His lifeblood to forgive our sins and His body of divine incarnation to absorb the penalty of death, we may be reconciled to God as we believe that His righteous work of suffering was not in vain. This chapter's study of Scripture reveals the purpose of Jesus' pain and death. May our hearts be moved to greater faith and our minds toward insightful understanding and transformation, even in the midst of our own suffering. The "birth pains" of the Kingdom of God are all around us. Therefore, let us not lose heart while we discover the fulfillment of the Lord's redemptive ministry that inspires trust and obedience through adversity.

Prelude

People have speculated about whether God is the author of suffering or if God simple allows it in the current order of things with the ability to use it for our ultimate good. From the time of Adam and Eve's fall, suffering has been the result of mankind's disobedience, a consequence of sin. God did not author sin, but planned for the possibility of sin as we were given free will. God does not author suffering directly, but has allowed suffering to exist as the consequence of rebellion and sin. The nature of sin is interwoven between humankind as it affects our relationship with God, one another and creation. Therefore as one person suffers, so do others suffer as a result. Just as one person commits sinful actions that produce suffering for others, so does God desire to break the chain of suffering that has resulted. Suffering therefore serves a purpose in that it arouses our awareness of wrongdoing, poor judgment and the spiritual existence of a rebellious force counter to God. Suffering does not have to be the final experience resulting from sin. In fact, God can work through suffering to draw us near to Him so we may receive His healing, comforting, restorative, redemptive presence and power.

The existence of evil arose within the angelic realm from Satan and his minions, and they are actively seeking to promote further rebellion from God among humankind. This spiritual realm, that has evoked the righteous judgment of God, affects the interwoven physical realm that we dwell in. Suffering is therefore a "wake up call" for seeking help with the condition of sin. Sin is involved with disease and brokenness within both spiritual and physical realities. God has given way for suffering to exist so that we may seek to discover His compassion, mercy and provision. Jesus accepted suffering as a result of bearing with our sinfulness and giving His life to heal the brokenness of humanity. Christ encountered people who were suffering; He responded with the heart of compassion and the healing touch of God's love. In Christ's own suffering people beheld a pure and bright image of God's love. Since then, God has worked through believers who suffer to reveal Christ's light and hope.

When God saw that the people of Israel were suffering under the bondage of slavery in Egypt, He was concerned. God set forth a plan to prepare Moses as a servant who would lead them out from the land while the Lord's hand delivered them from their suffering. Jesus' disciples learned that suffering was inevitable for the Messiah to endure for the sake of our salvation.

They too would suffer for the sake of God's Kingdom, but the Lord gave them courage to "take heart" for He would be "with us always until the end". The promises of God consummate in an end to suffering. God's Kingdom is coming in a radically transforming way to eliminate pain and grief, that the "old order" of things will pass and that there will be a "New Creation". This is reason to have hope, to endure suffering for the sake of the Kingdom of God.

There are times when people have questioned whether Jesus was truly a historical figure. They wonder if He was who He claimed to be and if what others recorded about Him was accurate. Was He the Beloved Son of God, one with the Father Creator God, having been with God from the beginning of time? If so, why did He suffer when He came in human form? Why was He rejected? What purpose did all this accomplish? Why hasn't God's Kingdom come in the fullness that is still hoped for and promised in Scripture?

The fact of Jesus Christ's historical being is verified through Jewish historian Josephus, and is also clear through Roman historical records.[17] The Bible itself is a historical document with multiple accounts and witnesses. Yet beyond the question of history is the amazing story of how this person Jesus lived, died, and rose again. Suffering was part of God's plan, and through such suffering God is even at work today among those who place their faith in the risen and triumphant Lord Jesus Christ who will come again in glory and power.

Scripture Passages:
Matthew 21:33-46

³³ "Listen to another parable: There was a landowner who planted a vineyard. He put a wall around it, dug a winepress in it and built a watchtower. Then he rented the vineyard to some farmers and went away on a journey. ³⁴ When the harvest time approached, he sent his servants to the tenants to collect his fruit. ³⁵ "The tenants seized his servants; they beat one, killed another, and stoned a third. ³⁶ Then he sent other servants to them, more than the first time, and the tenants treated them the same way. ³⁷ Last of all, he sent his son to them. 'They will respect my son,' he said. ³⁸ "But when the tenants saw the son,

> I. Jesus Predicted His Suffering in a Story
> (Matt. 21:33-41)
>   A. A Parable about Israel (33)
>   B. God's servants have suffered. (34-36)
>   C. God's own Son will suffer (37-39)
>   D. God will hold Israel into account (40-41)

---

[17] *Josephus, The Essential Works*. Paul Maier, Kregel Publications. Grand Rapids. 1995

they said to each other, 'This is the heir. Come, let's kill him and take his inheritance.' ³⁹ So they took him and threw him out of the vineyard and killed him. ⁴⁰ "Therefore, when the owner of the vineyard comes, what will he do to those tenants?" ⁴¹ "He will bring those wretches to a wretched end," they replied, "and he will rent the vineyard to other tenants, who will give him his share of the crop at harvest time."

⁴² Jesus said to them, "Have you never read in the Scriptures: "'The stone the builders rejected has become the capstone ; the Lord has done this, and it is marvelous in our eyes' ?

⁴³ "Therefore I tell you that the kingdom of God will be taken away from you and given to a people who will produce its fruit.

⁴⁴ He who falls on this stone will be broken to pieces, but he on whom it falls will be crushed."

⁴⁵ When the chief priests and the Pharisees heard Jesus' parables, they knew he was talking about them. ⁴⁶ They looked for a way to arrest him, but they were afraid of the crowd because the people held that he was a prophet.

Matthew 21:33-46 (NIV)

II. Jesus Predicted His Triumphant Kingdom (Matt. 21:42-46)
A. He is the Cornerstone of God's Kingdom (42) (Isaiah 28:14-16)
B. He is Lord for God's Kingdom (43)
   1. He will exercise judgment
   2. He will specify and magnify salvation
C. He is the foundation of God's Kingdom on earth (44)
   1. Judgment from Jesus testimony (Isaiah 8:11-14)
   2. Judgment in Jesus return in Glory (Daniel 2:34-35)

---

¹¹The LORD spoke to me with his strong hand upon me, warning me not to follow the way of this people. He said:¹²"Do not call conspiracy everything that these people call conspiracy°; do not fear what they fear, and do not dread it. ¹³The LORD Almighty is the one you are to regard as holy, he is the one you are to fear, he is the one you are to dread,
¹⁴and he will be a sanctuary; but for both houses of Israel he will be
a stone that causes men to stumble and a rock that makes them fall.
And for the people of Jerusalem he will be a trap and a snare. (**Isaiah 8:11-14**)

³⁴While you were watching, a rock was cut out, but not by human hands. It struck the statue on its feet of iron and clay and smashed them. ³⁵Then the iron, the clay, the bronze, the silver and the gold were broken to pieces at the same time and became like chaff on a threshing floor in the summer. The wind swept them away without leaving a trace. But the rock that struck the statue became a huge mountain and filled the whole earth. (**Daniel 2:34-35**)

Psalm 22

For the director of music. To the tune of "The Doe of the Morning." A psalm of David.
[1] My God, my God, why have you forsaken me? Why are you so far from saving me, so far from the words of my groaning? [2] O my God, I cry out by day, but you do not answer, by night, and am not silent. [3] Yet you are enthroned as the Holy One; you are the praise of Israel. [4] In you our fathers put their trust; they trusted and you delivered them. [5] They cried to you and were saved; in you they trusted and were not disappointed. [6] But I am a worm and not a man, scorned by men and despised by the people. [7] All who see me mock me; they hurl insults, shaking their heads:
[8] "He trusts in the LORD; let the LORD rescue him. Let him deliver him, since he delights in him." [9] Yet you brought me out of the womb; you made me trust in you even at my mother's breast.
[10] From birth I was cast upon you; from my mother's womb you have been my God.
[11] Do not be far from me, for trouble is near and there is no one to help. [12] Many bulls surround me; strong bulls of Bashan encircle me.
[13] Roaring lions tearing their prey open their mouths wide against me. [14] I am poured out like water, and all my bones are out of joint. My heart has turned to wax; it has melted away within me. [15] My strength is dried up like a potsherd, and my tongue sticks to the roof of my mouth; you lay me in the dust of death. [16] Dogs have surrounded me; a band of evil men has encircled me, they have pierced my hands and my feet. [17] I can count all my bones; people stare and gloat over me. [18] They divide my garments among them and cast lots for my clothing. [19] But you, O LORD, be not far off; O my Strength, come quickly to help me. [20] Deliver my life from the sword, my precious life from the power of the dogs. [21] Rescue me from the mouth of the lions; save me from the horns of the wild oxen. [22] I will declare your name to my brothers; in the congregation I will praise you. [23] You who fear the LORD, praise him! All you descendants of Jacob, honor him! Revere him, all you descendants of Israel!
[24] For he has not despised or disdained the suffering of the afflicted one; he has not hidden his face from him but has listened to his cry for help. [25] From you comes the theme of my praise in the great assembly; before those who fear you will I fulfill my vows. [26] The poor will eat and be satisfied; they who seek the LORD will praise him-- may your hearts live forever! [27] All the ends of the earth will remember and turn to the LORD, and all the families of the nations will bow down before him, [28] for dominion belongs to the LORD and he rules over the nations. [29] All the rich of the earth will feast and worship; all who go down to the dust will kneel before him-- those who cannot keep themselves alive. [30] Posterity will serve him; future generations will be told about the Lord. [31] They will proclaim his righteousness to a people yet unborn-- for he has done it. **Psalms 22:1-31 NIV**

> III. The Prophesy Fulfilled (Psalm 22)
> A. The suffering of Christ (1-2)
> B. The faith of Christ (3-5)
> C. The rejection of Christ (6-8)
> D. The trust of Christ (9-11)
> E. The crucifixion of Christ (12-18)
> F. The deliverance of the Christ (19-21)
> G. The declared hope of the Christ (22-24)
> H. The praise and promise of the Christ (25-31)

Exploring the Scriptures

When Jesus confronted the Pharisees He revealed God's plan and the destiny of Israel's temporal religious leaders. Jesus spoke to Israel as a whole while He personally warned the Scribes and Pharisees of the consequences of their rejection and lack of faith. Because they often did not receive His word directly, He spoke to them in parables. This parable in Matthew 21 encapsulated the history of humanity and the history of God's chosen people Israel. The rejection and mistreatment of the prophets, from the Old Testament up to John the Baptist, was evidence of humanity's sin and stubbornness. The landowner is God and the vineyard is the earth, with specific symbolism to the Vine of David and the land of Israel. The tenants were the abusive political and religious power mongers of humanity and the nation of Israel. The servants who were mistreated were the prophets, and the heir of the landowner who arrives to bring accountability is Jesus.

As Jesus tells this story, the Pharisees were dimly dull to miss the symbols Jesus used and the point Jesus was making. They did not immediately understand that the parable's proclamation of judgment and warning was upon them. They had the opportunity to repent and believe in Jesus, but as prophesied, they would reject His authority as the Son of God. Jesus actually asked the Pharisees what their response would be to the rebellious and ungrateful tenants if they were the land owner. Their response was an indictment of themselves. ""*He will bring those wretches to a wretched end*," they replied, "*and he will rent the vineyard to other tenants, who will give him his share of the crop at harvest time*." Jesus, astounded by their blindness, asked if they really understand the meaning of the prophet Isaiah's proclamation in Isaiah 28:16 "*See, I lay a stone in Zion, a tested stone, a precious cornerstone for a sure foundation; the one who trusts will never be dismayed.*" They probably didn't recall what proceeded this in verse 14: "*Therefore hear the word of the LORD, you scoffers who rule this people in Jerusalem.*" Jesus directly confronted them by saying that they were the ones whom the prophet Isaiah spoke of. The consequence of their rebellion and disobedience was then revealed by Jesus in Matthew 21:43. The Kingdom would be taken away from them. Jesus disclosed the consequence of future rebellion and disobedience for all mankind in verse 44. All who defy and work against God's Anointed One shall fail and be destroyed. When Jesus comes again in power and glory, His Kingdom will crush and replace all earthly kingdoms. As Jesus spoke to reveal this truth, their hearts were hardened. The religious leaders wanted to kill Jesus; they dared not to at that time because of the believing crowds.

This leads one to consider a historical prophecy from Psalm 22, which is an amazing portrait of the suffering Jesus went through in His Passion as the Messiah. Though David wrote this while in pain and suffering himself, it was as though he was given a vision of the suffering of God's coming Son, the servant King. David spoke of the coming Savior with a vision of One who would take upon Himself the iniquity of us all. Jesus would recite this very Psalm upon the cross. Jesus was the One who would have His hands and feet pierced. Likewise, His pierced side would pour forth water upon the land. Roman soldiers would encircle Him and would divide His clothing and cast lots to determine who would own His meager garments. The details of this event in Psalm 22 are unmistakable even though it was written many centuries before Jesus' crucifixion. In fact, crucifixion was not invented until after David wrote this vision down. Throughout this Psalm, the trial of suffering is countered by the Anointed One's resolute determination and faith. The Suffering Servant expressed His hope and trust in God. Jesus would likewise cry out to His Father God. His trust and obedience secured the divine gift of salvation and new life to all who will believe and receive Him as Savior and Lord.

Bridging into Today

People still reject Jesus. Religious and political leaders, philosophers, scientists, television talk show hosts, economists and a host of self-help gurus still teach in ways antagonistic to the truth and message of Jesus. People often deny His Lordship and dismiss the promise of His future return as King. The outcome is different for those who do believe, who receive Him. They are granted salvation and citizenship in God's eternal Kingdom. Those who oppose God's plans will eventually perish physically and spiritually. Those who unrepentantly oppose or resist the will of God shall be held into account at God's judgment seat. Those who submit themselves in faith and obedience to Jesus Christ shall be redeemed by the grace and merciful love of God. Believers can face suffering and pain with the perspective of Jesus. Even as He died for our sins on the cross, Jesus saw the greater good of God's Kingdom to come. Inevitably, those who oppose God are beating themselves against the rock of truth; those who assume they are in control will someday discover that God is in control. These passages are not an indictment upon Israel alone; they speak to humanity as a whole. Faith in Jesus Christ is essential for inclusion in God's Kingdom.

The Apostle Paul wrote to the Church in Thessalonica with a knowledge that they were suffering. He too, writing from prison, was suffering. The indomitable joy of Paul in the midst of his trials is inspirational. Paul's vision of Christ at the center of God's Kingdom plan gave him a prevailing hope. Paul wrote to encourage the church:

1 Thessalonians 1:4-7 (NIV)
^{4} For we know, brothers loved by God, that he has chosen you,
^{5} because our gospel came to you not simply with words, but also with power, with the Holy Spirit and with deep conviction. You know how we lived among you for your sake. ^{6} You became imitators of us and of the Lord; in spite of severe suffering, you welcomed the message with the joy given by the Holy Spirit. ^{7} And so you became a model to all the believers in Macedonia and Achaia.

May believers in Christ encourage one another (and those who doubt), not simply with words, but through prayer and kindness. We are called to imitate Jesus Christ in the way we handle suffering, in the way He forgave others from the cross, in the way He trusted in the promises of His Heavenly Father. God shall establish justice and righteousness within the coming of His Kingdom. Joy in the Lord sustains us through trials and pain by the presence and power of the Holy Spirit. Believers are transformed to become examples, models of Christian love and understanding, truth, righteousness and grace.

Questions for Class Discussion

1. How did God use the suffering of Israel and the prophets before Jesus? Name a few examples of people God used (ex. Job).

2. How was Christ's suffering used by God the Father? What purpose did it serve?

3. How has God used suffering and sacrifice in your life?

Closing Idea and Story

The next time someone rejects your Christian faith, don't take it personally. Realize that they are rejecting Jesus. Pray for them and ask God to forgive them for their rebellion and sin. Show God's Kingdom through mercy and loving sacrifice, even if that means suffering rejection or scorn.

Consider how glass is made from common sand that is heated to a high temperature. The result is a substance that can be shaped by the glassmaker for objects of beauty and strength. When the weather beats upon your glass windows, be thankful that the glass is tempered to protect you. People of faith will go through times of tempering (suffering), the result is not only a greater inner strength of character but also a lasting inner beauty of faith, hope and love if one is open to be molded by God's Spirit.

When I was a boy scout we built a campfire and tried burning many things in the fire pit. One of the guys found a long metal pipe made of magnesium. After a while the magnesium pipe started to sparkle and burn brightly. The scoutmaster explained that magnesium is one of the ingredients in fireworks. Not only did the pipe burn brightly, it also stayed bright for a long time after it was taken out of the fire. Years later I find a lesson for application as I consider the role suffering has when we go through the heat or pain of life. There are those who will melt with fear and give way to doubt, blaming or despair. However, with help from God we can be like magnesium to shine, sparkle and glow. I think of Jesus while He was suffering for our sins on the cross. He identified with our doubts and fears as He took our sins upon Himself. In that hot moment when the forces of evil had hurled insult upon insult, nail upon nail, pain upon pain, rejection upon rejection; our Lord and Savior took pity upon us and demonstrated God's perfectly refined love. He forgave us. He completed the work of suffering and did so in a way that burned brightly. A Roman Centurion overseeing Jesus' crucifixion was so moved by the presence of God's love shown in Christ that He declared: "Certainly this was the Son of God."

15

THE KING WHO IS VICTORIOUS

(John 20:1-18;   Psalm 91)

> ### Key verse:
> ¹⁷ Jesus said, "Do not hold on to me, for I have not yet returned to the Father. Go instead to my brothers and tell them, 'I am returning to my Father and your Father, to my God and your God.'" ¹⁸ Mary Magdalene went to the disciples with the news: "I have seen the Lord!" And she told them that he had said these things to her. - John 20:17-18

Purpose of study

When something completely new happens to us in life do we easily grasp what is going on? The purpose of today's study is to more firmly comprehend the truth of the resurrection of Jesus Christ. Not only was Jesus Christ raised from the dead. He had conquered evil and given believers victory over sin. He was triumphant in the battle for our salvation. Let's explore how Christ's resurrection brings new life in a new day for God's people of faith.

Prelude

In what way was Jesus victorious through His death and resurrection? At Jesus' birth God's Kingdom directly invaded the darkness of sin. In Jesus' death and resurrection He defeated the powers of evil through an exchange of perfect love that forgives sins, casts out fear and overcomes hate. Jesus' death and resurrection brought the critical defeat that spelled ultimate condemnation for Satan and his host of spiritual darkness. Christ the King won the decisive battle through His death and resurrection. Faith in Jesus Christ is necessary for salvation; this is what is involved for one's personal and pivotal victory over sin and death. God was faithful in His promise of redemption. Through Jesus we are given a covenant of grace, peace and hope. From now on we may place our trust in the power and authority of Christ Jesus the living Lord. Not only is Jesus an all sufficient Savior and King, through His authority we are equipped and empowered to be victorious over sin and death.

In life there is a spiritual battle, and ultimately we are promised the complete fulfillment of God's Kingdom when our Lord Jesus returns to earth. His Kingdom begins in our hearts as we believe that He died and rose again and then acknowledge that we need Him to forgive us and come live in our hearts. Jesus gives true believers new life for an eternity with God. Jesus welcomes and prepares repentant sinners for inclusion into the everlasting reign and realm of God's Kingdom. The world has changed and will be completely transformed because of Jesus. Praise God!

Scripture Passages
John 20:1-18

I. A New Day in God's Kingdom (John 20:1-10)
A. First Day of a New Day (1a)
B. Evidence for a New Day (1b)
C. Confusion of a New Day (2)
D. Excitement of a New Day (3-4)
E. Amazement of a New Day (5-10)

[1] Early on the first day of the week, while it was still dark, Mary Magdalene went to the tomb and saw that the stone had been removed from the entrance. [2] So she came running to Simon Peter and the other disciple, the one Jesus loved, and said, "They have taken the Lord out of the tomb, and we don't know where they have put him!" [3] So Peter and the other disciple started for the tomb. [4] Both were running, but the other disciple outran Peter and reached the tomb first. [5] He bent over and looked in at the strips of linen lying there but did not go in. [6] Then Simon Peter, who was behind him, arrived and went into the tomb. He saw the strips of linen lying there, [7] as well as the burial cloth that had been around Jesus' head. The cloth was folded up by itself, separate from the linen. [8] Finally the other disciple, who had reached the tomb first, also went inside. He saw and believed. [9] (They still did not understand from Scripture that Jesus had to rise from the dead.) [10] Then the disciples went back to their homes,

¹¹ but Mary stood outside the tomb crying. As she wept, she bent over to look into the tomb ¹² and saw two angels in white, seated where Jesus' body had been, one at the head and the other at the foot. ¹³ They asked her, "Woman, why are you crying?"   "They have taken my Lord away," she said, "and I don't know where they have put him." ¹⁴ At this, she turned around and saw Jesus standing there, but she did not realize that it was Jesus. ¹⁵ "Woman," he said, "why are you crying? Who is it you are looking for?"   Thinking he was the gardener, she said, "Sir, if you have carried him away, tell me where you have put him, and I will get him."   ¹⁶ Jesus said to her, "Mary." She turned toward him and cried out in Aramaic, "Rabboni!" (which means Teacher). ¹⁷ Jesus said, "Do not hold on to me, for I have not yet returned to the Father. Go instead to my brothers and tell them, 'I am returning to my Father and your Father, to my God and your God.'"

¹⁸ Mary Magdalene went to the disciples with the news: "I have seen the Lord!" And she told them that he had said these things to her.   **John 20:1-18** (NIV)

> II. A New Revelation of God's Kingdom (John 20:11-18)
> A. Angels give comfort (11-13)
> B. Jesus stands in compassion (14-15)
> C. Jesus speaks in love (16)
> D. Jesus reveals His Sonship (17)
> E. Mary shares the miracle (18)

Psalm 91

¹ He who dwells in the shelter of the Most High will rest in the shadow of the Almighty. ² I will say of the LORD, "He is my refuge and my fortress, my God, in whom I trust." ³ Surely he will save you from the fowler's snare and from the deadly pestilence.
⁴ He will cover you with his feathers, and under his wings you will find refuge;
   his faithfulness will be your shield and rampart. ⁵ You will not fear the terror of night, nor the arrow that flies by day, ⁶ nor the pestilence that stalks in the darkness, nor the plague that destroys at midday.
⁷ A thousand may fall at your side, ten thousand at your right hand, but it will not come near you. ⁸ You will only observe with your eyes and see the punishment of the wicked. ⁹ If you make the Most High your dwelling-- even the LORD, who is my refuge—¹⁰ then no harm will befall you, no disaster will come near your tent.
¹¹ For he will command his angels concerning you to guard you in all your ways;
¹² they will lift you up in their hands, so that you will not strike your foot against a stone. ¹³ You will tread upon the lion and the cobra; you will trample the great lion and the serpent. ¹⁴ "Because he loves me," says the LORD, "I will rescue him;   I will protect him, for he acknowledges my name. ¹⁵ He will call upon me, and I will answer him;   I will be with him in trouble,   I will deliver him and honor him.
¹⁶ With long life will I satisfy him   and show him my salvation."   **Psalms 91:1-16** (NIV)

> III. Affirmation of Salvation Fulfilled (Psalm 91)
> A. God is our refuge (1-4)
> B. God is our strength (5-8)
> C. God is our deliverance (9-14)
> D. God is our hope for salvation (15-16)

Exploring the Scriptures

Mary Magdalene was the first to behold the empty tomb and the risen Christ (Mark 16). According to the gospel of Luke, at a time earlier in Mary's life, Jesus had cast out seven demons from Mary Magdalene:

> ^{1} And it came to pass afterward, that he went throughout every city and village, preaching and shewing the glad tidings of the kingdom of God: and the twelve *were* with him, ^{2} And certain women, which had been healed of evil spirits and infirmities, Mary called Magdalene, out of whom went seven devils,
> **Luke 8:1-2 (KJV)**

. Perhaps this deliverance explains her undying loyalty and courage; she was there in hope from the foot of the cross to the darkness of the early morning garden tomb. Her faith, hope and love are inspiring. She would be rewarded by experiencing the early dawn of the miracle that changed the world. Her initial confusion is understandable in that the stone was rolled away and the tomb was empty. Where were the Roman soldiers? Their life depended upon being on guard. She was convinced that a miracle had taken place and so she immediately ran to tell the disciples. Peter and John raced there quickly, and John indicates in his account here (John 20) that he arrived first. His caution and pensive position is evident in that he bent over to look inside. He only saw the strips of cloth used for wrapping the body. Peter, pushing John aside, boldly went inside the tomb. Peter saw that, in addition to the linen strips, the head cloth was there as well. If anyone did take Jesus' body they surely would not have been so careless to have left this shroud which could be used to keep people from identifying Jesus in transit. This cloth was nicely folded, according to the account. One may then wonder who folded it. If someone had taken Jesus in haste or hurry, why would they take such care? Who folded it then? Was Jesus alive? If so, was it Jesus or one of the angels they found out about later who folded it? In either case, it was God's plan that they would find the cloth there. This was no accident. Mary Magdalene and the disciples were meant to find the empty tomb, the linen and strips of wrapping and the head cloth inside. Jesus had triumphed over the grave. The evidence would soon give way to the revelation of the risen Lord. Wonder and anticipation was building.

Jesus came to them and appeared in fullness of life. He started reaching out to Mary as she was crying in confusion and concern in the garden. The other disciples believed Mary about the empty tomb, and while they had seen the evidence for themselves, they were still in shock. They took off to tell the others. While the disciples had left, Mary could not leave without a firm answer. Jesus first appeared to her in humility; Mary thought Him to be the gardener of the cemetery. One may imagine Jesus planting an olive branch, a mustard seed or pruning a bush. In all fairness to Mary, she was blurry-eyed with tears and her heart was beating with excitement. Jesus approached her, His familiar voice called out "Mary". "Rabboni, is it you?" Mary finally recognized Him and wanted to understand and be taught by Jesus what all this meant. Though Jesus tells her not to touch Him, (why not is a bit of a mystery that Jesus explains has something to do with his preparation as resurrected Lord), we can be sure of the truth He proclaims and the connection with God the Father that He affirms. (After all, who else in the history of mankind has so verifiably died, had their tomb guarded and then was risen three days later?) Jesus commands Mary to tell the other disciples while also revealing to her that He is first going up to commune with God the Father. As a matter of celebration and joy, Jesus has affirmed that God His Father was involved and sovereign through all these events. God has demonstrated His love through His Son's own faithfulness and act of redeeming love. A sweet face to face reunion of Father and Son is in order.

The implications of this are profound; the hope of the resurrection was in God's will and Kingdom design for our redemption and salvation. Later on, during that resurrection day, Jesus would come back to appear to His disciples. Apparently the timeframe of Heaven may involve a different dimension that allowed Jesus to go to the Father and then return very soon to our earthly realm in a new, transformed, resurrection body. Upon His return it is clear that Jesus had been bestowed with a distinctly new type of body. While previously Jesus had humbly exercised His authority and power, now He validates that He has been given all authority and power from God His Father. Jesus will lead and send His disciples into all the world in His name with the Gospel of God's Kingdom. When Jesus returned to the Father, it was not only as a matter of celebration but also as a means of coronation and commissioning. Can you imagine that joyful moment of triumph when Jesus entered the gates of Heaven and was embraced with joy by God the Father and the Heavenly Host? Jesus was then sent back to inspire and equip us to bring more into the Kingdom of God.

Following Christ's resurrection, the disciples and many others would discover that Jesus was alive. Jesus would appear to them in many situations and in plain view. He touched them, caught and cooked fish breakfasts, restored their faith, confronted their doubts, renewed their joy and reminded them of their calling and responsibility. Then Jesus left them a Great Commission to preach the Gospel to all the nations and to make disciples of all people on earth. He promised them that He would "be with them always until the end of the age". Inspired and moved, the disciples were indelibly changed. Jesus had revealed God the Father's truth, grace, peace and joy. Jesus gave them further encouragement and instruction, and more importantly, the fullness and empowerment of the Holy Spirit.

Bridging into Today

God honors those who believe in His transforming truth and love. God blesses all who genuinely, courageously, wholeheartedly seek His Kingdom and righteousness. This is not to say that His blessings are not also given mercifully to people who don't deserve to receive them. God is gracious and desires not that sinners perish, but that all may come to salvation. Such was the case for Mary Magdalene; she had a mixture of experiences that would not be a source of acceptance for many who watched her come close to Jesus. Her dedication to follow Jesus involved a deep sense of being forgiven, and of the hope of being a part of God's Kingdom. Mary trusted in the saving power of Jesus because she had been forgiven of her sins by the Lord's own authoritative words of grace and life. Even after several days of grieving in the upper room with the disciples and others who followed Jesus, she felt that the new life she had received was still aflame. While Jesus had been crucified and buried, she could not deny her remaining hope. Mary Magdalene must have believed that the story was not over, that God was yet to do something great. When one is aware of the leading of the Spirit to go and do something others believe is crazy or dangerous (going early morning to a guarded tomb); it reflects a faith that is born of God's truth and grace. For believers today, to love and serve the Risen King and Savior, Jesus Christ, takes the same essence of faith, hope and devotion.   God's transforming and unconditional love is given to all who believe and to all who have trusted the unseen, and yet very real, Spirit of God that leads them to an encounter with the Living Christ. The Spirit of God led Mary to the tomb and inspired her to believe the revelation of Christ. Not only had the soldiers fainted and left their posts, the tomb itself was empty. Though at first she thought someone had taken Jesus' body away, and while angels then told her that Jesus had risen, it was not until Jesus revealed Himself personally to her that she began to rejoice in sheer wonder. Her first inclination was to worship Jesus for she knew without a doubt that He was the Son of God, the Savior and Lord of mankind.

From Mary's testimony we note that there is something life-changing about a genuine faith encounter with the resurrected Lord. What is realized in the moment of belief?   Jesus has complete authority to save us from sin and death. He is the triumphant Son of God! Jesus is destined to reign on earth in His future coming as the King of Glory. For now, He reigns upon the hearts of all who believe and obey Him. He abides with all who long and hunger for His words and presence. Believers seek His work of righteousness and mercy so that they may prepare for His coming Kingdom. This is the perspective of living one's life of faith as a "prelude" by sharing the beautiful music of the Kingdom with a lost world. "Prepare Ye the way of the risen Lord...".

The Psalmist affirmed God's plan of salvation in Psalm 91. God is indeed our refuge, strength, deliverance and hope for salvation. Through the ages God has revealed Himself through words of promise and through a reliable continuum of intervention. Jesus came to fulfill not only the promise of God's salvation; He also came to fulfill the powerful work of God's redeeming love. The cross symbolizes something quite different now. The cross is the bridge where human sin meets God's grace. Death does not have to be the final destination. The grave is no longer our end because God's Word of Life has opened up Paradise. There is hope and life eternal for all who believe in Jesus Christ. The world may often not "get it", or think that Christians are "fooling themselves".   Yet what can be said regarding the multiple witnesses of the resurrection? Why would Roman guards faint were it not for the awesome appearance of some strong angels? Mary had good reason to wonder, and yet, her faith was rewarded as Jesus came to show her how deep our Father's love is for humanity. Jesus would go to the Heavenly Father before coming back to show Himself more fully to the disciples. The implications of Jesus' resurrection were just being considered. Eventually, upon further revelation, this turning point in history would become the start of a community that was centered on the Living Savior and King of Glory, the Son of the Living God, Jesus.

Questions for Class Discussion

1. What evidence exists for Jesus resurrection?

2. What are the character strengths of Mary? How does Jesus bless her?

3. What can we learn about the new relationship we have with God through Jesus conversation with Mary following His resurrection?

4. With Peter and John's excitement, what do we learn about them that helps us see that they were very much like us?

5. How are we like Mary or the other disciples?

Closing Idea

When believers share the story of the resurrection of Jesus, they can tell others that just as Jesus called Mary by name, the risen Christ is also calling them by name. What will our response be? When a person believes, their heart will be blessed through a flood of joy and peace. This is the gift of a new life given by God through faith in Jesus Christ. This is what it means to be "born again". Jesus is alive and revealing Himself constantly by the work of the Spirit of God, in creation, in Scripture and through His Body the Church. God the Father and the Host of Heaven call us to celebrate the decisive triumph of Jesus over sin and death. May we prepare for the coming glory of God in Jesus' return as King. Our lives take on a greater purpose in telling others and preparing the way for God's Kingdom through our actions of faith, hope and love.

On a personal note, I realize that because of the experience of healing that I received through an encounter with the risen Christ, I am more apt to emphasize the power of Jesus. This is a reality that moves my heart to rejoice and continue to express, often in writing, the wonders of God's grace. God provides opportunities to share the Gospel, from Sunday morning sermons to personal visits with people at hospitals, homes, cafés and chemotherapy clinics. What I desire most is to describe the healing love and bright glory of Jesus. His awesome power swept through me as I was available in prayer. Each time I share Jesus with others, I desire to see Him in splendid bright glory once again. Yet even as strong as this desire is, my greatest joy is to witness how Jesus will change the lives of others who will come to faith and grow as disciples. I feel compelled to tell people of the love of Jesus Christ. I pray that I may not let Him down through neglect, diversion, selfishness or complacency. The work of God's Holy Spirit keeps me in step with the needs of others, God helps to guide me in how His message or ministry through Christ may be applied. For this reason, I must pray and be still. Consistently, I must stop and listen deeply in order to understand and hear the heart of God for a person, group or situation. Jesus commissions all believers to use their gifts as a prelude to His Kingdom work. This work of the Kingdom involves a surrendered heart and a committed will. This is how we may live out the character and message of the Gospel.

Selected Reading

"The New Testament church stood in a peculiar mid position between what had been done and what was awaited, between the present age which was dying and the new age struggling to be born. It was confident that the victory over all the dark powers of the old aeon had been won if Christ, so much so that the Kingdom of God could be spoken of as a present thing. Yet is was all too painfully aware that the Kingdom remained an unconsummated thing of the future which had yet to come in its power. In tension between the two the New Testament church lived and waited. It was a tension between the victory won and the victory anything but won, between the Kingdom which is at hand and the Kingdom unseen and unrealized, between the power of God and the power of Caesar, between the church militant and suffering and the Church triumphant. To that tension, that dilemma, we must now return; for in it we, too, must stand – as the New Testament church."

Bill Bright. *"The Kingdom of God"* (244-245)

16

INVITATION TO GOD'S KINGDOM PARTY

(Matthew 28:18-20; Matthew 22:1-14, Psalm 93)

> **Key verse:**
> *Therefore go and make disciples of all nations, baptizing them in the name of the Father and of the Son and of the Holy Spirit, [20] and teaching them to obey everything I have commanded you. And surely I am with you always, to the very end of the age." -*
> Matthew 28:19-20 (NIV)

Purpose of study

God is preparing a big party! Why? What's the occasion? The occasion will be the coming of Jesus Christ again to earth to establish the manifest and completed reign of God. In the Old and New Testaments this event is compared to a "Wedding Feast" between God and His people. Symbolically, where once Israel was seen as the Bride of God, this is expanded through Christ to include all Gentiles who receive salvation from Him.

This chapter's study is focused upon five action points for the church to apply from Jesus' teaching in Matthew 28:18-20; 22:1-14 and in Psalm 93:

1. <u>Encourage</u> the Body of Christ to go out and make disciples
2. Affirm that God has a plan for His Kingdom to come about in its fullness upon the earth.

3. <u>Cast</u> a vision for the diversity of people God will accept in His Kingdom.
4. <u>Uphold</u> that entrance into God's Kingdom is received by faith and salvation in Jesus Christ.
5. <u>Represent</u> Jesus Christ in our actions, relationships and responsibilities.

These five action points require that we use the Spiritual gifts that God has given us to express God's truth and grace in words and actions of witness to the world. God is preparing a "New Heaven and New Earth" through the coming reign of His Son Jesus. The church is to spread the word about what people need to do to be ready, prepared, included and involved. Believers are called by Jesus to "SHINE". An acronym I use for SHINE is: The "Spirit Helps Inspire Needed Expression."[18] God will use the Spiritual gifts He has apportioned us through Christ with the empowerment of the Holy Spirit. In this way, God reveals His presence and promise. Jesus indeed calls us to shine and stand fast in faith as we extend the gospel message of His Kingdom. We join Jesus and Heaven in praying for the increased harvest of people being saved. Believers long for that day when the banquet table of the Kingdom will be spread before us as God's children shall all reunite in the wedding feast of the Bride (the Church) and the Lamb (Christ).

Prelude

In a day and age when the governments and corporations of man seem determined to work out all their problems through political meetings, debates, economic summits, monetary manipulation, feeble peace initiatives and sadly enough, military means; a time is coming when Jesus shall reign and establish true and lasting peace. The birth pains that precede the coming of God's Kingdom are evident all around us. Some of these birth pains are being experienced now; others will come sharply close to the Second Coming of Christ. Everything that believers do now in preparation for Christ's coming is essential in extending the invitation of salvation to the nations. While there will be wars and rumors of war, famines and earthquakes in various places, and challenging trials for those who believe in Jesus Christ; the faithful are not to be discouraged. For God has given us a promise that the Great Tribulation will

---

[18] <u>SHINE: A Celebration of Spiritual Gifts</u>. Scott Arnold and Brad Parrish. Shine Publications, Quincy, MI. Createspace. 2011

give way to the great occasion and celebration of Christ's return. Even for those who don't believe, they too shall be humbled prior to their own judgment. Paul wrote, *"Every knee shall bow and every tongue shall confess that Jesus Christ is Lord"* (Romans 14:11). Until this Day of the Lord comes we are to prepare ourselves and others. The Church's mission is to go out and invite people to God's "Wedding Party". The Church is to go and secure the commitment and deepening of faith in people. This is disciple-making, and it involves a shared, wholehearted, joyful journey on the part of God's people.

Recently I was part of a team that conducted a survey in which over thirty American Baptist Churches in Michigan identified and rated the top two ministry challenges they were facing. At the top of church leaders' concerns for ministry were:[19]

1. **<u>Missional Outreach and Evangelism</u>**: Ministry in the local context must become creative, compassionate and consistent in response to the needs of the community in order to communicate the gospel of Jesus Christ.

2.**<u>Discipleship and Spiritual formation</u>**: Discipleship in the commitment and growth of mature and faithful followers of Jesus Christ is increasingly difficult to achieve, especially for new members and upcoming generations.

This welcome response indicated interest in deepening and spreading the message of the Gospel of Jesus Christ. The priority of evangelism and discipleship are still deemed essential for the Church. The concern is, how can the Church adapt to the needs and demands of people in our changing times? Before we assume a prescriptive set of programs and previously ineffective actions, we must have a better understanding of our actual adaptive challenges. Only then can we become more creative, compassionate and consistent to adapt to change with the leading of God's Spirit. We need to describe and analyze the condition of the church and society in order to design and implement effective ministries. What will it take to better communicate the Gospel in a world that speaks so many languages? We are trying to function in a "global Babel" that involves so many cultures and worldviews. Furthermore, how can we better make disciples who are more than skin deep in their faith?

To follow up with further analysis, Adaptive Challenge Teams were formed to describe the underlying challenges that are at the heart of the

---

[19] Transformed by the Spirit Initiative. A Survey of Michigan American Baptist Churches to identify and rate "Adaptive Ministry Challenges". January 2012.

existing reality of the church. Each group looked at Scripture and prayed for God's mirror of truthful confession. Here is what they came up with:

MISSIONAL OUTREACH/EVANGELISM: Contemporary American culture has been inoculated against Christian faith by the church itself. At the same time, the church's understanding of itself and its mission is faulty and maybe broken - we do not seem to understand ourselves as people on mission. When it comes to bringing/sharing the good news of Jesus Christ, we currently face the dual challenge of the culture's low view of the church and the church's low view of its mission.

DISCIPLESHIP/SPIRITUAL FORMATION: Despite our best efforts and intentions, the status of discipleship in today's church is too often characterized by:

A. Self-centeredness: Faith that is evidenced by a predominant concern for our own needs and desires being met than that we seek to live by the will and purpose of God.

B. Superficiality: An emphasis upon outward and minimal observance of the Christian faith with little substantial and lasting spiritual transformation.

C. Disconnection: Life is increasingly fragmented as we are out of touch with the presence and power of God through His Word in Scripture, His Son Jesus Christ, and the presence and power of the Holy Spirit.

While we confess this is the reality of the church now, we place our hope in the transforming power of God to break down the barriers that would keep us from going deeper in our discipleship with Jesus Christ.[20]

At a time when there are so many demands upon time and energy, the Church has a challenging mission. Many churches also face an increasing gap between generations in the way people communicate, worship, relate to one another, make commitments and think about life. A Post-Modern worldview tends to pull people toward thinking that morality is relative, commitments are transient and faith is primarily personal. Jesus came with a message for all people that is timeless and true, personal and corporate, peaceful and yet powerful in bringing people together. When we trust and follow His leading into "all the world" we can be sure that we have the backing of the Holy Trinity (God the Father, Son and Holy Spirit). Since God created the community of man from His own Divine Community (the Trinity), the Bible likewise teaches that His redemptive plan is for all things to be reconciled into His perfect and coming Kingdom community. Those who have gone ahead of us into Heaven are praying for us.

---

[20] Transformed by the Spirit Initiative. Adaptive Challenge Teams - "Adaptive Challenge Statements", American Baptist Churches of Michigan. April 30th, 2012.

Scripture Passages

Matthew 28:18-20

[18] Then Jesus came to them and said, "All authority in heaven and on earth has been given to me. [19] Therefore go and make disciples of all nations, baptizing them in the name of the Father and of the Son and of the Holy Spirit, [20] and teaching them to obey everything I have commanded you. And surely I am with you always, to the very end of the age."

> I. The Kingdom Preparations Start Now! (Matt. 28:18-20)
> A. Jesus is the host with the most. (18)
> B. Jesus calls us to reach the nations (19)
>   1. Go and invite
>   2. Convince them to believe and come (Make disciples)
>   3. Help them commit and celebrate (Baptize)
>   4. Teach people obedience (20a)
> C. Jesus promises His presence and saving power (20b)

Matthew 22:1-14

[1] Jesus spoke to them again in parables, saying: [2] "The kingdom of heaven is like a king who prepared a wedding banquet for his son. [3] He sent his servants to those who had been invited to the banquet to tell them to come, but they refused to come. [4] "Then he sent some more servants and said, 'Tell those who have been invited that I have prepared my dinner: My oxen and fattened cattle have been butchered, and everything is ready. Come to the wedding banquet.' [5] "But they paid no attention and went off--one to his field, another to his business. [6] The rest seized his servants, mistreated them and killed them. [7] The king was enraged. He sent his army and destroyed those murderers and burned their city. [8] "Then he said to his servants, 'The wedding banquet is ready, but those I invited did not deserve to come. [9] Go to the street corners and invite to the banquet anyone you find.' [10] So the servants went out into the streets and gathered all the people they could find, both good and bad, and the wedding hall was filled with guests. [11] "But when the king came in to see the guests, he noticed a man there who was not wearing wedding clothes. [12] 'Friend,' he asked, 'how did you get in here without wedding clothes?' The man was speechless. [13] "Then the king told the attendants, 'Tie him hand and foot, and throw him outside, into the darkness, where there will be weeping and gnashing of teeth.' [14] "For many are invited, but few are chosen."

> II. The Kingdom Party Parable (Matt. 22:1-14)
> A. The wedding to come (1-2)
> B. Declined invitations (3)
> C. Poor excuses (4-5)
> D. Consequences for evil (6-7)
> E. Open invitation (8-10)
> F. Proper dress required (11-13)
> G. God's choice of grace (14)

Psalm 93

¹ The LORD reigns, he is robed in majesty; the LORD is robed in majesty and is armed with strength. The world is firmly established; it cannot be moved. ² Your throne was established long ago; you are from all eternity. ³ The seas have lifted up, O LORD, the seas have lifted up their voice; the seas have lifted up their pounding waves. ⁴ Mightier than the thunder of the great waters, mightier than the breakers of the sea-- the LORD on high is mighty. ⁵ Your statutes stand firm; holiness adorns your house for endless days, O LORD.

> III. Worship in God's Majestic Reign (Psalm 93)
> A. God's Eternal Reign (1-2)
> B. The response of creation (3-4)
> C. The Words of God endure (5a)
> D. The beauty of God's dwelling (5b)

Exploring the Scriptures

The key passage in this study is the "Great Commission" given by Jesus (Matthew 28:18-20). Following His resurrection, Jesus gave His disciples direct instructions about their mission. They were to go and make disciples. This seems simple and direct, yet it is actually quite complex and profound. Their own journey in following and believing in Jesus was filled with adventure, excitement and miracles.   But they also experienced anguish, anxiety and trouble. (One might think of J.R. Tolkien's "Fellowship of the Ring" as they overcame great obstacles and forces of evil in order to prepare the way for the return of the rightful king.)[21]

Through it all, the disciples of Jesus had developed a growing admiration for the one who loved them perfectly; their devotion grew in recognition that Jesus went to the cross to forgive and die for their sins. In resurrected glory, and with Divine authority, Jesus spoke purpose into their lives with a sense of urgency. They were to "GO!" The imperative of Christ led to direct involvement in God's Kingdom work. There is nothing indicated that any disciple could "save" others, for indeed salvation is a gift received through faith in Jesus Christ. What is implicit, however, is that they were to be intentional and courageous in their commission. In sharing their faith and

---

[21] Tolkien, J.R. "The Lord of the Rings", "The Two Towers", "The Return of the King". These classic works of fiction present a story of symbolic parallel to the biblical story of God's redemption and the coming of God's Kingdom in Christ.

believing that God would use their witness, God used their Spiritual gifts to reach people with the "Good News" of the risen and triumphant Savior King. Discipleship involves helping people decide to follow Jesus, but this decision is incomplete unless it is followed by a process of spiritual growth that is Biblical, relational, practical, knowledgeable, theological and transformative for the character of a believer.

True conversion and repentance are a work in progress. The re-making of people into disciples of Christ takes time, patience, faith and love. Jesus painted a beautiful big vision that gave them hope beyond their limitations and immediate lifetimes. The disciples were infused with faith to give their best trusting that God would bless their efforts and continue to work through the people that they would reach. In Christ, they had joy and a new life. The unfolding blossom of hope helped them to believe in the emergent eternal Kingdom of God. God's revelation in Jesus Christ helped them to serve in order to reap the first fruits of God's Kingdom. The New Jerusalem was represented and revealed in the witness of the disciples as they shared the Gospel and witnessed to the living Lord and Savior Jesus Christ. The message of the Old Testament was the Scripture of the Early Church that supported Jesus' Gospel, affirming from Genesis to the Prophets that God's Kingdom is supreme and Christ's rule is destined to replace all human kingdoms and any principality or power. Therefore, believers can handle persecution because they know that the Lord their God shall hold all temporal rulers into account and eventual judgment.

The parable of the wedding feast from Jesus expresses the historic truth of God's appeal to Israel and the rest of humanity for inclusion and participation in God's Kingdom Covenant. The basis for inclusion is a faith response to the invitation of Christ. The received blessing of God's saving grace comes through faith and not by human effort or an imitation of righteousness. Jesus tells a story about God's Kingdom banquet, prior to His death and resurrection, as a way to help them relate to God's invitation of love for humanity. Jesus is the "Groom", and the people who respond are a collective "Bride". Together we may look forward to the consummation of this incredible union. The occasion of celebration shall be the inauguration of the Kingdom of God that shall be manifested one glorious day upon the earth. The Covenant that God pursues with humanity is not one based upon our goodness (symbolized by the garment worn by the man thrown out), but by the garments of salvation received through a response of commitment and faith (symbolized by the wedding garments worn by those who responded in faith). The man who thought he could sneak in without being re-clothed in the righteousness of God was mistaken, and Jesus may have had the unrepentant Pharisees in mind. The guest list had started with the people of Israel, but went on to include people from around the world. The description of people who respond, who are gathered, includes an odd lot. People are there who have often been outcasts, they are loved by God but rejected by the world. The qualification of inclusion is not their works or outer appearance, but their inner faith response to God's invitation.

All who respond, the good, bad, lame, ill, rich, poor, educated, uneducated, famous, not famous, the "have's" and the "have not's", they are all precious to God because they genuinely believed and humbled themselves in worship and faith. God will transform all who truly believe in His Son Jesus. Believers are remade to become inwardly beautiful through the power of God's love. While it is true that those in God's Kingdom will be rewarded according to their faithfulness of service, what is more important is that God's grace will be sufficient to complete the initial work of salvation. Each soul in Christ shall be transformed and resurrected in a new body. Through faith and Christ's redemption, believers shall partake in God's Kingdom banquet and coming reign. Worship is designed by God to prepare people for, and anticipate, this great consummation and reunion in God's Kingdom. Then, we shall know God fully even as we are fully known (I Corinthians 13). There shall be a complete and sweet communion upon the fulfillment of God's benevolent covenant with us through Jesus Christ.

Psalm 93 was a Psalm of Worship that came out of the writer's experience on a vessel that sailed the seas. His observation was that God rules over all. The Psalmist noted that the power of the sea is a reminder of the splendor and majesty of God's creation. God reigns over all of creation, and over all peoples. God is robed in majesty and splendor, and the creation itself even gives us a witness to this fact. God is mightier than all we see, and we may trust that He is enthroned above in Heaven. God's word of instruction and truth given by the words of His law, the prophets, and Jesus Christ shall endure forever. God shall fulfill His plans and purposes as surely as His Kingdom is secure and His majesty is eternal. Because of this, we are drawn by the Holy

Spirit to worship God and seek Him daily. We are called to trust in God's awesome power and Christ's saving love.

Bridging into Today

Called to be ambassadors, disciples of Jesus Christ are to bring hope to this troubled world in the message and ministry of reconciliation. This is the tangible and real witness of new life from Christ our King. We do this to glorify God our Heavenly Father who sent His beloved Son. We go out into the entire world trusting that Jesus is alive; He fills and equips believers with the Holy Spirit. Being guided and empowered God, believers then share the message of the Gospel, confident in its potential for changing lives. Until this Great Commission is fulfilled, and the Gospel has gone into all parts and to all peoples of the world (Mark 16:15), believers are to remain diligent and faithful in proclaiming the message of the cross. This Gospel announces the forgiveness of sins and invites people to new life born of God's grace received. This Gospel announces the presence of God's Kingdom and the opportunity to become active citizens through Christ's Lordship. Faith and Spiritual rebirth shall lead to healing, holiness and good works.

Receiving and sharing the message of God's Kingdom involves celebrating the commitment of those regenerated in Christ. The way to do this, according to Jesus, is through believer's baptism. Through baptism, one proclaims Jesus' death and resurrection. Their own personal salvation is accomplished through faith in Christ's sacrifice and victory. Baptism proclaims that we die to sin and are raised to new life in Jesus Christ. Can there be a better symbol of our conversion in Jesus Christ? Baptism affirms the transformative work of God in Christ through which we are born again to be redeemed as the glorious children of God.

When it comes to the Kingdom of God, there will be all sorts of people and types of personalities who will gather from every nation. There will be those who are good natured who believe and those who are ornery who come to faith. The Kingdom of God includes both the wise and the simple. The issue of acceptance or inclusion is not based on social status, knowledge, education, peer acceptance, popularity, culture, or of being educated and trained. The issue for being welcomed into God's Kingdom is also not a matter of nationality, race, lineage or religious denomination. The issue for salvation and inclusion into God's Kingdom is one of having faith in Jesus Christ, who alone makes us right (reconciled) with God. We who are invited and included by grace are to go and bring more in to the banquet hall via the same gift of grace that we received through faith. Those who respond in faith to Jesus Christ are re-clothed in the garments of salvation. The old has gone, and the new has come. Anything else, in terms of spiritual clothing (false religiosity or self-righteousness), may look good to us but are visible to God's righteous scrutiny as being like "filthy rags" (Isaiah 64:6; Philippians 3:7-9). In Jesus Christ, God has set forth a means for our salvation and redemption. In Christ, we are re-clothed in the garments of salvation that He alone can fit us with.

VISION: Lifted up to be cleansed and re-clothed

In 1998 I had a dream one night about the rapture of God's elect from the earth. I was driving along an expressway and had begun to get off at a cloverleaf interchange when there was a loud trumpet sound and brightness in the sky. I and others stopped their vehicles and stepped out to look up into the heavens. There were angels descending, coming to earth. In that moment everything else faded from importance and the shackles of concern began to lighten. As if I had been freed from a weight that held me to earth, I now stepped on air. There were also many others all around me who also were stepping up into the sky to where angels were escorting us into the clouds. In a last glimpse back to earth I saw green trees, building roofs, the highway and cars and people still below who had stopped to look. Putting my concerns behind me, I stepped up with the assistance of the angels who carried us to towers that were amidst the clouds. The tower that they brought me to was plain and simple, with a doorway. One by one each person went into the doorway. As my turn came I was escorted into a small room that was dark and warm. The door shut behind me and then I felt a cleansing power sweep over me, taking away sadness, grief and pain and filling my soul while remaking me in some way physically. Then a doorway opened from within the warm darkness and a beautiful light streamed in. I walked through into the glorious light. While I could see people all around me dressed in beautiful colors, I looked down to see that I too was dressed in clothing that was unique and representative of my personality. Filled with joy and wonder, I then woke up.

Perhaps this will be what it shall be like when Jesus gathers His people prior to the time of great tribulation. In any event, the vision He gives us is of hope and salvation, cleansing and transformation.

Beyond the hope of the reception of God's elect (in a rapture), in Jesus Christ our Savior and King there is a promised future time of His second coming and reign on earth. This is the culmination of God's process of judgment and salvation. When that day comes will you be among the redeemed who gather for the greatest wedding banquet of all time? Many are invited, but comparatively few will choose to reprioritize their lives, repent, be saved and be prepared to come. To accept this invitation a decision and commitment is required that leads to a process of preparation. To be ready we must allow Jesus to cleanse us within and prepare us with the robe of His righteousness. Likewise, we are to go and share this salvation and invitation with others. Like the Psalmist who looked forward to beholding God in His majesty, glory and power, so too believers look forward to the reign of God transforming this world. Jesus shall reign in majesty and glory. He invites us to come and be made new because this is how we shall be included in God's Kingdom.

Until then, we are given a window of time to believe and invite others to come to Jesus and be saved. God calls us to see time as being in His hands and resources as being within His providence. God calls us to see all of life as being sacred. Each life is to be valued for the redeeming work of Christ who loved us and gave His life for the salvation of humanity and God's creation.

Questions for Class Discussion

1. Who is the Great Commission for?

2. Describe what is involved in making disciples?

3. In what ways has the Lord worked through you to invite others into His Kingdom?

4. How has Jesus changed you so that His salvation is apparent from the outside?

5. How does worshipping God through observing His creation prepare you for direct worship before His Kingdom Throne?

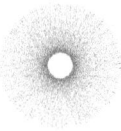

Closing Idea

Imagine who will be seated at the great wedding banquet of Heaven. You will be there, not because you were a good person, but because you accepted the gift of God's saving grace through Jesus Christ. Who will be there as a result of your faithful witness to Jesus Christ? Think about how you can make the joy of the Lord complete by bringing people into the family of God by sharing your faith in Jesus Christ. Think about how important it is to daily show others your dedication and love for Jesus and them. When the church shows its love for Jesus it is like a bride telling everyone how much they love and honor their fiancé. People are attracted to come to weddings that are a reflection of love, truth and grace. So too, the church that is genuinely and sacrificially telling the world about its love for Jesus is compelling and contagious in its devotion. Others want to also come and experience the love, truth and grace of the Savior King.

Recently, a football player in the National Football league was criticized for their open devotion to Jesus Christ. Tim Tebow was being told to "tone down" his public display of prayer and his words of faith to honor Jesus Christ

His Lord. At a press conference the quarterback replied: "People would not criticize someone for expressing their love for their spouse. Jesus is the primary love of my life. I cannot stop expressing my faith and devotion to Him." What makes the quarterback's faith most persuasive is his ongoing work to reach children who are crippled or have been orphans. Even non-believers can see that there is something different, genuine and compelling about this man's faith. Nonetheless, when Tim Tebow was traded by the Denver Broncos to the New York Jets, people were quick to be critical. At a Yankee baseball game in New York the fans booed him. Such a response indicated a level of distain the world has with Christians who have uncompromising faith to follow Jesus Christ.

Selected Reading

"Is the Kingdom of heaven to be entered merely by taking the name of Jesus upon one's lips and making a verbal confession? Is the blessing of life to be received by believing in the resurrection and deity of Christ? Can a creed save me? Can the utterance of three words: "Jesus is Lord," bestow life upon me? What does it mean to confess Jesus as Lord? – to believe in the Lord Jesus? The answer may be found in the demand of the Kingdom of God. The Kingdom makes one fundamental demand: the demand for decision. In Christ, the Kingdom now confronts us. The life of The Age to Come now stands before us. The One who shall tomorrow be the Judge of all men has already come into history. He faces us with one demand: decision. Bultmann is right when he says that Jesus proclaimed the nearness of God as The Demander. Jesus' message was, "Repent, for the Kingdom of Heaven is at hand." The basic meaning of "repentance" is to turn around, to reverse direction of action, to turn and to embrace in decision the Kingdom of God."

George Eldon Ladd. "*The Gospel of the Kingdom*" (96)

17

THE RETURN OF THE KING

(Revelation 1:1-8; 22:7 and Psalm 96)

> **Key verse:**
> 7 *"Behold, I am coming soon! Blessed is he who keeps the words of the prophecy in this book."* - Revelation 22:7 (NIV)

Purpose of study

Jesus Christ is coming back to reign on earth as the Messiah King, the Son of God. This concluding chapter reaffirms this Scriptural truth and promise. The prospect of Christ's return provides a message of hope for believers while also providing a warning for all who are alienated from God and needing reconciliation. The warning here is to prepare for God's judgment because there shall be personal accountability before our Creator/Redeemer. God offers reconciliation and renewal through repentance which leads to the reception of His gift of grace and spiritual rebirth. In the fullness of time, the Lord of Life shall make "all things like new". For this to happen, old things (our old nature and the corrupt ways of mankind that affect all of creation) shall come to an end. Our acceptance into, or rejection of, the coming full Kingdom reign of God is contingent upon faith in Jesus Christ.

Prelude

There have been many books written and sermons preached about the end times. While there are many interpretations of the Scriptures, there is common agreement among Christians that Jesus will return in power and glory. What has not been agreed upon is when this will happen and in what sequence the Kingdom of God shall be manifest. There is agreement (to Jesus' own teaching) that in some significant way the Kingdom of God is a reality within people who believe and obey the Lord and Savior of life. There is also agreement that the Church, in some significant way, represents the Kingdom of God on earth. These beliefs affirm that Jesus did establish the Church and holds the Church accountable for its collective witness and service to His Kingdom. There is also agreement that a time of tribulation and trial is coming when God shall consummate both salvation and judgment for humanity.

There are, however, different understandings about the Great Tribulation, the rapture, the millennial (thousand year) reign of Jesus and a final battle between Christ and the forces of evil. Still, if one believes in Jesus, even with various interpretations of Scripture and understandings of the working of God's Kingdom, there is a shared hope in Jesus' promise: "Behold I am coming soon!" His coming may seem long-delayed in human standards. However, in God's time and standard of grace, love, mercy and patience, this delay is necessary and purposeful. Jesus will come in power and glory; this should lead the faith-filled to be constantly ready and joyfully serving now. Someday it will be too late for people to change their minds about the nature and purpose of Jesus and the validity of the Gospel. Therefore, urgency in sharing the Gospel and inviting people to new life in Christ is always in season.

In studying the revelation given to John the beloved disciple, as he was exiled on the island of Patmos, may we also pray to have hearts that are open to receive the urgent message of the Gospel. God calls us to repent of our sins and believe in Jesus. This revelation not only encouraged John, it was the ordained message of hope that reinforced the Old Testament prophets and teachings of Jesus with an inspired vision of God's Kingdom to come. God has given more than sufficient evidence for the coming of His Son Jesus throughout the Old and New Testaments. Furthermore, Jesus lived and taught with a perspective that integrated the past, present and future work of God's judgment and salvation. Jesus was the fulfillment of the law and the prophets in that He came to give His life as the perfect atoning sacrifice for the whole extent of human sin. Jesus was the incarnate and very present reality of God in our midst. People beheld Him and wondered who He was, and Jesus made it plain that He was the Son of God, that as we know Him we also come to know the Father God who sent Him in love. Jesus will come again in the fullness of God's timing to complete the work of salvation and redemption that He began. The Kingdom of God will be consummated in glorious fulfillment because of Christ's humility. God's grace is fulfilled in Christ's sacrifice. God's judgment is fulfilled in Christ's holiness. God the Father's redemption is fulfilled through Christ's power to "make all things new."

Revelation 21:5 (NIV)
^{5} He who was seated on the throne said, "I am making everything new!" Then he said, "Write this down, for these words are trustworthy and true."

God's Holy Spirit reaches out to convince our hearts and minds to believe in God's Son Jesus Christ. Note in Rev. 21:5 that it is the Triumphant Christ who is given authority to sit and speak upon the Throne of God's Kingdom. The process of "making everything new" has begun within those of faith, and it shall extend to all of creation. The importance of writing down the words of Jesus is clear; His message of hope and salvation is not to be forgotten, dismissed or distorted. Faithfulness and diligence to God's Word is the responsibility and trust of the Church. Likewise, the Church is called to be faithful in its witness to the world while moving in its pilgrimage to God's promised New Jerusalem. This is more than metaphorical; the Revelation gives way to us actually participating in God's Story of redeeming His creation. Those who follow Jesus shall fulfill the will of God and represent His Kingdom until He comes again in power and glory.

Just before Jesus tells John about the transformation of all things, there is a passage here in Revelation that gives us a vision of the New Jerusalem to come. God has prepared a city that is designed for our life together. One may even consider that this Holy City is currently existent, above us, being prepared and dressed up for the consummation/wedding day for Christ and the Church.

Revelation 21:1-4 (NIV)
^{1} Then I saw a new heaven and a new earth, for the first heaven and the first

earth had passed away, and there was no longer any sea. ² I saw the Holy City, the new Jerusalem, coming down out of heaven from God, prepared as a bride beautifully dressed for her husband. ³ And I heard a loud voice from the throne saying, "Now the dwelling of God is with men, and he will live with them. They will be his people, and God himself will be with them and be their God. ⁴ He will wipe every tear from their eyes. There will be no more death or mourning or crying or pain, for the old order of things has passed away."

Jesus had an awareness of the City of God and its proximity. He spoke to His disciples with specific knowledge of Heaven's personalized architecture and of His Father's own big house. Jesus explained that He would go ahead to Heaven before His disciples to prepare this awesome place for them. The way to the place would be through Jesus Himself. Quite simply, only the Savior King comes back for our salvation. The resurrection is the first sign and revelation of Christ's victory for us and of His coming return for our salvation. This return of Christ is a personal promise for the soul when a believer's body dies (Jesus promises to come and take us to be with Him). Also, prior to the end of this age, Christ will appear in the clouds, and believers shall be rescued from the Great Tribulation. The Rapture is a "taking up" of the elect in Christ prior to, in the midst of, or after the Great Tribulation (I personally favor "pre" or "mid" tribulation perspectives). Whatever we may think or interpret from Scripture, God is the one to decide how and when. The promise of Jesus is that He will be the one bringing us into the Kingdom of God and the New Jerusalem that He is preparing.

John 14:2-4 (NIV)
² In my Father's house are many rooms; if it were not so, I would have told you. I am going there to prepare a place for you. ³ And if I go and prepare a place for you, I will come back and take you to be with me that you also may be where I am. ⁴ You know the way to the place where I am going."

Jesus assured His disciples: *"I am the way, the truth and the life. No one comes to the Father, except through Me"* (John 14:6). This is not only a message of future hope, but also a present tense clarification of daily discipleship. To live as a citizen of the coming New Jerusalem, the City of God, one must begin to repent and follow Jesus in this life. There is no other way than that of Christ Jesus that shall lead people to God the Father of life and to the Kingdom of Heaven.

Scripture Passages:

Revelation 1:1-8

¹ The revelation of Jesus Christ, which God gave him to show his servants what must soon take place. He made it known by sending his angel to his servant John, ² who testifies to everything he saw--that is, the word of God and the testimony of Jesus Christ. ³ Blessed is the one who reads the words of this prophecy, and blessed are those who hear it and take to heart what is written in it, because the time is near.

⁴ John, To the seven churches in the province of Asia:

Grace and peace to you from him who is, and who was, and who is to come, and from the seven spirits before his throne, ⁵ and from Jesus Christ, who is the faithful witness, the firstborn from the dead, and the ruler of the kings of the earth.

To him who loves us and has freed us from our sins by his blood, ⁶ and has made us to be a kingdom and priests to serve his God and Father--to him be glory and power for ever and ever! Amen.

⁷ Look, he is coming with the clouds, and every eye will see him, even those who pierced him; and all the peoples of the earth will mourn because of him. So shall it be! Amen. ⁸ "I am the Alpha and the Omega," says the Lord God, "who is, and who was, and who is to come, the Almighty."

Revelation 22:7

⁷ "Behold, I am coming soon! Blessed is he who keeps the words of the prophecy in this book"

I. Jesus Christ Reveals Good News (Revelation 1:1-3)
  A. Hope for all servants of the Gospel (1a)
  B. A revelation to John the disciple (1b-2)
    1. An angel escort
    2. God's Word from God's Throne
    3. The testimony of God's Son
  C. A revelation to know (3)
    1. Read it as prophecy (knowledge)
    2. Read it to be blessed (inspiration)
    3. Read it for preparation (urgency)

II. John Delivers the Good News (Revelation 1:4-8)
  A. Blessing the churches (4)
  B. Blessing the Lord Jesus Christ (5-6)
  C. Blessing believers with hope (7-8)
    1. Jesus is coming in great glory
    2. For all to see and be humbled
    3. To hear His Name proclaimed
      a. Alpha and Omega (Greek)
      b. Aleph and Tav (Hebrew)
      c. The Almighty

III. Jesus Declares His Eventual Return (Revelation 22:7)
  A. Expectation of joy (7a)
  B. Call to faithfulness and hope (7b)
    1. Blessing in believing God's Word
    2. Blessing in following God's Word

Psalm 96

¹ Sing to the LORD a new song; sing to the LORD, all the earth. ² Sing to the LORD, praise his name; proclaim his salvation day after day. ³ Declare his glory among the nations, his marvelous deeds among all peoples.
⁴ For great is the LORD and most worthy of praise; he is to be feared above all gods. ⁵ For all the gods of the nations are idols, but the LORD made the heavens. ⁶ Splendor and majesty are before him; strength and glory are in his sanctuary. ⁷ Ascribe to the LORD, O families of nations, ascribe to the LORD glory and strength. ⁸ Ascribe to the LORD the glory due his name; bring an offering and come into his courts.
⁹ Worship the LORD in the splendor of his holiness; tremble before him, all the earth.
¹⁰ Say among the nations, "The LORD reigns." The world is firmly established, it cannot be moved; he will judge the peoples with equity.
¹¹ Let the heavens rejoice, let the earth be glad; let the sea resound, and all that is in it; ¹² let the fields be jubilant, and everything in them.
   Then all the trees of the forest will sing for joy; ¹³ they will sing before the LORD, for he comes, he comes to judge the earth.
   He will judge the world in righteousness   and the peoples in his truth.

> IV. Rejoice for the King is Coming (Psalm 96)
> A. Sing a new song (1-3)
> B. Splendor in God's presence (4-6)
> C. Giving glory to God (7-9)
> D. Jesus reigns on the earth (10-13)

Exploring the Scriptures

John was a faithful disciple of Jesus, and for this he was entrusted with a revelation that exposed a spiritual and symbolic map of the future plans of God for salvation and judgment. God's promise was for the eventual coming and consummation of His Kingdom through Christ Jesus His Son. Those who thought they could hinder the spread of the Gospel by placing this ardent disciple on a deserted island were wrong. In fact, they placed John exactly where God could show him this revelation. It took an angel, likely Gabriel, to guide him into this experience of drawing near to God, and of seeing Christ revealed within the vision of future events that unfolded before his eyes. Though John recorded what he saw through a combination of descriptive narrative that had symbolic reference, there is ample evidence within his writing that an intense encounter had taken place with Christ, God the Father, and with angels. The only other possible explanation would be to say that John was out of his mind or had suffered hallucinations. What John sees is extraordinary in the fact that it all fulfills the teachings and promises of Jesus as given by the Old Testament prophets. This is not simply a revelation for the Elect, Christians and Jews alone. This revelation is for all people on earth, given to John to pass on regarding the proclamation of salvation and judgment.

Though there are many people who would try to interpret Revelation to fit their own projections or timelines, it is essential that we do not presume to blaze the trail. This leadership is reserved for Jesus who is the "pioneer" and "perfecter" of our faith (Hebrews 12:2).

[1] Therefore, since we are surrounded by such a great cloud of witnesses, let us throw off everything that hinders and the sin that so easily entangles, and let us run with perseverance the race marked out for us. [2] Let us fix our eyes on Jesus, the author and perfecter of our faith, who for the joy set before him endured the cross, scorning its shame, and sat down at the right hand of the throne of God.
Hebrews 12:1-2 (NIV)

The key to understanding and appreciating the book of Revelations is that of focus and devotion. Jesus is to be our Lord and we are to trust Him as our Savior. He will mark out a course for us to race. Along the way we battle sin and are called to overcome temptation. The wiles of the devil can easily entangle or hinder people if not dealt with through prayer and perseverance. The spiritual battles highlight the need for disciplined focus and a greater depth of faith. Salvation is not by our will power alone, or by any intellect. Salvation comes from believing and following Jesus, even to the point of following Him to whatever crosses He will help us endure. We can find solace in Christ's peace and strength in that we are not alone. The writer of Hebrews takes joy in knowing that we are also surrounded by the Host encouraging us from Heaven.

John sets the tone of invitation within Revelation by greeting the Church in Revelation 1:1-3, making it clear that they will be blessed if they listen and heed Christ and His message. The person who reads the letter is blessed to believe in Christ and share the hope that is given. Those hearing it will be blessed if upon receiving this news shall take it to heart. One might imagine how circuit readers in the early church were sent to bring and read this revelation to the churches that were listed. These churches represented a diversity of cultures with believers having various experiences of faith. Some churches were persecuted while others were able to function in relative peace. In either case, the churches were being called by the Lord Jesus to grow into deeper devotion, dedicated service and heightened trust in the grace and truth of God.

What motivating factor would help them to move forward in faith and obedience? The amazing revelation that John was given not only contained a vision of Jesus Christ that would enliven people's worship of God, this vision served to reinforce and reveal the good news of God's forgiveness and redeeming love in Christ's work on the cross. The fulfillment of what Christ did shall extend into the coming manifestation of salvation and redemption in God's Kingdom on earth. Jesus reaffirms His return and the need for people to be ready several times in the book of Revelation. The reference to Daniel's vision of looking to the clouds will be fulfilled by Jesus when He returns to reign on earth.

> ^{13} "In my vision at night I looked, and there before me was one like a son of man, coming with the clouds of heaven. He approached the Ancient of Days and was led into his presence. ^{14} He was given authority, glory and sovereign power; all peoples, nations and men of every language worshiped him. His dominion is an everlasting dominion that will not pass away, and his kingdom is one that will never be destroyed. **Daniel 7:13-14 (NIV)**

Every person who surrenders in faith to serve Christ is consecrated by our Lord to become a "priest" of God. Each believer is therefore called to represent Jesus and the Kingdom of God to the world, to stand in a role of mediation and communication. Graciously and personally, God gave us the Word, His Son, who was made "flesh" (human), and this Word (Jesus the Christ) will return again in Divine power and glory. Until then, believers are equipped and empowered through the Holy Spirit to follow the counsel of our Savior and fulfill the commission of His Kingdom. Jesus is the beginning and completion of God's work for man's reconciliation and creation's redemption. In Revelation 1:8, John is faithful to transmit the very words that Jesus spoke to him for us to hear. Jesus spoke to John upon the throne of Heaven: ***"I am the Alpha and the Omega," says the Lord God, "who is, and who was, and who is to come, the Almighty."*** Such a message cannot be lightly treated. People may speculate as to whether John was in his right mind or that he was delusional. His responsibility was to relay God's message and raise an essential question: Who will trust in Jesus as God's Son and believe to receive salvation?

Our response is vitally important for salvation and to live as God intends. We are called to trust and prepare for Christ's returning reign as King eternal.

Psalm 96 functions as a song of preparation and celebration for the Kingdom of God. There is a new song in the hearts of believers during this time of prelude to the Kingdom of God's coming. Among the nations God has placed His servants to give witness to His majesty and to declare His glory. The song takes a significant shift when the focus is placed upon coming into the courts of God's temple. Worship at this point is not simply an activity but a life changing experience in the midst of God's presence. God will someday reveal His full splendor, His Holiness, to all the earth and its peoples. God shall reveal His glory through Christ's reign and judgment upon the earth. Heaven and earth, indeed all of creation, shall be still at the coming of Christ to judge the earth in righteousness. All will tremble before Christ, and the Lord will faithfully bring salvation to all who rejoice in God's Son and believe.

The consequence for those who shall not believe in Jesus and the Gospel of the Kingdom of God will be severe. Going back again to Revelation 21, we note that the judgment at the coming of the Kingdom of God is a story that reflects people's various positive or broken relationships with God. If people overcame sin and death with faith in Jesus Christ the outcome is inheritance into God's eternal Kingdom. If people chose to deny Jesus as the way, truth and life so as to believe the lies of Satan through cowardice, disbelief, rebellion and willful actions of sin, the consequence is the "second death" of the soul. Without faith one will not be included in God's Kingdom. The issue of finality for the soul occurs through judgment, destruction and being cut off from the source of life.

> [7] He who overcomes will inherit all this, and I will be his God and he will be my son. [8] But the cowardly, the unbelieving, the vile, the murderers, the sexually immoral, those who practice magic arts, the idolaters and all liars-- their place will be in the fiery lake of burning sulfur. This is the second death." **Revelation 21:7-8 (NIV)**

Bridging into Today

When God impresses the importance of a message, we better take heed. The Gospel of Jesus Christ brought the hope of salvation, and a deep respect for the judgment of God, to John and the churches. In Revelation, John was given a symbolically veiled vision of God's Kingdom that is coming in the midst of the story of God's redemption in Human history. This bright and overwhelming vision is compelling and awe inspiring; God is giving birth to His Kingdom. Christ and His Church shall prevail through sacrifice and suffering; believers trust that God is bringing about a Kingdom of eternal proportions.

The importance of preparation and readiness must not be minimized. Believers are called to herald the gospel of salvation through prayerful and faithful humility and service. People are brought into the Kingdom of God through decisions of faith in Jesus Christ and with transformation from God's Holy Spirit. The time is coming when the trumpets of Heaven shall herald the return of Christ Jesus our King to reign upon this earth. God only knows when His Son must return. None of this is a makeshift plan, for it has been set into motion and partially revealed to us through John the beloved disciple. God is patiently, faithfully, deliberately and creatively working out this master plan. His Son is at the heart and center of this Kingdom. When Christ Jesus returns it will be with power and glory. All people will be humbled and filled with awe at Jesus Christ's glorified state. God shall establish His Kingdom on earth through His Son in complete and utter fullness and holiness.

For now, we are on a journey. At times believers feel the weight of the knowledge of this Kingdom to come while struggling with this fallen world. Jesus told us to take heart; we are to trust that He shall completely overcome the world of sin and evil by establishing the fullness of God's Kingdom. While we will at times be overwhelmed by the problems that beset us through humanity's pollution and corruption, there is hope in Christ who promises to make "all things new". The Holy Spirit is given to all who believe so as to counsel and guide us into God's truth and grace. We have not been left as orphans; we can discover how Christ works to give our hearts strength and courage. Come Lord Jesus, come.

Questions for Class Discussion

1. What does it take to be ready for Christ's return?

2. How ready are you for Christ's return?

3. How ready are your friends and family for Christ's return?

4. What role does worship, like that in Psalm 96, have in readiness for Christ's return?

Closing Idea/Story

In putting the finishing touches to this last chapter on my laptop computer, God touched my soul with a moment of encouragement. The final triumphant song from Howard Shore's "Return of the King" played through my home desktop computer's music player which was on random "shuffle". With over 37 days of music to select from (over 10,000 songs), the timing could not have been more providential. Immediately, I felt God's peace and joy rush through my heart. I lifted my hands in praise as I thanked God for the hope that is ours in Christ. He shall return.

In the meantime, we will have challenges to overcome, and adventures that lead to that moment of His triumphant return. Be strong of heart to live boldly for the sake of Christ. His Kingdom is not far away, it is close and near. In fact, if you trust Christ Jesus and follow Him, you can be sure that "The Kingdom of God is within you".

Selected Reading

"Now when every evil authority and rule has been abolished from among us and no passion dominates our nature any longer, it follows inevitably that with no other master over us everything will be subjected to the power which is over all. Subjection to God is total separation from evil. When we are all free of evil in imitation of the first-fruits, then the whole mass of our nature will be comingled with the first-fruits and we shall become completely one body which accepts the Lordship of the good and of that alone. So the whole body of our human nature will be comingled with the Divine and uncompounded nature; and therein will be achieved in us what is called the subjection of the Son – for the subjection which is established in His body is being rightly ascribed to Him who makes the grace of subjection effective in us."

Gregory of Nyssa. *"Sermon on I Corinthians 15:28,32-44"*

Three Key Principles of "Prelude"; Living as Citizens of God's Kingdom:

1. **Receive salvation** and citizenship in God's Kingdom by faith in the authority and sacrificial love of Jesus Christ. As the Servant King He forgave and ransomed us on the cross, and rose three days later victorious over sin and death.

2. **Become an ambassador (sign)** of God's Kingdom as you follow, grow, and serve the Lord Jesus Christ as disciples.

3. **Give glory to God** the Creator/Father in **service** His Kingdom as ambassadors of reconciliation and agents of righteousness through faith and obedience to Jesus Christ.

ABOUT THE AUTHOR

Scott gave his life to Jesus Christ in 1974 when he was sixteen years old on an ordinary Sunday at his home church when he responded to God's calling and received the peace and joy of God's gift of grace through the Holy Spirit. Scott chose to follow Jesus Christ in believer's baptism while in college at Michigan State University. Following God's call to ministry he went to study in seminary in Chicago. While there he met his wife Marilyn in 1982, they have been blessed in marriage since 1983. Scott and Marilyn are also blessed to be the parents of three creative adult sons, Mark, Thomas and John.

Rev. Dr. Scott Arnold has been an ordained Baptist pastor since 1984. He received his Doctorate in Ministry with a project in discipleship from Luther Rice University in Lithonia, Georgia. Scott has a Masters of Divinity from Northern Baptist Theological Seminary in Chicago with a focus on Urban Ministry. While in Chicago, he also completed the ministry training program at the Seminary Consortium in Urban Pastoral Education (SCUPE). Dr. Arnold is a graduate of Michigan State University with a Bachelors' of Science degree in Urban Planning. He studied the visual arts at Delta College prior to M.S.U.

Scott enjoys travel, the outdoors, gardening, fishing, landscape painting, fixing old cars, writing songs, playing midi guitar, cooking with Indian spices, and eating at small ethnic restaurants. Scott has been in pastoral ministry in New England and the Midwest. Scott desires to further the cause of the Gospel of Jesus Christ so that the work of God's Kingdom is advanced through the Holy Spirit working in and through God's people.

Scott has authored "Soul Fruit: Bearing Blessings through Cancer", and ministers to people facing cancer as a fourth stage survivor of Non-Hodgkin's Lymphoma. "Soul Fruit" is the story of how the Lord miraculously brought healing to both Scott and his son Thomas. Scott has also coauthored a book with Brad Parrish on Spiritual Gifts called "SHINE: A Celebration of Spiritual Gifts". Scott is the author of "Come Follow Jesus", a book and Bible Study on formative discipleship. You are welcome to contact Dr. Scott Arnold directly at: scotteagle7@aol.com. Visit Scott's personal discipleship website at: www.comefollowjesus.com or go to preludekingdomofGod.com.

Current Books and Resources by Dr. Scott T. Arnold:

Current books:

"Soul Fruit: Bearing Blessings Through Cancer" 2009
> This is the personal story of how Scott and his son Thom experienced hope and healing through cancer. The fruit of God's Spirit is outlined as a blessing that comes through adversity. Scott shares how God intervened, worked through people, and even revealed grace and healing personally. This is written for all of us who face trials and adversity, so as to give hope, faith, and assurance.

"Come Follow Jesus" A Bible Study for Discipleship. 2009
> This is a basic easy to use Discipleship Study for small groups or discipleship triads. The main focus is on the gospels for practical insights into growing as a follower of Jesus Christ. "Come Follow Jesus" is set up for 10 weeks/lessons of study.

"SHINE: A Celebration of Spiritual Gifts" Scott Arnold and Brad Parrish, 2011
> Dr. Arnold joins up with his friend and a lay leader from his church to create a lively resource for churches to use as they explore how Spiritual Gifts are an integral part of God's revelation to the world through the witness of the Church, as the Body of Christ. Scott and Brad consider both the joys and the dangers of Spiritual Gifts and their use in the church. This study goes into more depth about why we have been given Spiritual Gifts and gives practical wisdom about making Spiritual Gift development a priority for the church.

"Prelude: The Kingdom of God: Salvation, Signs, and Service." 2012
> This is a Biblical/Theological study with applications, visions and personal stories. Questions are also included for group discussion and personal reflection.

Upcoming books:

"Faith, Friendship, and Fruitfulness: A Triad Discipleship Journey" 2012.
> This is a long term discipleship guide for small groups or triad groups. There are 26 lessons/studies of intimate and personal interaction from Biblical passages that cover a variety of Old and New Testament key texts.

"Clarke and Williams" 2014. A historical narrative account of Dr. John Clarke and Roger Williams. These two early colonial Baptists have left a legacy of Christian witness, principled faith, religious liberty and radical discipleship that has relevance for applying the Christian faith in any century without compromise.

"The Gospel Amidst Ruin: A Message of Salvation and Endurance for the Urban Christian", Paul's Letter to the Romans" 2013 Scott will examine the significance of the apostle's theology of God's redemptive purposes over the reality of ruin that exists in the creation's bondage to decay. The Gospel gives hope to those who receive the gift of grace and believe in the power of God's eternal love. It is essential to explore the practical implications of living with the hope of the gospel while living in an imperfect world. This world is increasingly urban, giving a glimpse of the New Jerusalem to come on one hand, but also reflecting the vivid corruption of mankind and how the community of God's Kingdom exists in tension with evil principalities and powers. The dystopia of man is not our end, but shall be replaced by the coming New Jerusalem ushered in through Jesus Christ.

Bibliography

Barclay, William. *The King and the Kingdom*. 1968. Westminster Press, Philadelphia, PA

Bright, John. *The Kingdom of God*. 1981. Abingdon Press, Nashville, TN.

Jones, Robert Griffith. *The Gospel According to Paul*. 2004. Harper Collins, New York, NY

Ladd, George Eldon. *The Gospel of the Kingdom*. 1959. Eerdman's, Grand Rapids, MI

Ladd, George Eldon. *A Theology of the New Testament*. 1974. Eerdman's, Grand Rapids. MI

MacCulloch, Diarmaid. *Christianity: The First Three Thousand Years*. 2009. Penguin Group, New York, NY

Snyder, Howard. *Community of the King*. 1977. Inter Varsity Press, Downer's Grove, IL

Wiles and Santer. *Documents in Early Christian Thought*. 1975. Cambridge University Press, Cambridge, England

www.ingramcontent.com/pod-product-compliance
Lightning Source LLC
Chambersburg PA
CBHW081454040426
42446CB00016B/3240